# Van Life

## by Seb Santabarbara

## Van Life For Dummies®

Published by: **John Wiley & Sons, Inc.,** 111 River Street, Hoboken, NJ 07030-5774, www.wiley.com

Copyright © 2022 by John Wiley & Sons, Inc., Hoboken, New Jersey

Published simultaneously in Canada

For general information on our other products and services, please contact our Customer Care Department within the U.S. at 877-762-2974, outside the U.S. at 317-572-3993, or fax 317-572-4002. For technical support, please visit https://hub.wiley.com/community/support/dummies.

Wiley publishes in a variety of print and electronic formats and by print-on-demand. Some material included with standard print versions of this book may not be included in e-books or in print-on-demand. If this book refers to media such as a CD or DVD that is not included in the version you purchased, you may download this material at http://booksupport.wiley.com. For more information about Wiley products, visit www.wiley.com.

Library of Congress Control Number: 2022943422

ISBN 978-1-119-88623-5 (pbk); ISBN 978-1-119-88625-9 (epdf); ISBN 978-1-119-88624-2 (epub)

SKY10035736_081922

# Contents at a Glance

# Table of Contents

# Introduction

Are you ready to pack up your life into a tiny home and travel the world? Perhaps you're watching the clock eagerly in anticipation of heading out on the road, or maybe you're just excited to convert your very own camper van and are already wearing your protective goggles. The notion of traveling and exploring is, for many of us, a craving that can't be ignored. I for one get itchy feet quite often, and I imagine if you're holding this book in your hands and reading this introduction, you're already keen to flip through to Chapter 1 to discover how you too can live and travel in a van full time.

But what is van life? How do I live in a van? How do I wire up a USB socket, and what is the best method for insulating a camper van? If those are the questions that are currently flitting around your brain like a loose ping-pong ball, then you've come to the right place.

Now, you may be thinking that there's no way you can learn how to build and live in a camper van with zero knowledge of DIY or any idea about parking up in remote locations. Don't worry; that was me a few years ago, and now here I am, giving you all the tools, hindsight, tips, tricks, and hacks that I've picked up along the way (along with a lot of laughs at my expense) to help you get started on your van life adventure.

## About This Book

I've been lucky enough to have spent many years documenting the van life movement over the globe, getting up close and personal with the digital nomads, weekend warriors, and thrill-seeking wanderers who make this movement what it is. Not only that, I have both lived and traveled in a van during this time, calling my tiny house on wheels my full-time home and the entire world my front garden.

In my time working as a writer and van life journalist, I've read a lot of books and articles about how to convert a camper van, all of which have had a rather convoluted view about building a camper. What you hold in your hands is a simple and effective guide on how to choose a van and turn it into a camper from scratch. Not only that, but this is one of the only books I've come across that tells you how to then go on and live your best van life, covering everything from how to stealth camp, cook on a tiny stovetop, and take your job on the road to how to empty your portable toilet.

I designed this book as the ultimate van life guide — a one-stop-shop for all the information you need to both build your camper van and live off grid. While this book is designed to be read from start to finish and followed a little like a manual, there's no reason why you can't skip ahead or back to previous chapters if you're keen to learn about certain elements of your build first. (I get it; I'm impatient too!)

I also made sure that no matter whether you live in the United States or the United Kingdom, you'll find the relevant measurements, costs, and equipment names for you to use when making your build. There might be the odd bit of Yorkshire slang thrown in here or there from time to time to help you brush up on your British-isms, but for the most part, I made sure to use vocabulary you'll understand no matter from which side of the pond you're reading.

# Foolish Assumptions

While writing this book, I worked on the assumption that you, dear reader, know nothing about camper van conversions. Not only that, I assumed that you've never held a soldering iron or a drill in your hands either. I know; it's a sweeping generalization, but it's not as if I'm calling you a dummy or anything. I was in the exact same spot as you when I embarked on my camper-building journey, which is why I tried to lay everything out in as simple a way as possible.

Don't worry though; if you *do* know your midi fuses from your blade fuses and have a good grasp of how to use a jigsaw, then the following information is laid out in a way that you can skip straight to the instructions and follow my easy-to-use guides on how to fit everything from false walls to 12-volt refrigerators.

I also worked on the assumption that you've never spent a night in the wild in a camper van either. As you discover throughout this book, living in a converted camper van is my favorite way to travel and the best way to see everything the world has to offer. Again, if you have spent some time in campers thus far, there's still a plethora of information that I've picked up from living life on the road full time that you may find useful for your future travels!

# Icons Used in This Book

Throughout this book, icons in the margins highlight certain types of valuable information that call out for your attention. Here are the icons you'll encounter and a brief description of each.

**TIP**

Whenever you see the Tip icon, it's more than likely going to be a piece of useful information related to something that I learned the hard way while building my camper. That's the beauty of hindsight; you benefit from all the mistakes I made along the way. These tips will definitely make your life easier in the long run, so don't skip past them!

**REMEMBER**

They say an elephant never forgets, but humans do quite a lot. When you see the Remember icon, it means I'm hammering home a point that you really need to keep in mind.

**TECHNICAL STUFF**

The Technical Stuff icon sounds like something you should initially switch off from, but don't be fooled. When you see this icon, there's usually a little fact or juicy piece of information that will both help your van build and impress your friends at parties. You're welcome.

**WARNING**

When you see the Warning icon, I want you to pay full attention. You're going to use lots of sharp tools and electrical items as you go through the steps in this book, so stay focused and proceed with caution whenever it arrives. I want you to have all your fingers intact when you finish your van build, so pay attention!

# Beyond the Book

In addition to the abundance of information and guidance related to van life that I provide in this book, you get access to even more help and information online at Dummies.com. Check out this book's online Cheat Sheet. Just go to www.dummies.com and search for "Van Life For Dummies Cheat Sheet."

# Where to Go from Here

Ideally, from here you'll either go straight on to purchase a van after reading Chapter 3 or head out on the open road. As I said earlier, this is a book that you'll able to take with you after you finish building your camper van. It's not just a

conversion guide; it's a guide to living van life, a mysterious scroll of great importance that you can pass on to your children and grandchildren.

In other words, it's a great value for the money.

While I clearly want you to start with Chapter 1 and read my comical quips about
the birth of van life, Chapter 3 is a great place to dive into if you're desperate to
discover some tips and tricks when it comes to purchasing the right van. Already
living in your van? Head to Chapter 14 and get swotting up on how to prepare you
and your tiny home for the adventure of a lifetime!

For now, I want to give you a warm welcome to *Van Life For Dummies* and thank you
for buying this book. Now, go and make a cup of coffee; things are about to get
deep very quickly!

# 1
# Getting into Van Life

Discover why van life has become such a popular movement and what brings the vibrant and bustling van life community together.

Understand how to think like a vanlifer and what you need to do to start downsizing and adopt a minimalistic state of mind.

Determine how long you want to be on the road: as a weekend warrior or as a full- or part-time vanlifer.

Explore the options for traveling solo or with a partner, and how you can bring your pet along for the adventure.

Figure out how to make van life work for your family and discover how expensive (or not) this lifestyle can be.

# Chapter **1**

# What Is Van Life?

All good adventures start somewhere, and yours is about to begin right here, right now, in the very first chapter. You've seen all the pictures and dreamed about opening that sliding van door onto an ever-changing paradise, and now you've taken the plunge and officially embarked on your van life journey.

In this chapter, you explore the origins of van life and how this global phenomenon has captured the hearts and minds of people everywhere. I show you how to begin thinking like a vanlifer and — most important of all — how to begin downsizing for your new minimalistic way of life.

## Introducing Van Life

Van life might be all over your social media feed and spread out across your desktop screensaver like an ode to wanderlust, but the concept of living in a vehicle equipped with basic amenities full or part time has been around a lot longer than you might have originally guessed.

Many think the pinnacle of van life occurred during the Swinging Sixties and the Summer of Love, with Brian Wilson and the Beach Boys wishing for California Girls while cruising down Big Sur toward the golden sands and twinkling ocean. Still, you have to go even further back to find the roots of this movement, back even before the illustrious 1950s when the camper van was widely believed to have been invented.

So who do we have to thank for sparking this unique movement?

Back in 1855, a certain traveling medic from Scotland called Dr. William Stables designed the first-ever touring caravan. He named it "The Wanderer," and while they say that not all of those who wander are lost, the two horses that pulled The Wanderer probably spent most of their time trying help it out of a ditch rather than finding great spots to boondock along the glorious sights of the North Coast 500. (I've thrown a wrench in the works already by mentioning boondocking in the very first chapter, but stick with me; in Chapter 16 all is revealed!)

Fast-forward to today, and Dr. Stables's Wanderer has paved the way to a world of exciting adventures in all manners of different vehicles from off-grid truck campers to beautifully converted panel vans, Volkswagen busses, travel trailers, and many more. One thing is for certain, however; the concept of van life and the freedom it brings has forever remained the same.

Van life is more than just a means of exploring the planet we call home. It's that feeling you get when heading out on the type of expeditions you just can't buy from a travel agency, hitting the open road in search of excitement and adventure, and searching the unknown for unique memories that will last a lifetime. It's more than just grabbing the ultimate picture by the beach or the obligatory forest campfire; van life is that all-encompassing feeling that grabs young and old, rich and poor alike, those who are seeking a life that doesn't revolve around Black Friday sales or the latest air fryer with added egg-cup holder. It's a call to the explorers, the curious, those who strive for more.

That's van life in a nutshell.

Of course, if you want a more literal explanation of van life, you don't have to delve too far into the name itself for an answer. Moving your life into a van is an incredibly rewarding experience, whether you plan on just heading out to your local campsite for the weekend, driving into the mountains for a month-long retreat in the summer, or exploring the world full time after leaving the daily grind behind.

More time spent outdoors; what's not to love?

If you're anything like me (and the fact that you're holding this book in your hands suggests you are), then I imagine you're already bursting with questions about solar panels (Chapter 9) and window placements (Chapter 7). Perhaps some of you have just gulped incredibly loudly and are now finding the whole concept of living in such a small space a little daunting and confusing, but don't worry. I guide you through the whole process from start to finish and get you on your way to fulfilling your true travel potential.

# Why Van Life Is Such a Popular Movement in Today's World

Van life, and "vandwelling" in general, are more than just movements that have been ticking away in the background since The Wanderer clunked over its very first pothole. It's safe to say that van life is a cultural phenomenon, and one that isn't showing signs of slowing down any time soon.

No matter where you live around the world, the general idea of "the dream life" is changing. Whereas at one time getting a perfect job with the local firm and securing a mortgage would have been the ultimate goal for many people, the concept of working to live rather than truly living is slowly dying out. People are sitting up and realizing that there is more to life than waiting patiently for the next paycheck to arrive.

There is a whole world out there to discover, and for many, the idea of being tied down by mortgages and contracts just doesn't sit true. For many of the people I've met on my van life journey, living in a van has allowed them to call any country or state home, waking up to oceans or deserts outside their front room without the worries and stresses of a "conventional life."

Sounds pretty good, right?

# Joining a Global Community

Okay, I know what you're probably thinking: "This is just a phase that lazy hippie kids go through, isn't it?" And while I admit it's true that there is an element of "rebelling against the norm" with van life, there are so many different reasons that bring this vibrant and bustling community together.

I've had the pleasure of meeting vanlifers of all ages and from all walks of life, and I have chatted with them at length about their stories and reasons for taking the road less traveled. For some, van life is a means of living a more self-sustainable, eco-friendly lifestyle once the workweek ends, while for others, van life means having the chance to fulfill a lifelong dream now that their kids have flown the nest, leaving all their possessions and their nosey neighbors behind for a slower pace of life.

And speaking of community, the van life community is made up of some of the nicest people you'll ever meet. What bond could be greater than one forged with people with whom you share the same ideals and life plans? We help each other on the road, recommend places to camp and eat, look out for one another when the going gets tough, and always have supplies hidden away in the back of our vans to fix everything from a leaky roof to a squeaking hinge. In essence, van life is like having the whole world as your neighborhood!

Alternative living isn't just something your grandpa will tell you layabouts used to do "back in the day" anymore. House prices are skyrocketing all over the world, and unlike during the 1970s when buying a house was a plausible notion, today many people struggle to get the funds together to buy a home of their own.

I spent £3,000 (around $3,600) buying my first van and around the same amount doing it up. It was my full-time home for four and a half glorious years, which makes it the longest-occupied abode I've lived in since leaving my parents' house all those years before. Getting on the property ladder is incredibly tough, but buying a school bus and converting it into a tiny home . . . now that's much more achievable!

# Becoming a Vanlifer

Do you just wake up one morning and decide to become a vanlifer? Can you catch the wanderlust bug like you would the number 52 bus into town?

For me, it was less of a eureka moment than you might think. I was working at a music venue in Yorkshire, U.K., not entirely sure about my current career and feeling a little lost. I'd spend hours scrolling through pictures of people embarking on van life adventures on Instagram, just wishing that I could work from the cusp of a beautiful forest or on the edge of a glistening lake like the smiling people staring back at me.

You might not believe it, but I couldn't even drive when the idea of van life first hit me, which I think we can all agree was a major flaw in this potential new life plan. I'd spent my life thus far taking trains, taxis, and busses everywhere I needed to go, and I was more comfortable behind a pair of rubber-coated handlebars than behind the wheel of a car.

So at the age of 27, I found myself purchasing my first ever vehicle: the long-wheelbase panel van that I would end up converting and driving all over Europe. Most people buy a rickety, old Ford Fiesta or something small like a Mini Cooper as their first vehicle, but not me. Try doing your first ever three-point-turn without your instructor sitting beside you in something that most people rent when moving house. Might as well jump straight in at the deep end, right?

**REMEMBER**

Still, becoming a vanlifer isn't just as easy as rolling out of bed and straight into a brand-new way of life. Van life is as much about changing your mindset and opening yourself up to new possibilities as it is parking up in beautiful locations with the wind in your hair.

**WARNING**

This lifestyle can be challenging and is often demanding. You've got to make sacrifices and give up certain home comforts; get used to sleeping, bathing, and going to the toilet all in one room; and, if you're traveling as a couple, learning to work together while living in a tiny space.

If you're planning on living off-grid, then there might be cloudy days when your solar panels aren't charging your batteries as quickly, and without a constant water supply, you'll need to plan visits to filling-up spots while on the move. Don't worry though; there's always a solution at hand, and I go over many of them in Chapters 14, 15, and 16, but it's important to remember that being a vanlifer involves a certain amount of forward-thinking.

But trust me; it's worth it.

**REMEMBER**

Now, I don't want you to get disheartened so early on; I just want you to be fully prepared for what's about to come. The initial journey might well be tough, and yes, your toilet might overflow at 1 a.m. while you are miles away from the nearest town. But you know what people say; nothing worth having is ever easy. Though those people didn't have this book to help them, did they?

## Downsizing

But how is it possible to take your entire life and squish it into 80 square feet of living space? That's smaller than most people's bathrooms, which means you're going to have to start being a little picky about what you take with you on your next trip away or on your new lifelong adventure. Do you really need to keep your DVD collection or the singing fish that Auntie Mabel bought you eight years ago? What about that signed picture of Michael Caine? And is it necessary to have 15 variations of the same coat?

We accumulate so much stuff over the course of our lives that we quite often forget what we've even got in the first place, carting belongings from house to house and adding to the ever-growing in the understairs cupboard. I gathered 13 bags of belongings to take to the local charity shop before moving into my van, sold my TV and games consoles to put money toward my travels, and gave other bits and bobs away to friends on permanent loan. Although if you visit Adara Tattoo Collective in York, U.K., the mirror on the wall was only supposed to be on temporary loan until my friend Josh painted it black. Never leave your possessions with a goth, kids.

Looking back, I think the last shower I took in my rented house was the longest on record and caused the whole street to lose water pressure; sometimes you've got to make the most of the little things, and I'll never forget that shower.

**TIP**

To start the process of downsizing, first consider what are the most important things to you in life, and then think about what you want to get out of your van life experience.

Okay, so you enjoyed watching soap operas and asking your SmartHub to dim the lights on in the evening, but are they worth giving up for a brand-new life of adventure? I think we all know the answer here, but just in case you're confused, it's *yes*.

I know a lot of people who travel with a TV in their van, but would using a laptop suffice instead? How vital is it to have a shower on board when there are hot springs and freshwater lakes aplenty on the open road? These are all things you'll need to consider when drawing up plans for your trundling tiny home.

Next, I want you to consider what things bring you joy, and I mean *really* bring you happiness, things that you can't ever possibly imagine living without. Now, if those things are essential for life on the road or are memorable items that are small enough to implement into your build like a figurine of Bob Ross or a special item of furniture, then put them to one side. If they're too big or have no use right now, then consider putting them into storage or passing them on to a family member or friend. Your new space will soon feel incredibly cluttered with lots of excess items inside, so choose wisely.

**TIP**

There's also the factor of weight to consider as well. In many countries around the world, if a camper van weighs over the allotted weight classification that you're allowed to drive as stated on your license, then authorities can ask you to remove items until you are back under the legal weight limit. In short, you don't want to have to hand over a singing fish to a policeman to try and save on weight. Plus you'd need to learn how to say "singing fish" in a dozen languages, and that's the sort of pointless information that would push something else useful out of your brain.

# Adopting a minimalistic state of mind

That's right; I'm already using the M word and it's only Chapter 1.

More than thinking about where you'll put stuff in your camper or calculating the weight of every DVD in the collection that you still can't whittle down, this process of downsizing is a chance to declutter your mind. I know I'm on the verge of sounding what your grandparents might call "new age," but it's true. I can't begin to tell you how amazing it was the first time I sat in my van with only the things I actually needed rather than tons of useless bric-a-brac that served zero purpose.

Rather than having 18 plates, I now had 2. Instead of multiple drawers and cupboard space for clothes I never wore, I now had one drawer with the essentials in it. You start to realize what you really need to feel comfortable and content, and that happiness isn't a slicing-and-dicing food processor or a reclining leather sofa. Happiness *is* a Bialetti moka pot and a Nintendo Switch, however; I'm a minimalist, not a savage!

In Chapter 2, I get more into what it means to get into the mindset of a tiny home dweller and talk about how to mentally prepare yourself for this change, but hopefully you've already started to think about what it means to live small and benefits it can bring.

# Chapter **2**

# Knowing Whether Van Life Is for You

What does it mean to be a tiny home dweller, and can everyone make the change from living in a house to living in a converted panel van? Speaking from experience, getting into the mindset of a tiny home dweller isn't something that happens overnight; it takes a lot of thought, compromise, and self-evaluation about what you want to get out of your new lifestyle before you can fully commit to this way of life.

Luckily, I've already done all that thought-provoking soul-searching and got the T-shirt to prove it, and while you can't physically borrow said T-shirt as it isn't real, I *can* help you kickstart the process with some useful advice about what it takes to become a vanlifer. Over the course of this chapter, you discover how to think like a tiny homeowner, decide how long you want to travel, and most important, whether you think van life could be the lifestyle for you.

# Getting into the Mindset of a Tiny Home Dweller

Don't worry; I'm not going to ask you to sit down and meditate or chant some mantras (though by all means, feel free if you've had a busy week so far). Getting into the mindset of a tiny home dweller does, however, take a little bit of inner reflection and a willingness to change your outlook on the world.

**WARNING**

Living in any kind of tiny home takes a little bit of adjusting time. To go from a house with two bedrooms, a bathroom, kitchen, living room, and dining room, to a house with one room and a toilet cupboard (in the case of a van), is a massive change. You're about to give up a lot of the things you rely on daily, things that have become commonplace like a dishwasher, a flushing toilet, your guitar amplifiers, a flushing toilet, your shower . . . oh, and a flushing toilet.

Why did I mention the toilet three times? It's the one thing people most often tell me that stops them from living the van life. Giving up the luxury of a flushing toilet is too much of a change from their normal routine. When I first started building my tiny home, I had a lot of these same reservations. Would I be able to manage? How would I feel in such a small space? Could I really give up the TV? Honestly, and I genuinely mean every word here, I did not miss any part of living in a house. Sure, emptying the toilet down another toilet while I lived in a van in Yorkshire and the new routine of showering at the gym took some getting used to, but after a few weeks it just became the new normal.

Now, I'm going to get a little deep here, so you might want to make yourself comfortable for this next bit . . . .

What is the most important thing to you in life? Is it working hard and saving up for a house or a big trip? Is it getting out into the open and spending time with your family? Is it living within your means in order to have more time to spend working on a passion project that you might want to turn into a career? In some respects, tiny home living can help with all three of those choices.

I worked full time while living in a van for over a year, saving my wages every month for my European travels. Equally, I know people who have done the same thing and put their money toward buying land in a different country. Living small certainly gives you more time to spend doing the things you love too, whether that's heading out on a trip with your loved ones, or working less and putting your energy into writing a book or honing your photography skills.

TIP

I can best summarize the feeling that made me want to live in a tiny house as "wanting more." You've got to want that change more than anything else, to be prepared for things to get a little bit tough at times, to live a life that can be uncertain but with infinite rewards and exciting discoveries every day.

## Life in the slow lane

I think one of the best parts of living the van life — and this is a theme I come back to throughout this book — is the lack of rushing around or the need to do anything to a timescale. There's no *should* in the van life vocabulary; you do what you want, when you want, making your own hours if you work on the road or just enjoying life on your own terms.

Say goodbye to the stressful morning commute or eating your breakfast while watching mind-numbing morning television shows if you're taking your job with you. Say goodbye to waking up listening to the next door neighbor's toilet cistern rumbling through the wall or the sound of the garbage truck reversing down your street. Every day feels more relaxed when you wake up in a new place, listening to the ever-changing sounds of nature or sometimes no sounds whatsoever.

For a lot of people, this lack of structure and routine can feel a little like freefalling. Again, it's no real surprise; since around the age of 4, most of us have gone to school at a certain time, eaten meals at set times, gone to university and eventually to work in a preplanned structure laid out for us. To go from this to a life where you make the rules can be freeing for some, but make others feel lost.

## A motto to live by

TIP

Here's something I want you to think about, and this is something I tell people who are thinking about living the van life on a daily basis: *There is no dress rehearsal for life, so don't waste time dreaming about your perfect life when you could be out there living the dream.* Admittedly, I'm not a philosopher and I haven't had many public speaking gigs thus far in my career, but I think you get the general idea.

If you're reading this from the office instead of sending emails, then don't wait until you're retired to give travel a go. If you're retired but thinking about waiting for the right time, throw caution to the wind and get out there and give van life a go. I know too many people, young and old, who have sadly passed away before getting to live their traveling dreams. Don't wait for tomorrow; make that decision to live a different life today.

I'll now wait 30 seconds for your applause before carrying on with the next section.

# Deciding How Long You Want to Be on the Road

I think we can all agree that you're now fully committed to giving van life a try, what with buying this book and my rousing speech earlier. The next question you need to ask yourself is: How long would you like to be on the road away from home? Or, and here's the million-dollar question: Do you want to take your home on the road with you?

Before I go any further, I know that while it's physically possible to "up sticks" and live the van life full time, not everyone can or wants to give up the life they have built to live on the road. For some, it's just not viable due to work locations, while others might love their jobs and not fancy the thought of giving up the empire they have built. That's why, almost as if I had preplanned that little paragraph earlier, I describe three categories of van life travel in the following sections to help you figure out what kind of van life lifestyle you might want.

## Weekend warriors

Weekend warriors lead a secret life. You might have one in your office but not even know it, a person who clock-watches every Friday while sitting in a Rab jacket or who stirs their coffee with a miniature kayak paddle–shaped spoon. These wanderlust aficionados work through the week and head out on the open road every weekend, putting the pedal to the metal as the clock hits 5 p.m. on a Friday and making the most of every second of their weekend until it's time to punch back in again on Monday morning.

The beauty of van life and being the owner of a camper van is that you can keep your vehicle stocked up and ready for adventure at a moment's notice. And, as you get further through this book, you discover some of the different outdoor activities that complement the lifestyle.

As the name suggests, weekend warriors simply travel over a weekend. Whether frequenting campsites or wild camping in the hills, scheduled short trips away give you something to look forward to, a chance to live as free as a bird on the weekend while still maintaining a steady work/life balance through the week.

**TIP**

I've spoken to lots of people over the years who have used weekend trips away in their vans as a starting point to determine whether they can manage full-time van life. Twelve months of weekend camping should give you an idea of what living on the road is like and what parts of your conversion might need adapting or changing for longer trips away.

If you're thinking of joining the ranks of the weekend warriors, then don't wait until 4:30 p.m. on a Friday to decide where you might want to go that weekend. When the clock hits 5 p.m., the only thing you want to think about is following that satnav arrow to your destination. Do the planning through the week and pack the night before to make the most out of your time away.

One way to make sure you're always ready is to draft a list of essential items that you know you'll need every time. Pack a kit bag with everything on a Thursday evening and make sure all your gadgets and power banks are charged up in advance. Do your food shopping the night before too so you have everything ready for that first Friday night park-up.

## Short-term: One to six months

Planning a short-term adventure of one to six months could be a more manageable way of fitting van life into your current life. So many people buy a van and convert it as a cheap way to see the world, always knowing that it won't be with them forever. Some countries, such as Australia, have systems set up for people driving North to South in a camper and then selling the camper to someone else so that that person can drive it back up North again, continuing the cycle.

Perhaps you could chat with your employer about a sabbatical or career break. It's a surefire way of discovering if you're a valued employee or not, and if the answer isn't to your liking, you might as well take a little break and have some fun before finding a new job!

Maybe you're about to hit your gap year before university or your first job, or perhaps you're a little disillusioned with your career. Maybe you're up for a promotion at the end of the year that is going to be much more demanding and leave you with less time, or perhaps you know you're going to be made redundant and fancy getting away and rebooting your brain before changing jobs. Short-term travel can provide the reset your body and brain need. All you need to do is decide how long you want to be away and if you actually want to come back!

Six months is a long time to take in a big chunk of your country or continent. Traveling in a van is also the cheapest and most convenient way of traveling too as your accommodation goes everywhere with you and you don't have to carry it around on your back. Ticking off countries has never been easier, and with a place to dry clothes and make a cup of tea after a long, wet hike, it's never been more comfortable too.

Of course, there's nothing to say that building a van for short-term travels can't lead to weekend excursions later down the line or a potential move to full-time travel if you decide to take your job on the road with you, something that could be highly probable after reading Chapter 17.

**REMEMBER**

Don't be too hasty to get rid of your van when you get back from a short-term trip. I know you might need the money or initially think that you don't have room to park it anywhere. Don't make any rash decisions; give yourself a little time to think about it before making that sale. Camper vans are incredibly useful when it comes to heading out to see friends, going on impromptu trips, or even having a place for your parents to stay when they visit and you don't want them snoring in the spare bedroom. Their snores on the street may attract wild animals, but at least you can sleep in peace.

## Full-time travel

Making the jump to full-time travel was something I had in the cards from the very beginning of my camper conversion. This was the dream that drove me to convert my van every evening after work and wake up at 7 a.m. on weekends for six months.

Obviously, if you're thinking about traveling full time, then you need to either be in a position where you are financially stable or plan on working on the road. I managed to travel full time working two days a week writing articles, and budgeting costs accordingly along the way. You can find out more about how much I spent per month and some of the things that you'll need to account for along the way in Chapter 20.

Believe me, full-time travel becomes normal incredibly quickly, so much so that when you do find yourself having to stop for any length of time due to a breakdown, you'll be itching to set off again!

**REMEMBER**

The information you'll glean throughout the rest of this book comes from a perspective of living in a van and traveling full time. I'm not saying I'm biased (okay, maybe I am a little), but this is my main reference point as I jumped straight in at the deep end and dedicated my life to full-time travel.

# A Global Movement for Everyone

As I sit here writing this chapter right now, the van life movement is growing. From narrowboat marina-style living arrangements designed for vans to park full time to companies that solely exist from a traveling Volkswagen bus, more and more people are discovering van life in one of its many guises and finding out that travel doesn't have to be an expensive pipe dream.

**REMEMBER**

Van life isn't always what you see on social media. This topic, and indeed this fact, crops up a lot throughout this book because it's important for you to be given the truth before we crack on with planning your conversion and later planning your van life adventures.

Unfortunately, the main bulk of the van life hashtag content on Instagram shows a very small minority of people who are in fact part of a global movement built for everyone. I've had the pleasure of speaking to vanlifers from all different backgrounds and cultures while covering the movement in my wider work. I've spoken to members of the BIPOC nomadic community striving to make a change in diversifying van life, LGBTQ+ vanlifers championing safe spaces for all in mobile meet-ups over the globe, and people from all walks of life breaking away from cultural traditions in order to pursue a life they choose rather than one that is expected of them.

Van life is a movement that does not discriminate; it's not a members only club, and it's certainly not something that you have to prove your worth to be a part of. I've never known a collective group of people to be as caring and considerate, who always look out for one another and switch from strangers to neighbors to lifelong friends over the space of a couple of hours as the van life community.

Who knows? You might meet your new best friend, partner, or hopefully both combined when setting off on your van life adventures.

## Enjoying van life when you have a disability

Adventure doesn't stop when you live with a disability. If anything, van life is one of the easiest ways to plan adventures based on your specific needs, enabling you to create a conversion that works with you rather than trying to make a pre-existing camper fit your lifestyle.

How many of you are thinking, "But I'm in a wheelchair, I can't possibly travel around the world." If that's you, then stop right away. There are countless ramps and lifts available that can be implemented into your van build to accommodate entry in and out of the vehicle, and while the industry needs to do more to accommodate accessible users on the whole, changes *are* being made for the better.

I've interviewed a wheelchair user with a pull-out living room that slides out the back of their van, and another who built all of their worktop spaces lower down to accommodate cooking and opening cupboards from their chair. The beauty of building and designing your own conversion is that it can be to whatever specifications you need, with multiple options to suit couples if they are traveling together and both the driver's seat and living quarters.

**REMEMBER**

No matter where you are in the world, you can buy automatic panel vans to convert. What's more, vans can be adapted with hand levers for breaking and accelerating instead of pedals. If you're traveling with a non-disabled partner or friend, then the pedals can still be kept but tucked out of the way when not in use, meaning you can still share the driving and, more important, both get a chance to kick back in the passenger seat and watch the world go by. Always remember that there is a solution for everything, and nothing is out of reach.

Of course, not all disabilities are physical. Throughout this book, I mention how van life can help with your mental health and well-being too, freeing up more time for meditation and mindfulness, a chance to relax down and work on *you*. While traveling isn't a cure for anxiety, you might well find that having less pressure from jobs or social obligations helps you to center yourself a little more.

Whether you have ME/CFS, muscular dystrophy, autism, OCD, a prosthetic limb, or any other disability, you can still enjoy van life. And, while I can't account for every type of conversion in this book, there is a thriving community of accessible nomads and adventurers on social media sites such as Instagram with a plethora of information, experiences, tips, and tricks ready and waiting for you to discover.

## Wandering the continent, regardless of age

Whether you're 18 or 81, the world is out there waiting for you to grab hold of it. And, while I advised you crack on and live in the moment earlier on, the fact remains that it's never too late for adventure.

Maybe you've lived your entire life as part of a nomadic family, embracing the thrills of travel from a very young age. Maybe you've just turned 60 and bought a camper on a whim after never thinking about leaving your village before. Whatever the reason you've decided to open this book, the main thing is that you do get out there and experience everything the world has to offer.

Now, I don't want you to think that I'm about to fall into the ageist trap of saying that older people can't climb mountains or do some of the stuff that younger people can. My mum walks eight miles a day some days and has more stamina than the kids I see playing games on their phones at the bus stop could ever dream of. (And yes, I'm well aware that I just turned into my grandad there for a second, but it's true.)

No matter what your age, ability, or mobility, van life can cater for all types of adventures, big or small. My 70-year-old uncle heads up into the hills most weekends with his camper, traversing peaks and staying as fit as a fiddle. Equally, he sometimes finds a campsite near a river or lake and just relaxes with a pint of beer and a good book. Van life promotes an outdoor lifestyle, but there's nothing to say that you have to be the next freeclimbing expert or a surfing extraordinaire.

## Seeing the sights as a solo traveler

Would you go out and see the world on your own? You certainly don't have to be in a relationship to head out and explore the globe. In fact, many people choose to travel on their own so that they can follow their own itineraries and adventure agendas, heading off to a new place at the drop of a hat without having to worry about whether their partner can come or whether they'll agree to the next destination.

For solo travelers, every stranger is a potential friend, every invite or chance meeting an opportunity to experience something new and exciting. You can choose to alter your travel path and join up with new friends for a time or go your own way completely, exploring as much or as little as you choose.

TIP

Of course, there is a safety aspect to traveling on your own that unnecessarily puts people off solo adventures. If you walk for the bus at night or head to the capital city of your country on your own on a train, then there's no reason why you can't travel on your own. It's the same thing but just in a different city or country, and with language apps available on every phone, tablet, or laptop, there's no reason why you can't navigate your way around any situation, big or small. In Chapter 16, I discuss some of the safety features you can take with you on the road and some of the things you can look out for when it comes to going with your gut when arriving at a parking spot for the night.

WARNING

Not everyone enjoys being on their own, and for many people, it's their worst nightmare. If you haven't spent a lot of time living on your own in the past, then suddenly finding yourself without your housemate, partner, or parent on the other side of the world in the midst of a thunderstorm might be quite a lot to handle. My advice is to get your own place for a little bit; you need to be comfortable with your own company and not reliant on other people for your happiness. Try this in your home city where people know you and can provide support before booking that ferry ticket.

# Bringing Your Pet Along for the Adventure

If you live with a pet, then you can hardly leave your furry friend at home and go out on an adventure on your own. Just think how annoyed your pet would be at having missed out on all that excitement while you were paddleboarding along rivers and running through forests while they had Uncle Derek coming round once a day to put some food down and let them out into the garden.

Let's talk about dogs. I have a little pup named Bilbo, though if you're reading this in the future he's probably not so little anymore. He's a great companion and always eager to get out and explore, a little like his owner. Dogs are another heartbeat when you live on your own, a source of comfort and companionship when you're feeling low, and have a surefire way of feeling more excitable when you do.

Depending on where you live, you might have to make some necessary arrangements for taking your dog abroad, especially if you live in the United Kingdom now that the U.K. has left the European Union. Certain countries have restrictions as to when you can travel with a pet depending on when they had their vaccinations and other essential treatments, and many require that you obtain a certificate from their vet before traveling. If in doubt, speak to your vet and check the government website of the country, state, or region you are traveling to for more information.

If you live in the E.U., taking your pup along is as simple as obtaining a pet passport from your vet, which is valid for your pet's lifetime so long as its rabies vaccinations are kept up-to-date.

If you're traveling across the United States as an American citizen, then it's important to double-check whether the state you are traveling into requires a pet health certificate on entry. Some states like Hawaii also require your pet to be quarantined. It's also advisable to make sure your dog has had all its vaccinations.

**REMEMBER**

Do a Google search for the government website or contact the relevant local authority for the country, state, or region that you are traveling into to determine what papers you need or criteria you need to meet to bring your pet on the road with you.

But what about cats? Well, I've met a lot of people traveling with cats over the years too, but the problem is that cats tend to enjoy taking walkabouts and don't have the same urges to stick with their owners as dogs do. If anything, they probably spend most of their time wondering why humans are joining them on a van life adventure and not the other way around!

**TIP**

As well as microchipping your cat (something you should do for all pets on the road), keep a GPS tracking device on their collar or harness at all times. That way, you can keep tabs on them using your phone and always know where they are. The GPS tracker will need charging from time to time, so set an alarm on your phone to top it up every day or couple of days as necessary. There's no point in your pet walking around with a drained tracker, so keep on top of it in case the worst happens and your cat or pooch does wander off.

**WARNING**

Your dog might have always been well-behaved in the local park or while wandering through your local woods, but anything can happen while exploring new places. Many European farmers let goats, sheep, and horses roam around acres of wild land, and while you can usually hear them from the telltale sound of the bell around their necks, your dog might easily go into fight-or-flight mode at either the sound of the bell or the sight of an animal it hasn't seen before. Likewise, the U.S. has the added danger of bears and mountain lions, and you don't want little Fido getting mixed up with them! While there's always the temptation to let dogs run off the lead in new places, always check out new locations with them on a lead first so that you can get the lay of the land before letting them roam free.

Beaches are a great place to take dogs as they usually don't have any livestock or animals that might want to eat your four-legged friends for dinner around. I did once see a man on a white horse galloping back and forth along a beach in Spain while smoking a cigar, so maybe keep an eye out for him, just in case.

**WARNING**

If you have no other option than to leave your pet in your van for any length of time, make sure the van is cool and shaded inside. Leaving a pet in a hot van can be fatal, so use air-conditioning or create a through draft using window ventilation to maintain a nice temperature, and always ensure that they have plenty of water in their bowl. And it goes without saying that on hot days, you should keep the time your dog is on its own to an absolute minimum.

**TIP**

Consider investing in a digital thermometer that you can access from your phone to monitor the temperature in your van while you're away.

# Figuring Out How to Make Van Life Work for Your Family

One comment I get quite a lot from people is, "I wish I could travel, but I've got a family now." Traveling with kids is more than just possible; it's a viable option and a way of life that many vanlifers successfully manage across the globe. During my travels and while writing about van life, I've met a Russian couple traveling full time with a baby, a family of five who have covered a quarter of a million miles on the road together, and lots of other couples who head out with their children and loved ones on the weekends.

I never did much traveling as a child; my parents couldn't drive, so if we went anywhere, it usually had to be by taxi. To me, the notion of taking a child on the road and teaching them the value of a simple life filled with adventure is a fantastic idea and one that would be infinitely rewarding. Maybe someday I'll get to give it a go!

## Roadschooling

But what about school? Won't my child miss out on lots of opportunities?

Arguably, when your whole world is a massive classroom, the possibilities for learning are infinite. Why learn about things in a textbook when you can get out into the real world and see them firsthand?

Homeschooling, or *roadschooling* in this sense, requires prior planning and a lot of patience, but it's a great chance to share new discoveries together. It gives kids a chance to pick the subjects they want to learn and choose topics that really inspire them, alongside key online curriculums for math and other core subjects required to pass national tests. Plus, as the van life community grows, so too does the roadschooling community, with parents and children meeting up with other nomads on their travels for socializing and group teaching sessions.

## Planning your build for a family

From sprinter vans with built-in sleeping pods to bunk beds and cozy pop-top roof platforms, there are many different ways to accommodate multiple family members in one van. Granted, the more family members you have in a tiny space, the more crowded it might feel, but with clever planning and maximum usage of your van's internal space, there's no reason why a family of five can't travel together and have a great time out on the road.

**TIP**

When thinking about your initial build, consider sleeping arrangements such as a drop-down bed that stores away up against the ceiling or a chair that folds down into a single bed. Hammocks are also a fun option and great for stowing away during the day. Get creative and involve your children in the build process so that they can get excited about their new way of life.

## Having time to yourself

No matter how much you love your family, you're going to want some time to yourself. The trouble is that, unlike in a conventional house, you can't close yourself off in a different room or take the newspaper to the toilet for half an hour while you do the crossword. The important thing here is to schedule "you time" into the equation. I know that you might have thought about van life because you want a free and easy lifestyle, but you can still create a structure that doesn't involve you waking up at dawn every day.

**TIP**

Build a camper routine from the get-go. Make time for joint family play in nature, board games, exploring, and learning on the go, but also instigate quiet time where you or your spouse can read, the kids can play Mario Kart or draw, or just kick back and listen to music on headphones. Even just an hour a day will help everyone to recharge their batteries, which will only help for the next day's activities.

**REMEMBER**

You don't have to be adventuring all the time; in fact, it's physically impossible to be on the go 24/7. Don't feel guilty for having down time, and spend time explaining the benefits of relaxation to your family too. Though, if you're traveling with teenagers, I imagine they won't need much persuading.

# Is Van Life Expensive?

If you're looking for a dedicated breakdown of estimated costs while traveling in a van, don't worry; that's coming a little later on in the book. Still, I want to take a minute to answer this very simple question.

No, van life is not expensive.

There, that was easy!

I don't want this book to turn into "Seb Santabarbara's Travel Diary" (spoiler alert — it will in some parts), but I traveled full time for about a third of the money I was spending on a house in York that didn't move or offer differing sliding-door views and free energy.

As you soon find out, the costs of full-time van life included fuel from driving between locations, entry to some attractions, and all the day-to-day costs that come with running a vehicle as your home. Working a couple of days a week and having enough time and money to enjoy five-day weekends is how life should be, after all.

# Wandering when you feel like it

**TIP**

Here's a little van life tip that I want to share with you in the spirit of getting into the mindset of a tiny home dweller:

*Move onto the next place when you feel like it. Drive when you want to, not when you feel you should.*

Now, I know that sounds like the kind of limp philosophical quote that might come out of a Christmas cracker, but it's true. One of the best things about van life, especially if you're traveling for an undetermined amount of time, is that you don't have to be constantly on the move. If you're boondocking or wild camping and there aren't any specific parking restrictions, then it doesn't matter if you stay put in a place for two days or two weeks. So long as you have water and power, you can head out on the open road when the feeling is right, thus elongating your time away and reducing the amount of time you spend at fuel/gas stations filling up your tank.

Opting for a slower driving pace certainly helps to keep costs down, but it also means that you can wander around on foot when and as much as you feel like. Parking by the beach gives you the option to get out into the waves every day for a week before moving off to do more city-tripping sightseeing adventures. Or, you can mix your time in the surf with heading out into the hills and forests, exploring the local area and discovering hidden gems like abandoned ruins and coves with glittering golden sands.

**TIP**

Something I will undoubtedly say a lot throughout this book is that exploring on foot is one of the best ways to see everything an area has to offer. Getting on a plane and traveling to a resort you found in a holiday brochure is all well and good, but you only get to see a very specific part of your chosen country this way and in turn receive a very "cookie cutter" experience in the sense that it will be the same as everyone else's. By taking a camper out into little towns or local forests, you get to see real life, experience the people who call the country home all-year round and not just in busy tourist seasons to earn a living. You also get to taste traditional food cooked the right way and not for holiday-goers with mild tastebuds.

**REMEMBER**

Wandering when you feel like it provides a life with more flavor, more excitement, and more money in your pocket at the end of the week.

**TIP**

Traveling when you feel like it also means you can avoid toll roads and take longer routes, helping to keep costs down. These routes are often more scenic too, so you get to see even more of the country in the process.

# Motoring around the countryside 24/7

Not everyone has the luxury of taking it slow, however. Some people have a strict itinerary and stick to it, ticking off the miles every day in order to reach specific destinations on time. There's a certain kind of thrill to a timed trek around the globe — just you and your very own Passepartout heading around the world in 80 days . . . or more likely around North America in 150, but you get where I'm going with this.

There is, however, a lot of pressure with this method of travel, mainly the pressure to be places on time, especially if you've booked ferries or attractions in advance.

The costs of motoring around the countryside 24/7 are, as you might have guessed, much higher than if you take your time and stay in places for longer periods of time. You'll go through fuel at a quicker rate than my dog goes through gravy bones, so make sure you budget accordingly. Likewise, you'll probably end up taking more direct toll routes to get to places more quickly so that you can spend more time while you're there, thus racking up extra costs in the form of toll payments.

**REMEMBER**

There is another cost to fast-paced travel that isn't monetary. Constantly thinking about the next place you need to be and the rate at which you are burning through you budget can quite easily make you feel stressed, meaning you won't enjoy your time at your current park-up as much. My advice is to not overdo it when you're planning your route.

Let's say, for argument's sake, that you have three months to travel. Don't try to fill every day with a different activity in a different place. You'll end up missing so much around you and tire yourself out in a matter of weeks.

Aim to spend a minimum of three nights in the majority of the places you put down on your route. Can you imagine going to Yosemite for one day or hoping over to Sardinia for 24 hours and trying to take in everything? For starters, there simply aren't enough hours in the day, and you would spend most of your time in the driver's seat and not enough out in nature. It's much better to see all there is in one area rather than zooming through only catching a brief glimpse, so pick the places you really, *really* want to see and concentrate on immersing yourself in everything those places have to offer.

**TIP**

Driving is tiring too, so allow yourself a little relaxation time before you get back behind the wheel.

# 2
# Building the Perfect Camper

Discover the different types of camper vans from Mercedes-Benz Sprinter vans to Volkswagen Caddys to the all-American RV to truck campers.

Determine how much you want to spend on your new four-wheeled home and decide if financing or buying outright is best for you.

Find out how to build your perfect camper van from choosing and laying your flooring to building the internal structure to adding insulation, cladding, windows, skylights, and even a hole for a chimney.

Understand what components you need for your electrical system and how to put it all together.

Determine what type of bed you want in your van and create useful storage solutions.

Connect up all the utilities you need to live off-grid: gas, water, and heating.

**IN THIS CHAPTER**

» **Costing out your new rolling home**

» **Discovering how to get the most out of your camper**

» **Picking the right vehicle**

» **Finding out how to deal with dealers**

# Chapter **3**

# Buying the Right Van

N ow that you've decided van life is for you, it's time to get over the biggest hurdle — buying your very own van. Just like choosing a house to buy or rent, there are so many different factors to consider when picking out a van, though thankfully, location isn't one you'll need to worry about anymore.

Far from being a case of "any old vehicle will do," in this chapter, I give you information and tools to help you purchase your first van — new or secondhand — as well as tips on picking the right van for you and successfully navigating the sneaky world of "the dealer."

## Knowing What You'll Spend on a Four-Wheeled Home

Money makes the world go round, but it is possible to travel around the world without bags of it stored away under your bed for that perfect van conversion. Still, when it all comes down to it, the initial budget you have to start your van life journey ultimately dictates what kind of vehicle you purchase and its overall condition.

Whether you have £3,000 or $30,000, there's a vehicle out there for you that will do the job perfectly. It's all about shopping around for the right van that fits your needs, but don't worry if you don't know your ProMasters from your pop-tops. By the time you get to the end of this chapter, you'll be able to walk into any dealership or up to any private seller and purchase a vehicle that's just right for you without any scary hidden dangers jumping out to surprise you.

# Saving for Your Van

So you've just made the decision that you want to purchase a camper. For the purposes of this section, I assume that you haven't spent the past four years saving up your wages just in case a future eureka moment strikes. The truth is, there are many ways to bolster your funds for your future trundling home. Perhaps your parents have sold the family home and given you some of your inheritance early, or maybe you're planning on taking on an evening job in order to store away the pennies.

**TIP**

I can imagine that at this point you're already raring to go and scouring the Internet for vans in your local area. The main tip I can give you here is to take a deep breath and relax; don't rush into this purchase like a bull in a china shop. Your initial idea on the perfect camper might change half a dozen times throughout this chapter alone, so take a step back and assess all the variables before you hit that "Buy Now" button.

Prior to purchasing my van, I was never very good at saving money. In a world of same-day delivery and online bargains tempting us in, it's hard to keep cash to one side and to stop buying those little extra things that we want but don't necessarily need. The trick I used was to keep my sights set firmly on what goal I wanted to achieve from my van life adventure. Remember the change of mindset I spoke about in Chapter 2? Well, I want you to stay in that frame of mind throughout the rest of this book and hopefully for the rest of your van life journey.

The first thing you need to do is to look at where you can start saving money. Now, I'm not talking about feeding the family bread and jam for the next six months or wearing four jumpers to save on heating, but you'll be surprised how quickly costs rack up.

Van life is about making sacrifices, some short term, some much longer. Can you live with two take-out meals per month instead of two per week? Do you need to keep purchasing those holographic marbles on eBay when you're about to move into a small space? Little changes like these can make a big difference on how much money you have left over at the end of the month, and it's all going toward something that could change your life forever.

Selling unwanted items is a great way of saving up for your van conversion too. By the time I moved into my van full time, the only furniture I had in my house was two camping chairs, and they were going with me in the van anyway!

Selling unwanted items doesn't mean pawning off your grandmother's priceless heirlooms or auctioning off your first-edition *Harry Potter* book. Think about things that you can live without in your new life, things that I like to call "dust absorbers." If you haven't used something for a long time and it's taking up space, then get it on your chosen online marketplace and add that money to the van life pot.

Speaking of pots, let's talk about banking.

Whether you're thinking about purchasing a van on your own or with a partner, opening a savings account at a bank with the ability to create specific savings pots, or accounts, is a great idea to visually see your dream becoming a reality each month. Online banks like Monzo or Ally are great for this. Centered around a mobile banking app experience rather than actual branches, online banks offer the option to make different labelled pots to syphon your money off into.

If you have the ability to create a separate savings pot, then get one labelled "Van Life" right away. There, that wasn't so painful, was it?

The next thing you need to decide on is how much of your wages you could comfortably drop into your savings account each month.

Don't leave yourself short for bills or everyday essentials, but if you've already started to get into a more minimalistic or thrifty way of thinking from reading this book so far, then you should be able to comfortably tuck at least a couple of hundred notes away each month toward your new lifestyle.

# Buying Outright versus Financing

Now, I know I have just spent the past few paragraphs giving you advice about saving up for your van and not rushing into a purchase, but I know that you may be itching to get on with buying a van and may have just skipped the previous section entirely.

There are pros and cons to both buying your vehicle outright and financing, and depending on your individual income and how you like to manage your finances, I imagine that one of these options will automatically seem more appealing than the other. Let's start with buying outright.

## Buying outright

If you've saved up your money and found the perfect vehicle, then buying outright gives you the peace of mind that you fully own your vehicle and don't have to worry about any other monthly costs coming out of your bank account each month. If you're the kind of person who doesn't deal well with lots of different transactions bursting from your account every month and likes to know exactly where your money is going, then I would advise this method every time.

## Financing

Financing is an option if you don't want to use up all your funds at once. For the purposes of this section, let's suppose you are working a full-time job while saving up for your van. If you know that you have X amount of cash coming in each month and can afford Y for the finance payment, then there's no reason not to purchase your van on finance.

TIP

If you're self-employed and will be using your camper for work, such as in a role as a nature trail leader or a forester, then you can always consult your accountant about offsetting these payments toward your tax bill at the end of the year too.

WARNING

Don't rush into putting a van on a credit card. Always borrow money responsibly and don't get yourself into any unwanted debt. If you feel uncomfortable financing, then be kind to your mind and save up the old-fashioned way.

# Deciding What You Need from Your Camper

Before you put pen to paper and start sketching out the build for your van, it's important to figure out what you need from your camper and whether you plan on living in it full time or part time. That doesn't mean to say that your plans might change in the future; I know people who have changed the layout of their vans three times while traveling. Still, if you do some prior planning now, you can spend less time parked outside hardware stores and more time parked up in nature.

In this section, I outline the different amenities and features to consider for full- and part-time van life with the goal of helping you to pick the right vehicle for your individual needs.

# Full-time home

If you've been bitten by the wanderlust bug hard, then the chances are you're considering purchasing a van for a full-time home. As someone who's spent four-and-a-half years living in a van as his full-time home, I feel like I've got a good idea of what worked, what didn't, and what I would have added if I had the chance to do the build again. The important word to focus in on here is "home." Just because you are downsizing into a small space doesn't mean that it can't feel like home or that you can't replicate many of the same features that you had back in your old life.

Think about the core things you need from a home:

>> Somewhere to sleep

>> Somewhere to cook

>> Somewhere to relax

>> Somewhere to use the bathroom

For many vanlifers, the last two are completely optional. For around a year, I didn't have anywhere to sit in my van other than on my bed. Still, for long-term living, these are four of the key areas you should focus on to help you plan out what you'll need from your space.

## Sleeping

Let's start with sleeping. Picking a van with enough space for a comfortable bed is a must. When your home is on wheels, you need to make sure you're well-rested before heading off on a long drive.

There's an age-old argument in the van life community about having a fixed bed versus a rock 'n' roll bed (one that folds into a sofa during the day). You'll see throughout the course of this book that I'm firmly on the side of having a fixed bed in your build, especially if you're living in your van full time. Knowing that your bed is ready-made for you to climb into after a long day of working or hiking out on the trail is one of the best things that makes a van feel like a home. The same goes if you fall ill, which I'm afraid to say you will at some stage, just like you would in a conventional home.

## Cooking

If, like me, you like to cook up good food and often cook for others, then implementing a well-thought-out cooking space into your build is a must. In many homes, the kitchen is the focal point of a home, and while it's possible to live long term in a small space, it certainly helps to have a vehicle that you can stand up in while getting your cook on.

TIP

One thing I've come to realize from years of van living is that the bulkhead wall is a great place to put your kitchen set up. With the sliding door directly next to the bulkhead, it's a great position for letting steam out when cooking and provides easier access to gas and water storage for filling up. Having a long worktop also makes for a suitable area for preparing food.

## Relaxing

How many of you stretch out on the sofa when you come from work or sit in your favorite chair and reach for a book? When I removed the wood-burning stove from my build (more on this in Chapter 12), I put a bench seat in its place the same day. Not only did this give me more storage space underneath, but it also provided a comfortable place to sit while writing articles on the road and when eating at my pop-up table.

TIP

Many people also use bench seating as a means of storing their portable toilet. I actually dedicated a whole cupboard to my porta-potty which doubled up as (you guessed it) more storage space, this time for dirty laundry.

## Using the bathroom

There's a strong chance some of you bought this book simply to find out what the deal is with going to the toilet in a van, which is why I've dedicated a whole section to it in Chapter 15. Again, "to poop or not to poop" is one of the hottest topics in the van life world; it's all something that we do, which makes it an important necessity to consider when planning your build. Sure, you can shower in gyms or wash in lakes using eco-friendly products, but not everyone feels comfortable squatting in a bush to do their business.

Remember the key theme for this segment: home. While it's possible to visit restrooms in service stations or plan on stops at local attractions so that you can do your ablutions, having a toilet available to use as and when you need it is a home comfort that I think you *definitely* need for full-time van living. Porta-potties are small, they don't take up much space in your build, and you'll thank me for this tip when it's raining outside and you need to "go" in the middle of the night.

While we're on the subject of bathrooms, I want to touch upon shower units. The chances are that if you're buying a ready-made camper either outright or on finance, it will come pre-fitted with a shower. I've spoken with lots of people who planned van builds based on "needing" a shower on board. And to be honest, it's not a crazy thing to think, is it? Your morning routine for most of your life so far will have undoubtedly involved having a shower; it's ingrained into us and therefore something that's hard to change.

There are many different types of shower units that you can get in your camper, some with retractable heads that store away and pull-around shower curtain setups to prevent your belongings from getting soaked. In all honesty, there are much better solutions for keeping clean on the go than installing a shower in your van. If you're reading this now and thinking, "no way, this guy's mad," let me explain. I lived in my van for 13 months here in the U.K. before heading out on a European adventure. For the entire four-and-a-half-year stint, I never went without washing, but I did it all without having a shower installed.

**TIP**

Gyms open 24/7 are the best answer for showering while living on the road. Get a subscription for a gym near you or a chain that has multiple branches in locations you might pass through. Whether you want to work out or not is up to you; the subscription fee is worth the endless amount of hot water you'll be able to bask in.

**REMEMBER**

If you want to have a shower installed in your van, you'll need to carry more water to compensate for what you're going to use. This will require underslung tanks for your fresh and wastewater, which increases your overall weight too. Not only that, but you will have to factor in more fill-up stops while out on the road, preventing you from going as far off grid as you might have originally liked.

While on the road, there are plenty of opportunities to use showers in service stations, truck stops, and "aires," which are free-to-use facilities often found in park-up spots throughout Europe. And of course, don't forget the delight of factoring in a visit to a natural hot spring, the best refreshing hot soak a vanlifer can get. Plus, if you travel with a solar shower bag, you can always fill it up with spring water to take back to your van for a more secluded wash using your back doors as a privacy shelter.

## Part-time home

Of course, van life isn't just about full-time travel. For vanlifers who have jobs that are unable to be carried out on the road, then the life of the weekend warrior or campsite holiday maker undoubtedly looks pretty appealing.

In my experience, there are two different types of people who use vans as part-time homes: the off-grid explorers who don't mind roughing it, and the luxury campers who like to get away from it all in comfort. It doesn't matter which one of these categories you fit into, but depending on which lifestyle suits you best will determine how much you put into your camper.

For many, the idea of jumping into a camper and heading up to the lakes or into the mountains for some good old-fashioned camping at a moment's notice makes for the ultimate weekend away. With a place to sleep and somewhere to store a single-hob burner and a cooler, these part-time vans tend to follow the function-over-form principle. Still, if you're not worried about having a dedicated cooking space or dining table setup, it gives you chance to get more creative with natural materials, seating arrangements, and storage for outdoor gear.

If you're planning on using a camper as a means of somewhere just to cook simple meals and sleep while out adventuring, I would still opt for a static bed to give you ample "garage space" in the back. Even in smaller vans, it's possible to store outdoor equipment such as inflatable paddleboards, bike frames, climbing gear, and more under your bed and out of sight!

If the idea of roughing it isn't your style, don't worry. Whether boondocking beside the ocean or hooked up to power at the local campsite, there are plenty of options available for those who want a home away from home that will take care of your every need. It doesn't matter if you're opting for a Winnebago Mercedes-Benz Sprinter conversion, a VW California camper van with plush leather interior and rock 'n' roll bed, or the million-dollar EarthRoamer, there's no reason why you can't have a camper with all the same amenities that you're used to using at home. Crank up the microwave, turn on the TV, or even put a load of washing on if you have the space.

# Van Life Isn't One-Size-Fits-All

Now that you've decided whether you're going to live in a van full time or part time, it's time to find out what size of camper is right for you. There are so many different styles, sizes, and wheelbases out there that it can seem like a minefield if you don't know the lingo. Luckily for you, I compiled a list of all of the different vehicle classes for you for reference. Don't worry, there won't be a test later . . . or will there?

>> **Class A:** These campers are the large touring vehicles you might see rockstars traveling in on the way to a gig. They are large busses with multiple rooms inside and what I would definitely class as luxury campers. This is not exactly the type of vehicle for an off-road adventure, but definitely one for a comfortable stay in the wilderness.

>> **Class B:** Class B campers are mostly what I will be talking about over the course of this book. This class covers all conversions made within the pre-existing dimensions of a panel van such as a Ram ProMaster or a Mercedes-Benz Sprinter (see Figure 3-1). This is by far the most common class for DIY camper conversions.

>> **Class C:** These campers are what I like to call "traditional" campers — think snowbirds driving to sunnier climates in their Winnebagos when the first frost hits. Class C campers, an example of which is shown in Figure 3-2, often have a sleeping area in the bulkhead over the top of the cab area and the telltale fold-out steps for entering the living area.

FIGURE 3-1:
My Class B
camper, hanging
out near a hot
spring in Spain.

FIGURE 3-2:
The traditional
Class C camper
spotted in the
wild.

» **Truck camper:** This type of camper, shown in Figure 3-3, is perfect for off-grid enthusiasts and usually consist of a removable camping pod with a pop-top roof that slots into the truck bed itself. I've spent a lot of time traveling the United States in a truck camper mounted on the back of a Dodge Ram and that setup never, ever let me down.

**FIGURE 3-3:**
A truck camper with over-cab sleeping quarters.

» **The All-American RV:** If you watch a lot of movies, then chances are good you've seen families hitting the road in an all-American RV. And trust me, they're just as big in real life as they are on the screen. These are the type of vehicles that you might see trundling up to Glacier Point in Yosemite or cruising down to Big Sur in the summertime. Check them out in Figure 3-4.

» **Classic camper vans:** Whenever I hear the term, "classic camper van," there's only one vehicle that springs to mind — the Volkswagen bus (see Figure 3-5), and specifically, the T2 Splitty that is still the symbol of the swinging sixties. These are most often the subject of restoration projects and can make for beautiful busses, though they often soak up money like a sponge due to continual repairs.

» **School bus:** If you're used to canal boat living, then a school bus might be a good option for a faster-moving tiny home. With more space and plenty of light, they make a great blank canvas for a full-time home.

**FIGURE 3-4:**
The quintessential all-American RV — the classic road trip vehicle on so many people's bucket lists!

**FIGURE 3-5:**
There is no vehicle more iconic and eye-catching than the VW T2 Splitty.

Vans also come in four wheelbase sizes: short wheelbase (SWB), medium wheelbase (MWB), long wheelbase (LWB), and extra-long wheelbase (ELWB). The *wheelbase* is the measured distance between the middle point of the front wheels and the middle point of the wheels at the back of the van. The longer the wheelbase, the more room you'll have inside the main body of the van to utilize for your conversion.

# Picking the Right-Sized Camper for You

You now know that van life isn't a one-size-fits-all kind of deal, so what sized camper should you opt for? Well, it all depends on what you want to get out of your van life experience and how often you're going to use your camper van. And then again, it's also down to personal preference. As I said earlier in the section on full-time and part-time homes, whether you view standing up at all times an essential feature or whether you prefer to go under the radar when boondocking will have a great effect on your decision whether to buy a small or larger van. In this next section, I touch on some of the most popular camper van styles for people carrying out conversions and the benefits they can provide.

## Small campers and pop-tops

| Pros | Cons |
|------|------|
| Easier to park | Less space for a shower and kitchen |
| Easier to heat up and more fuel-efficient | More messing around with adjusting interior spaces |
| Better for stealth camping while boondocking | Not as well-suited for family trips |

Small campers and pop-tops cover everything from minivan conversions and VW Caddys to VW California campers and the epic Sportsmobile 4x4. These are campers that many people would class as "day vans" — campers people take to the beach or the mountains for one or two days at the most.

There's one thing for certain: Small campers and pop-tops are certainly easier to park in everyday locations. I've taken both out on the road on different trips, and smaller campers can usually fit under height barriers that would otherwise thwart bigger vans like Ford Transits and Mercedes-Benz Sprinters. That means you can get a lot closer to attractions and lakefronts, which is perfect if you're traveling with cumbersome adventure gear in tow or want to avoid competing for a motorhome parking space in tourist traps. It also means you can get under height barriers at most supermarkets!

A pop-top camper is a camper van with a roof that pops up when stationary (see Figure 3-6). These campers can either have whole segments that push up or more commonly, a roof that pushes up into a triangular shape revealing canvas walls.

**FIGURE 3-6:**
The Ford Transit Connect camper with pop-top and awning may be the perfect impromptu forest park-up.

Both small campers and pop-top vans tend to make use of a rock 'n' roll bed setup in which the bed doubles up as a sofa throughout the day and folds out into a bed at night. While this creates more living space, it does reduce the amount of garage storage in the boot of the camper, so that's something to think about if you're planning on living in a van for a long time.

Still, the added benefit of buying a pop-top camper is that the pop-top gives you extra space for standing and fills the camper with more light. It just depends on whether you mind setting up and packing down your living area every time you park and set off from a camping spot.

**WARNING**

Keep in mind that in bear country, soft-shell pop-ups aren't allowed as bears can easily rip into them.

Some classic examples of vans in this range to look out for:

>> Fiat Scudo

>> Ford Connect

- >> Ford Econoline
- >> Ford Transit (MWB)
- >> Ram ProMaster City
- >> VW Caddy
- >> VW California

## Maxi-roof and long wheelbase vans

| Pros | Cons |
|---|---|
| Better suited for a full-time home setup | Harder to park |
| Easier to fit a shower and toilet setup | Costs more to convert |
| Full-sized static bed for impromptu snoozes | Harder to blend in while wild camping |

Maxi-roof and long/extra-long wheelbase vans cover most of the larger Class B panel-van conversions that you will have come across on your favorite van life Instagram channels. They're the base vehicle type for many conversion companies across the world and are solid foundations for DIY camper conversions. These vans might be harder to park and tougher to take down those windy country lanes, but they are certainly better suited for full-time living than smaller vans that are designed for stealth camping or compact living.

Larger vans like these are easier to cook in too; having that extra height to stand up in makes cooking more labor-intensive meals like roast dinners, risottos, and even dishes like sushi much easier. What's more, you have more space to include an oven as well as a gas burner.

For me, having the option of creating multiple "rooms" inside your van certainly helps it to feel more homey. By creating a bedroom nook, a seating area, and a separate kitchen space, a small vehicle can suddenly feel like three self-contained areas, which is perfect if you're traveling with a partner or family members and want to have time to yourself.

Some classic examples of vans in this range to look out for:

- >> Fiat Ducato
- >> Ford Transit (LWB)
- >> Mercedes-Benz Sprinter
- >> Peugeot Boxer

>> Ram ProMaster

>> Vauxhall Movano

>> VW Crafter

# Knowing What to Look for When Buying a Used Van

The phrase "try before you buy" has never been more applicable than when buying a used van. Okay, so you can't take a van home with you and try living in it for a couple of months before changing your mind, but there are lots of things you can do to ensure that you're buying a vehicle that is perfect for you and to get a feel for whether you're buying something that is mechanically sound.

**WARNING**

Believe me when I say that buying a second-hand van without testing it is dodgy territory indeed, especially if you're planning on taking said van to the other side of the world as your full-time traveling home.

I also want you to think about one other phrase that my cousin Kev told me repeatedly when I was young: If you buy cheap, then you buy twice. In other words, if you buy something that is so cheap that it seems too good to be true, then it often is, and you end up having to spend either more on repairs or buying a whole new vehicle altogether.

The main thing I'm concerned with is making sure that your hard-earned cash is going into the right vehicle. I know it would be impossible for me (or my cousin

Kev) to be there with each and every one of you while you buy your vehicles, but if you follow the advice here, then I should be able to sleep soundly at night knowing that you aren't getting ripped off or spending money on unnecessary items.

## How to approach dealers

We've all been there at some stage in our lives: You walk into a shop and a customer service assistant approaches to ask if you're okay and what you might be looking for. If you've ever worked in retail like me, then you'll know that every person who walks through the shop door could be the sale that gets you closer to your daily target, which means there's always an element of gentle persuasion involved.

A van dealership can be a pretty daunting place, especially if you're looking to purchase your first vehicle. You see a sales team wearing smart clothes and holding clipboards and suddenly you feel like a rabbit in the headlights. All thoughts about what you want, how much you want to spend, your name, and what you need from your vehicle might go out the window.

TIP

The important thing to remember is that dealers are just people. You don't need to worry about being pressured into a sale and you certainly don't need to settle for a vehicle that is on offer or isn't the one that you initially looked at. Stay true to your original ideas and remember that the customer is always right. That's you!

REMEMBER

One plus point of purchasing from a dealership is that you'll more than likely get a warranty or money-back-guarantee for a limited period after your purchase. This is more for anyone buying a camper van straight off the bat instead of purchasing a panel van to convert. However, once you start cutting holes in the vehicle, any warranty will be null and void, so make sure you're completely happy with your van before you make that first modification.

Here are a few tips that I have found helpful when initially approaching dealers — advice that you can take into any retail situation, vehicular or otherwise:

>> **Make a plan before you go in.** Before you walk into the dealership, it's good to have a plan of what you're looking for. Do some research on prices and availability so you're armed with all the facts.

TIP

It's a good idea to make notes for you to refer to, and there's no need to feel silly taking these with you into the dealership for reference. If you're nervous about speaking to dealers, then there's no reason why you can't write out all the questions that you want to ask beforehand and read your notes like a script. Do whatever feels most comfortable to you.

>> **Take your time and don't be pressured into a sale.** Whether you've got an idea about the van you want or are open to negotiations, you need to feel confident enough to be able to walk away and take time to think about your decision. You'll find this step applicable for both dealers and private sellers; if you're being pressured into a sale, just walk away.

TIP

Spend as much time in the vehicle as possible and ask as many questions as you can think of. Buying a van isn't something you can do during your lunch break or before the school run. Set aside a whole day to look around at different vehicles and take some test drives.

>> **Beware of add-ons.** When I used to work in a shoe shop, the team would be given incentives with regard to selling add-ons like leather cream and extra laces. Well, the same thing goes for dealerships and add-ons that you might not have initially expected.

REMEMBER

There will always be "something extra" that you haven't accounted for, especially if you're purchasing a new van. Whether it's a premium seat package, upgraded suspension, off-road tires, or an expensive roof rack, the list of upgradable options will be vast, so keep your wits about you and don't say yes to things you're not sure you will need.

>> **Keep an open mind.** Still, if you really don't know what type of van you want to purchase and just want some solid advice, then a dealership *can* actually be one of the best places to get all the facts at once. Retail workers must learn about their products to give the customer all the relevant information to clinch the sale (especially with the threat of a mystery shopper snooping around), so keep your mind open and soak up some knowledge.

# How to approach private sellers

The world of the private seller is an ever-changing rollercoaster ride where you're never really sure what to expect. In most cases, deals with private sellers will be based on secondhand vehicles that they have either owned for a number of years or bought with a view of doing up and flipping on for a profit.

Head to eBay, Facebook, Craigslist, Gumtree, ConversionTrader, or any automobile trading site, and you'll see thousands of potential vans listed by people throughout the country.

WARNING

Now, I don't want to fill you with fear, but a private seller doesn't have the same rules and regulations to follow that a respectable dealer does. I like to think that people are generally honest and can be trusted, but there's nothing to stop a seller from "forgetting to mention" something that is wrong with a vehicle and offering no money-back guarantee.

I will never forget heading to look at a van that a private seller had up for sale and taking a look around with him. The phrase "I've seen some sheds in my time, and this certainly isn't one of them" will stick with me until the end of my days. However, calling that van a shed would have been unkind to sheds and storehouses all over the globe. Not only was it covered in rust spots that had been hidden with metal paint in a slap-dash manner, but the engine also made a high-pitched noise like a supersonic bee.

Thankfully, I used the tips from the Seven-Point Foolproof Checklist for Viewing Used Vans later in this chapter to quickly determine that this wasn't the van for me. But for the moment, I want to leave mechanical musings to one side and talk about some pointers to think about when heading to the sale itself.

Here are some tips to bear in mind when heading to meet a private seller and things to look out for when making that deal:

>> **Safety is paramount.** This is a pointer I wish I didn't have to make, but nevertheless, it's important to remain safe when heading to make a potential deal. Always make sure to meet the seller in a public place wherever possible, and if the sale is being carried out at a person's private property, let others know where you are going and take someone along with you.

>> **Keep your cool.** I know how easy it is to get over-excited about the first van you see. You're standing in front of a vehicle that might be the one that kickstarts your van life dreams, and suddenly you're smiling and saying how perfect it is. This is a surefire notice to a seller that you're interested, which will make them less likely to come down on the price or less willing to share information about things that might be wrong with the van. Keep your cool and don't show all your cards at once.

>> **Don't be afraid to negotiate on the price.** Providing that you've managed to keep your cool, don't be afraid to come in with a lower offer than the asking price for the van. Remember that the worst thing that they can say is no, and the best thing they can do is either say yes to your offer or come in with a counteroffer. I talk more about this a little later in the chapter.

>> **Take a mechanic with you.** Following the Seven-Point Foolproof Checklist offered later in this chapter will give you all the tools that you need to successfully figure out whether a van is mechanically sound, but if you want that extra piece of mind and don't feel comfortable with your own judgment, then don't be afraid to ask a mechanic to take a look at a vehicle with you.

Perhaps you have a friend with mechanical knowledge, or it might be that your local mechanic would be able to take a look over the vehicle either at the seller's location or back at their workshop. We have surveyors look over houses and canal boats, so there's no reason why you shouldn't have a second opinion on a van if you're really not confident with your own decision.

# Negotiating a price

I know that it's easier said than done, but you should always try to negotiate the price when buying a vehicle, especially when purchasing a secondhand van. Now, I'll be the first to admit that I never used to be the best at this in the past. I'd see programs about people who asked for money off the price of display television sets and home appliances and just wonder how they had the guts to go against the grain like that. But, just like when buying a house, negotiating a price in the automotive trading world is something that's not only acceptable, but it's also expected. Let's look at how to approach the notion of asking for a price reduction.

**REMEMBER**

In these situations, "cash is king." Simply put, if you have the money in your bank ready to go and don't have to wait for financing or a loan to come through and can make a guarantee that you will purchase the vehicle there and then, you are more than likely to get a bit of money knocked off.

So how do you go about figuring out how much money to ask off the price? More often than not, the actual price the seller is looking for is easier to spot than you might have first thought. Usually, sellers are looking to round down to round figures or meet in the middle at one. For sake of argument, let's look at my first camper and its eventual sale as an example:

When I first bought the van that I turned into a camper, it was listed for £3,250. I (and when I say I, I mean my friend Andy) managed to get it down to a round £3,000. That extra £250 was what I like to call "a negotiation buffer" and clearly there for this exact purpose.

When I eventually sold the camper four and a half years later for £11,500, I used a similar method. My lowest price was always going to be £11,000, with that extra £500 being my negotiation buffer.

The general rule of thumb is that the higher the price, the more a seller will be willing to take off. As I said previously, the worst thing a seller can say is no, but don't insult them by going in at a ridiculous price. If the price is under £10,000 ($12,000), use a 5 to 8 percent reduction as a ballpark figure. If it's over £10,000, then consider a 10 to 12 percent reduction and work from there.

And remember, be confident, friendly, and at ease with the negotiations.

# The magic mileage

One of the questions that I get asked the most on a daily basis is "what mileage should I look for when buying a secondhand van." If you're not from the U.K. or the U.S., then the same question applies with regard to how many kilometers a van has done too.

I've always bought diesel vans and cars throughout my life thus far. As long as they're serviced regularly, they tend to last longer and can put away more miles than a petrol vehicle. My general rule of thumb (and this is one that I picked up from a friend who worked for BMW for many years) is that if you're buying a petrol vehicle, anything around the 70,000 miles/110,000 kilometers mark is fine. For diesel vehicles, I suggest looking for anything up to 100,000 miles/160,000 kilometers.

I've known Mercedes-Benz Sprinter vans that have been looked after to still be running at 400,000+ miles. Make sure to keep your van moving rather than sat still for long periods, service regularly, keep the engine healthy, and you and your mobile home will have lots of adventures for many years to come.

# Seven-Point Foolproof Checklist for Viewing Used Vans

There isn't anything more terrifying than viewing a used vehicle when you have no idea what you're looking for, that is, unless Dracula is selling the vehicle; then the whole thing would feel much scarier. What's more, it's incredibly easy to get duped into buying a vehicle by pushy sales advisors that might not be all that it seems. I recently looked at an incredibly clean car with a sporty leather interior up top that was sitting on a chassis that looked as though it had been pulled from the wreckage of the *Titanic*.

As I mention earlier, take your time when checking over a used vehicle and don't be embarrassed to ask for five or ten minutes to look over the vehicle without the salesperson standing over you. And as always, if you're being pressured into a deal, just walk away. Let's get down to business and take a look at the tips and tricks you'll need to make sure you get the right van the first time.

1. **Never buy a van while it's raining or buy a vehicle that is wet.**

   I thought that I would start off with a tip that many of you might not have considered before now. Water droplets are very good at masking small imperfections in a vehicle's bodywork. These imperfections can be anything as small as dents or scratches or something much bigger like a weld line.

   A friend of mine once went to look at a car being sold by a private seller who had "just washed it" as a favor to seal the deal. After insisting there and then that he and the owner dried it down with leather shammies, my friend spotted a weld line where two cars had been chopped and joined together. If it's raining, come back or ask to see the vehicle in a workshop. If the seller is genuine, they'll oblige without any problems.

**2.  Carry out a vehicle history check.**

Before I go to view any vehicle, I always do a vehicle history check online. Here in the United Kingdom, by entering the registration number into a free online vehicle registration number checker on the Government website, you can check to see the vehicles previous Ministry of Transport (MOT) results from each annual test. This is a good indicator as to whether the vehicle has any problems and if those problems are recurring or getting worse with age. It's also possible to check other information such as how many previous owners have owned the vehicle and whether the vehicle is currently taxed or declared as SORN (Statutory Off Road Notification). In the U.S., prospective buyers can use CARFAX (www.carfax.com) for similar information.

**3.  Look underneath the vehicle at the chassis.**

As I mention earlier, a van might look clean and new up in the cab or the main storage hold, but you need to get down underneath the vehicle to check out all the bits that make it tick.

A van can still have only done 60,000 miles yet be riddled with rust if it hasn't been looked after properly. It pays to get on the ground and pop your head underneath to check out the underside of the van, the suspension, and the exhaust for any signs of rust or corrosion. You don't need to be an expert to know if something looks off; if it's flaky and brown or you see any big holes, then steer clear.

**4.  Make sure the engine is cold before starting it.**

If a dealer or private seller tells you that they've got the van going for you before you arrive, then ask to come back another day. One of the oldest tricks in the book is to get the engine nice and warmed up before you arrive so that the vehicle starts straightaway, which is a sure sign of transmission problems or a poor battery. You can usually tell whether the van has been on for a while prior to your arrival by placing a hand on the bonnet, or hood. You'll also know when you turn the key too as the temperature gauge will shoot straight up rather than slowly rising over a short period of time while driving.

While you're in the bonnet area, open it up and scan over the engine. Check for any signs of corrosion on the battery and any rusty pipes or broken hoses.

**5.  Check the exhaust fumes.**

A good way to tell whether the engine is in good working order is to place your hand close to the exhaust while the engine is running.

Place your hand in the exhaust flow for around five to ten seconds and then remove it. If there are any black spots on your hands, then it could be a sign that the fuel lines need cleaning or that the engine hasn't been looked after.

Don't place your hand directly on the exhaust pipe as it may be hot.

6. **Pay attention to general wear and tear.**

You've probably heard horror stories about people changing the milage clocks on vehicles before selling them. I would like to think that this doesn't happen half as much as you might be led to believe, but there are surefire ways to tell how many miles a vehicle has done.

One good trick is to check the seatbelt. Pull it all the way down and look for any excess fraying and wear. Check the seat, the steering wheel, and the door catch too. As an example, if you're a buying an ex-delivery van that has a tattered seatbelt but only 40K miles on the clock, then alarm bells should be ringing.

The same goes for paint spots on the outside of the van. Many people don't have access to a proper paint spraying kit, so the chances are that any noticeable rust spots will be covered over with some Hammerite metal paint dabbed on with a paintbrush. If you can make a dot-to-dot picture on the outside of the van, then give it a miss and go back to the drawing board.

7. **Take the van for a drive.**

I don't mean sit in the passenger seat while the dealer or owner drives it either. It's important to get a feel for the vehicle you're going to be purchasing before you drive it away.

Make sure you drive without the radio on too. Even if you're a new van owner, you'll be able to sense anything that sounds off such as clunky gears or dodgy acceleration.

Take the van through a variety of scenarios; use the handbrake, test the indicators, get out and check that all the lights are working while the engine is on, and so on.

# Chapter **4**

# A Beginner's Guide to Fiberglassing

You've probably heard the word *fiberglass* bandied about from time to time, but what exactly is it, and how easy is it to use? When applied correctly, fiberglass can provide a quick and easy fix for holes and cracks that you might come across in your camper van build. It's cheap to buy, simple to use, and incredibly effective. In this chapter, you discover what fiberglass is, how to keep safe while using it, and how to apply it to the body of your van.

## Figuring Out Fiberglass

Fiberglass, or glass fiber matting, is essentially a type of plastic matting that also has little glass fibers inside of it, all fused together into sheets of different shapes and sizes. On its own, fiberglass is quite flimsy and can be rolled and folded, but when combined with resin and a special hardener, it becomes incredibly tough and forms a secure covering suitable for most repair jobs.

Fiberglass has lots of uses in the automotive and construction industries. You can even use it to fix boats and make canoes out of it, though in this chapter, I'm only concerned with how it can help you fix up cracks, seal pesky holes, and cover up mistakes in your camper van build.

## Knowing when to use fiberglass

Fiberglass can be used to cover over small holes and cracks, which makes it great for use in camper van conversions. This is especially true if you're buying a secondhand vehicle and one that might already be a camper that you're planning on ripping apart and starting a van build from scratch.

TIP

It's impossible to see the entirety of a secondhand vehicle before you buy it, but with any van build, it's always a good idea to take all the factory-installed panels out and check the bare metal and the fiberglass roof of your van if your vehicle has one.

Perhaps a previous owner installed a gas drop-out vent that you don't want to be there, or maybe there are screw holes in the floor that you would like to cover up. Fiberglass is perfect for little jobs like these as well as covering up cracks that might be letting water in . . . something that I discovered in my own build.

Unbeknownst to me, the van I bought from a private seller for my conversion had a crack in the rounded corner of the fiberglass roof, which was letting water into the insulation. This can cause all kinds of problems, not least of all a horrible damp smell, which it's why it's always best to strip your van down to its bare bones and inspect every nook and cranny before starting your build.

## Sourcing fiberglass

You can buy glass fiber matting and all the necessary components to complete repairs in your camper van separately, but for general ease, it's much simpler to buy a fiberglass repair kit that contains everything you need for the job. These kits usually come with a tin of resin, hardener, a small mixing cup, an applicator brush, a mixing stick, glass fiber matting, and gloves.

One such kit is the Isopon Fastglas Glass Fibre Kit, which costs around $20 (£17) and is available at your local hardware store or from all online retailers. This kit comes with enough glass fiber matting to cover about 6 square feet (0.5 square meters), though other branded kits and different sizes are available. It's a good idea to have a couple of these kits on standby; you never know when you might need to make a quick repair!

# Using Caution When Working with Fiberglass

Before you rip open that box and get started making repairs on your van's body, there are a few important health and safety notes you need to be aware of. All of this information is common sense, but that still didn't stop yours truly from finding some of it out the hard way.

**WARNING**

First of all, fiberglass resin gives off incredibly strong fumes and should not be sniffed or inhaled under any circumstances. When you're working with fiberglass, make sure you're in a well-ventilated area and avoid confined spaces as much as possible.

**TIP**

Second, *always* wear a mask and gloves. The mask isn't just for the smell of the resin; the glass fibers inside fiberglass are incredibly itchy and can irritate your throat. Wearing gloves will prevent any rashes on your hands from the small fibers and stop resin from getting onto your skin. If you're extremely sensitive to these fibers then you might find it useful to wear safety goggles to protect your eyes too.

**WARNING**

Third (and this is the one that I wish I'd used my brain for), don't try to wash up your plastic container with hot soapy water after you've finished. Why I thought this would be a good idea I do not know, especially without a mask on. The steam produced by the hot water hitting the sticky resin inside the container billowed straight up into my face, and I spent most of the day afterward lying in a darkened room feeling incredibly dizzy and nauseous from the fumes.

So please, *don't* make the same mistake!

# Repairing Holes or Cracks with Fiberglass

You're almost ready to make your first fiberglass repair. In most cases, it's best to park your van outside in an open space, or if that's not possible, then somewhere with plenty of ventilation will suffice.

Keep in mind that each layer of fiberglass takes about 30 minutes to dry before you can add a new coat, and a good repair may require up to three layers, so be sure to budget enough time. A good repair shouldn't need touching up, so just take your time and follow the simple instructions that follow.

Things you'll need:

>> A fiberglass kit

>> Paintbrush

>> Mask (I can't stress enough how important this is!)

>> Plastic container to use as a mixing bowl

>> An open space with plenty of fresh air

>> Extra pairs of protective gloves (just to be on the safe side)

**REMEMBER**

If you're working outside and need to get to areas high up or on the roof of your van, pick somewhere that has enough room to safely erect ladders. I converted my camper on a terraced street outside my house and was forever having to put the ladder up and down as cars drove past. Not only is this quite time consuming, but it's also potentially dangerous for both you and drivers passing by.

**TIP**

Keep an eye on the weather if you're working on repairs outside; you'll need a dry day without any chance of rain while your repair is drying. And don't forget, if you're working in a workshop through bouts of bad weather, then it's a good idea to keep all doors and windows open to let fresh air in throughout the repair process. And remember, always wear a mask!

Let's get started. To repair a hole or crack with fiberglass, follow these steps:

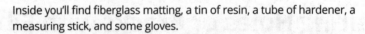

1. **Before you begin, make sure to clean the area around the hole or crack thoroughly so that there's no dust or debris anywhere.**

   When it's nice and dry, you're ready to start.

2. **Open up your fiberglass kit.**

   Inside you'll find fiberglass matting, a tin of resin, a tube of hardener, a measuring stick, and some gloves.

**TIP**

   Put the gloves and your mask on right away; you'll thank me for this later.

3. **Refer to the back of the box and measure out as much resin as it instructs you to use into a plastic container.**

   Use a container that you're not going to need for anything else again and especially not a bowl that you eat out of.

**REMEMBER**

   There's always temptation to pour out a lot of resin just in case you need it, but once the hardener is added, it can't be reused, so use it sparingly. You can always make more if you need to.

4. **Once you've measured out the appropriate amount of resin, add the appropriate amount of hardener (again, you'll find instructions for mixing on the back of the box), and then swirl the hardener around with your mixing stick.**

   It should soon turn pinky-red and start to feel more like glue.

   Now, it's time to cut your fiberglass matting.

5. **Using scissors (again, a different pair than the ones you use in the kitchen), cut out a piece that is large enough to comfortably cover over your hole or crack.**

   I recommend cutting about a half an inch bigger than the size you need for the repair to be on the safe side. Cut too big and you'll use excess mixture trying to stick it all down to the body of your van. Cut too small and your matting will sag through, ruining your chances of a solid and smooth covering.

6. **Dip a brush into the resin mixture and completely cover one side of your fiberglass matting in a thin layer.**

   Some fiberglass kits come with a tiny brush, but you're much better off using an old decorator's paintbrush, especially if you're using bigger pieces of matting for larger areas.

7. **Apply the fiberglass matting resin-side down onto your hole or crack.**

   Then, using the same paintbrush, gently dab the exposed side with a little more mixture until it's completely glued onto the body of your van.

**TIP**

   If the hole or crack that you're covering over is large, then don't go crazy with your mixture. You'll need to repeat the process a couple of times with more matting to really strengthen the repair up.

   Now it's time to take a break.

8. **Move away from your van and get some fresh air while you wait for your first layer to dry.**

   This should take around 30 minutes. Leave your side and rear doors open too if you can to let some of the smell out — it's strong stuff!

9. **Repeat Steps 5 through 8 as necessary.**

   If you're going to do something, then do it properly. I always recommend doing three layers of fiberglass to ensure all repairs are nice and strong.

**REMEMBER**

   If you have a crack somewhere that's likely to get a lot of exposure to water like the curve of a fiberglass roof, then make sure to repeat the process on the outside too. Just remember to always wait until one coat is dry before adding another.

**10.** **Once all the coats are dry, you're good to go.**

If the repair was on the outside or roof of your van, use a hose or watering can (or wait until it rains) to make sure that the repair is watertight. Then, once the area is dried off, you can paint over it for a nice finish.

**WARNING**

If you're planning on covering up a larger hole like a chimney exit, then there's a strong chance that fiberglass won't be suitable. For a chimney exit point repair, I recommend using a piece of ⅛-inch (3-millimeter) thick aluminum sheeting large enough to cover the hole, screwed down with self-tapping screws and rubber washers and sealed with a layer of Sikaflex sealant to make it watertight. For more information on how to do this, check out Chapter 12.

# Chapter 5

# Finding Your Footing with Flooring

One of the first steps in turning a metal box on wheels into a comfortable home is to keep that warmth inside where it belongs. There's nothing worse than a cold floor, a fact I discovered all too often in the early days of my van life experience. It might seem like a boring thing to consider, but the floor of your van is something you're going to look at every single day — depending on how messy you are with dirty laundry, that is.

In this chapter, I show you how to turn a bare metal floor into an attractive feature piece that adds character to your van. And most important, I make sure your feet thank me when it's cold outside. You're welcome, feet of the future.

## Insulating Your Floor

When you climb down from your bed in the morning or walk bleary-eyed across the floor to make a coffee, the last thing you want is sharp pains shooting up through your feet as your toes touch an icy floor. Yes, this is yet another thing that I found out the hard way. Still, me making all these initial mistakes and then learning from them is bound to save you a heck of a lot of time.

Just call me Captain Hindsight.

Naively, I thought that wooden boards and general-purpose insulation would do the job, but it was nowhere near enough insulation for colder climates. I had to resort to slippers at all times while camping in the mountains, which while practical, isn't a great look if you've got new friends coming round for a cup of tea.

By following the steps in this chapter, you'll be able to create a toasty floor space that will also help with sound insulation, all without taking up tons of space.

TIP

Some vans come with wooden boards already screwed down to the base of the van floor itself. If your van has these, then make sure you keep them to one side and congratulate yourself on a lucky win. If you just have a bare shell and no wooden boards, don't worry. I get to that in the coming sections.

# Installing Insulation and a Plywood Subfloor

It might look like a major job when you scan over all the instructions in this chapter, but trust me, laying your flooring is a piece of cake. It's a pain-free process from start to finish — so long as you don't accidentally glue your hands together along the way.

REMEMBER

The size and quantity of many of the items in the materials list that follows are based on the size of your vehicle. Softwood pine beams, for example, come in all different lengths, as do insulation board pieces. In these instances, I provide recommended thicknesses, but use your own judgment when it comes to buying the correct length for your chosen vehicle.

The first thing you need to do before even buying any flooring equipment, however, is to measure the entire floor space. Make notes on the following:

>> Overall width of your van

>> Overall length of your van

>> Width between the wheel arches

>> Measurements around the sliding door

**TIP**

Measure everything twice. You might notice that I repeat this advice as much as possible over the course of this book, and for good reason. Measuring multiple times is one of the best tips on how to prevent unneeded frustration and expense when building out your van.

The following instructions are based around installing vinyl flooring on top of a plywood subfloor, but the same principles apply for laying down pallet wood or parquet flooring.

Things you'll need:

>> Tape measure

>> Foam insulation board (such as Celotex or Kingspan)

>> Spray adhesive

>> Softwood pine beams (2-inches [50-millimeters] thick)

>> Polythene vapor barrier (optional)

>> Plywood (if you don't have an existing subfloor)

>> Jigsaw

>> Soundproofing tape

>> Gloves

>> Ruler

>> Marker pen

>> Stapler

>> Drill and drill bits

>> Screws

>> Workbench

Now that you have everything you need, let's crack on with prepping your van floor!

**1.** **Before cutting any wood or firing up your drill, check the floor of your van.**

If you bought a brand-new van, then chances are there won't be any holes or cracks in the metal floor. If, however, you're removing an existing wooden floor that was screwed into the base of the van or you bought a van that was previously used as part of a conversion, then now is the time to cover over any holes in the floor that might let in water and cause unwanted rust.

2. **If needed, cover over any holes in the floor of your van using the steps covered in Chapter 4 before you begin laying down your insulation.**

   When your repairs are dry, move on to Step 3.

3. **Lay soundproofing tape.**

   Van floors are usually made up of little peaks and troughs, almost like little metallic ripples (see Figure 5-1). Start by placing your soundproofing tape in the troughs along the length of the van to fill those gaps up and level out the floor space to prepare it for your insulation boards.

**FIGURE 5-1:**
Level your floor out a little by placing soundproofing tape in the troughs of your van floor.

The next step is to make a wooden frame for your insulation boards to sit in. Many foam insulation boards, such as Celotex or Kingspan, are already lined with silver general-purpose insulation, so they're ready to go without any excess faffing around.

4. **Make a frame for your insulation boards.**

   The thickness of your insulation boards determines the thickness of your pine beams. For the purposes of this instruction, I reference 2-inch (50-millimeter) thick Celotex insulation boards and 2-inch (50-millimeter) thick pine beams.

   As I mention earlier, the length of both your insulation boards and your beams depends on how long your van is, but both can be cut down easily enough to fit in any space. Refer to your measurements and size up accordingly to avoid waste.

REMEMBER

**5.** Once measured, cut your pine beams (long for the length of your van and small for the width) to make your frame.

When using a jigsaw, make sure you're cutting on a stable surface and wearing both goggles and ear defenders.

Here it is again — measure twice before making any saw cuts. You can always take extra wood off, but you can't add it back on!

**6.** Lay your pine beams down on the raised ridges of your floor lengthways.

You'll need around four or five pine beams.

**7.** Create a wooden grid on your van floor by laying smaller horizontal segments crosswise along the beams.

Imagine you're making three ladders. When finished, you should have made a wooden grid on your van floor ready for pieces of insulation to drop into.

**8.** Cut your insulation board to size.

You can cut Celotex relatively easily with a craft knife.

**9.** Using your ruler and marker pen, mark out the shape and sizes of each segment on your new wooden grid and cut your insulation boards to size.

**10.** Before placing the board into its specific segment, spray one side with adhesive spray to help secure it down.

**11.** Repeat with each segment of insulation board until the entire grid is filled in.

After laying down the insulation boards into your wooden grid, you're bound to find some gaps that you've been unable to fill. That's where expanding foam comes in.

**12.** Fill in the gaps with expanding foam.

Most vans aren't 100 percent square, unless you're converting a box van, then ignore that statement entirely.

This stuff is called *expanding* foam for a reason; you spray a little and it expands incredibly quickly, so don't go too hard on the trigger straightaway.

Expanding foam comes with a pair of protective gloves, and you should put them on straightaway. If the foam gets on your hands, then it's an absolute nightmare to get off. Likewise, tie your hair back out of reach and try not to get any on your face either . . . or your head if you're bald like me.

**13.** **Lay down a vapor barrier (optional).**

A vapor barrier is essentially plastic sheeting that goes underneath your plywood subfloor before you lay your chosen flooring. Simply roll it out and staple it down into your wooden grid to stop it from slipping and sliding around.

I included laying down a vapor barrier here as an optional step as some people swear by them and some people find no need for them whatsoever. If you live in a more humid climate, then this is a step you may want to consider for extra peace of mind.

**14.** **Create your plywood subfloor.**

Some vans come with a ready-made subfloor. In these cases, you can either use the existing subfloor or use the individual pieces as templates to draw around in order to create a new floor out of fresh plywood.

TIP

If your van hasn't come with an existing subfloor, don't worry. There are simple ways to create templates to make a floor, and one of the easiest is using carboard sheets. You can stick cardboard sheets on the floor of your van and then cut around intricate curves or spaces (such as the wheel arches). Once you have cardboard templates, transfer them to your plywood sheets and trace the template onto the sheets with a marker pen.

REMEMBER

Your floor is going to get a lot of action, especially if you like to do aerobics inside on a rainy day. I recommend going for 9- to 12-millimeter thick plywood sheets to provide a sturdy subfloor for your chosen flooring design.

**15.** **Using a jigsaw, carefully cut your plywood sheets to the shape of your van floor, moving slowly and following your pre-drawn lines.**

Don't push too hard when using your jigsaw; let the blade do the work and concentrate on making those clean cuts.

**16.** **Affix your plywood subfloor.**

There's a reason you made that clever wooden grid for your insulation boards to sit in. Once you've laid your subfloor down, use a wood drill bit to predrill holes down into your wooden beams.

**17.** **Using a counter-sinking bit, create a depression for your screw to sit into to avoid and lumps and bumps in your vinyl flooring.**

**18.** **When your plywood subfloor has been screwed down, fill in the depressions with wood filler and sand smooth for a level finish.**

Figure 5-2 shows the existing subfloor that I reused in my van.

**FIGURE 5-2:** After adding insulation, I screwed the subfloor back down and sealed over the joins with tape to make a smooth surface for my vinyl flooring to sit on.

# Deciding What Flooring Is Best for You

I said it before, and I'll say it again: It's surprising how much you look at the floor of your van. I know a floor is usually something you stand on in a conventional house or workplace, but in a small space, it's the little things like a floor design that stand out — especially if you have made a pig's ear of it.

Flooring is one of the first things you see when you open your camper door. Likewise, if you spend a lot of time sitting up on your bed, then you'll become pretty well-acquainted with your floor. And let's face it: If you're planning on setting up a social media account to keep your friends back home up to date with your adventures, then you want that floor to look like a work of art and not a back-alley pub in a dodgy part of the city.

When it comes to picking material for flooring, there are two obvious choices: vinyl flooring and wood. Following is an overview of both for you to get a feel as to which one might work best in your build.

## Vinyl flooring

It might seem like a bit of a cop-out to just lay vinyl flooring down, but trust me when I say that a lot of the vans with wooden floors you see on Instagram have done just that. It's amazing the effect that you can get with vinyl flooring these days, and it's supremely easy to fit and very cost-effective. It's also incredibly easy to clean too, as well as being lightweight. When you're making a van conversion, every gram counts.

Vinyl provides the look of a real wooden floor at a fraction of the weight, and you don't have to worry about sealing over the cracks to prevent food and dust from falling between wooden planks either.

You can buy vinyl flooring from most hardware stores or online, and there are a variety of different styles to choose from. I recently laid a parquet floor down on a narrowboat that took three days to fit, but convincing parquet vinyl could be laid down in a couple of hours.

## Natural wood

Of course, the pull of using natural materials inside a self-sufficient and sustainable tiny home is always going to be at the front of anyone's mind. While visiting one of the U.K.'s biggest camper van festivals, I met an artist who had painstakingly recreated a design on some tiles that he had seen onto wood, painting the design 69 times by hand to create a unique one-of-a-kind look. If you don't fancy going that in-depth, then stained pallet wood creates a great rustic vibe, as does parquet flooring.

REMEMBER

Don't forget that wood adds excess weight to your vehicle, so make sure to use thin boards wherever possible to keep that overweight down. (In the U.K., a camper van conversion driven on a normal license must be below 3.5 tons. Bear this in mind when adding wood to your build; it quickly adds up!)

TIP

If you're using wood for your van floor, make sure to sand it and seal it before adding any other elements into your build. Use a circular sander for a smooth finish and seal with a couple of coats of quick dry wood floor sealer. Give it a quick once over with a fine sanding pad afterwards and you're good to go!

# Laying Your Flooring

Remember how calm and collected you are when you're putting a new screen protector on your mobile phone? Well, that's the level of concentration I want you to have in this next section. The last thing you want is to make creases or dints in your flooring; mistakes like that will stand out like a sore thumb. While you're getting in the zone, here's a list of everything you will need to successfully lay your flooring. As I mention earlier, we're going to use vinyl flooring as that's what I installed in my van.

Things you'll need:

» Tape measure

» Vinyl flooring

» Vinyl adhesive

» Marker pen

» Craft knife

Now that you've collected everything together, let's start measuring your vinyl and preparing to make that first cut.

**1. Cut your flooring to size.**

If you're plumping for vinyl flooring, then it's usually possible for a shop to cut a sheet to your overall floor surface area. Just like when you're cutting wood, make sure your measurements are spot on. It's always easier to cut extra off if you're not confident about your measuring skills than it is to add it on if you measure too short.

**TIP**

It doesn't matter if the raw edges of the vinyl flooring meet the edge of your van walls as your cladding will eventually cover these up.

**2. Lay the vinyl down in your van before sticking it to your floor.**

Make sure that you do a dry fit before you stick your flooring down to your subfloor. Not only is this a good idea to make sure that your flooring will fit neatly, but it also gives you a chance to mark out where you will need to make slits for your wheel arches.

**3. Mark out where you need to make slits.**

Rather than pre-cutting the wheel arch spaces beforehand, it's a good idea to make little slits in the vinyl around the wheel arches so you can press it down around them, making it easier to slide over the bumps and create a tidier finish.

**TIP**

This might seem a little drastic, but trust me, it's much easier for you to make the floor look neater with a craft knife later on as long as your vinyl is lying flat against the main floor of the van. And as I mention earlier, cladding will cover over most of the raw edges, so don't worry too much if you mess up at this stage.

**4. Apply vinyl adhesive.**

At this stage, your vinyl flooring should be laid out flat on the floor of your van and tight up against your wheel arches thanks to the slits you made along your marker points.

5. **Lift one half of your vinyl lengthways and lightly fold to expose the underside of the material.**

TIP

You don't want to crease the vinyl flooring, so make sure not to fold over completely or press down on the bend in any way.

6. **Using your vinyl adhesive, spray the exposed underside and then return it back to its original position, pressing the flooring back down onto your subfloor as you go.**

7. **Repeat the same process with the other half of the vinyl.**

8. **Leave to dry.**

That's all that you can do right now. It's time to leave the floor to dry, and it's always a good idea to put something on top to help the vinyl bond with your subfloor. I covered my floor with packs of cladding overnight to help the sticking process, but if you haven't bought your cladding yet, then weights or camping equipment will do the job just fine.

# Adding Finishing Touches to Protect Your Flooring

Think about all the times you will be stepping into and out of your van once it's completed. The chances of you scuffing exposed edges of vinyl flooring are pretty high, so it's a good idea to protect those edges as soon as your flooring has stuck down securely.

The answer: *aluminum floor trim.* This can be picked up in various lengths and thicknesses from most hardware stores. Most pieces attach view a few screws, though some affix via adhesive tape. When using aluminum floor trim, simply attach a length of it to the exposed edges of your flooring at any door points, most commonly the sliding and back door entry areas, and you'll be good to go.

TIP

Another useful tip for anyone opting for a wooden floor is to use a quick drying floor varnish. Just your common-old-garden unbranded variety from the local hardware store will do, but just make sure that it's fast-drying; otherwise you'll be messing around for ages. Apply it using a paint roller, leave to dry, and then apply again, following the coverage guidance on the back of the pot. When finished, sand it down lightly with a fine sanding pad, such as 240 grade, before standing back and admiring your handiwork.

# Chapter **6**

# Building Your Internal Structure

Your flooring is in (and looking pretty good if you don't mind me saying), which means it's time to start building the wooden internal structure that you'll use to screw your cladding or boarding into. Things are about to start taking shape right before your eyes!

In this chapter, you find out what tools are needed to complete most of the wood-working tasks in your build, and then how to use them to create your internal wooden ribcage (which, once completed, might feel like being inside Moby Dick's stomach . . . if his ribs were made of wood, that is). You also discover how to build a false wall, how to prep your wall for building a cupboard, what general-purpose insulation is, and the benefits of cement board when installing a log burner.

## Getting the Right Tools

My mum has always told me that "if something is worth doing, then it's worth doing properly." There are many variations to this adage, some with Yorkshire slang that unfortunately I can't put into print, but I'm sure you get the general idea.

When you set out on a journey to make your rolling home, it's important to have the right tools for the job. It might seem a little daunting to go out and spend money on buying drills and jigsaws when you've never had any experience in the subtle art of DIY before, but I guarantee this won't be the last time you use power tools throughout your van life adventures.

**REMEMBER**

Just like when living in a traditional house, you might want to make changes to certain areas or repairs if you're a little heavy-handed, so it pays to purchase quality equipment.

Let's take a look at the tools that you will need to build the internal structure of your van and that will be useful throughout your van build as a whole.

# Drill

While it's easy to buy a cheap drill, this is one tool you don't want to skimp on. You'll use your drill not only to affix wooden beams to the metal ribcage in your van, but also to put up cladding or boards, cut holes in your floor using a hole saw, and many more crucial jobs both before you set off and while you are on the road.

I recommend you spend around $70 to $100 (£59 to £84) on a drill. Look for a drill with multiple speed settings, a lightweight design, and spare batteries so you don't have to stop when one runs out. I prefer using drills by Dewalt or Bosch.

# Drill bit set

Throughout your van build, you will be drilling into wood, metal, and stone if you're fitting a log burner, and using a variety of screw sizes to fix everything together. Rather than buying specific drill bits for every job, it's worth getting a sturdy drill bit set boasting multiple sizes to cover all aspects of your build.

**TIP**

If you're adding cladding to your walls, then you will likely go through multiple 3-millimeter wood drill bits. Sometimes they snap, and sometimes they just disappear off the face of the Earth with the drill bit genie or cladding goblin, so grab a pack and keep them in a safe place for when you need them.

# Countersink drill bit

You might get one of these in your drill bit set, but if not, a countersink drill bit is a piece of the kit you need in your arsenal. A countersink drill bit looks a little like a miniature mining drill shaft and is used to make depressions for your screws to sit in so that they sit flush with the surface of your wood.

## Screws

Screws come in all shapes and sizes. Essentially, screws are screws, but you'll use shorter ones for putting up cladding and longer ones for attaching cupboards together. For your internal structure, you'll need multipurpose screws long enough to get through multiple wooden beams, especially when making a false wall.

TIP

If you're putting up boards or cladding, bronze or gold screws blend in nicely with the color of the wood, especially when the wood is stained.

## Easydrive self-drilling wafer screws

I say "screws are screws," but these little things are lifesavers. Easydrive screws have a special tip that can screw straight into metal without drilling a pilot hole, which is useful when you're doing a lot of drilling into metal van parts. Grab a few packs in different sizes; you use 4-millimeter screws for most of the work in this chapter.

## Jigsaw

Like a good drill, getting a solid jigsaw that will be able to withstand some long stints in the workshop is crucial for your van build. You will be using your jigsaw to cut through wood and metal, so it's important to get a model that has a quick-release blade system to make changing those blades much simpler.

If you have the money, a Makita cordless 18-volt jigsaw is a good bet as, with a cordless jigsaw, you won't need to worry about being near a plug socket or trailing wires across your workshop or across the pavement in the front street. (If that last one sounds niche, that's because that was my working setup.)

TIP

If you're building on a budget, the Bosch PST 700 is also a great jigsaw with a sturdy quick-release system.

## Jigsaw blades

You will use lots of different jigsaw blades throughout the course of your van build. To build out your internal structure, you're mainly going to be cutting straight edges in pieces of timber, but as you progress with your build, you'll be chopping through metal, cutting cladding, and sizing up lots of different thicknesses of wood for different jobs.

Grab a couple of packs of jigsaw blades. Bosch offers a great set with multiple blades designed to cut different thicknesses of wood and other materials such as plastic and metal.

TIP

When cutting cladding, use a fine-toothed cladding blade. These will blunt after a while and might even break, but don't plump for a larger-toothed hardwood blade as it will just split the thin cladding. I know it can be tempting to just crack on with what you have when parts are missing, but you will only make more work for yourself in the long run, so stock up on jigsaw blades in case you need to change them midway through a job.

TIP

When cutting through fiberglass, use a fine-toothed metal blade made for cutting aluminum. The finer the tooth, the cleaner the cut will be.

## Tape measure

A tape measure could be the most important tool you use throughout the course of your van build. I know that's a little like saying that the pen is mightier than the sword, but it's true (on both fronts).

REMEMBER

Measure everything twice, three times, if possible, to avoid making mistakes when you're cutting and putting everything together.

TIP

As with the tools I discuss earlier, it's worth spending the money to get a reliable tape measure. You can't go wrong with the Stanley FatMax, a sturdy tape measure with a three-rivet hook that moves to compensate your 0-millimeter measurement accordingly whether you are taking measurements on the outside or inside edge of an object or surface.

## Masking tape

Now masking tape *really is* masking tape, so you don't need to get too much into the nitty-gritty here. Masking tape comes in handy when jotting down measurements, labeling beams for certain sections — the works. Don't just keep all your measurements in your head; write them down regularly.

## Spirit level

I'm not suggesting you perform a séance and increase the number of spirits around you to help you complete your build (although that wouldn't be a bad idea when working in the rain). A spirit level, also called a bubble level or just a level, is a useful tool for making sure surfaces are straight. If you have never seen one before, they are thick rulers with a vial of fluid in the center. The vial contains a bubble and is marked with two lines. When your surface is straight, the bubble sits in a central position between the two lines.

# Picking and Sizing Wood for Your Ribcage

Now that you have your power tools, screws, and trusty tape measure, the first step in building the main internal structure inside your camper is to pick the wood to use for your ribcage. In essence, the internal structure is the skeleton that will hold the main bulk of your build together. As well as providing a place to screw cladding or boards into, this structure also acts as an anchor for cupboards, spice racks, and other hanging objects you might place into your build.

**TIP**

I say *hanging objects* because I added a hanging fruit basket in my build to help save space — it was a real useful item that looked nice too. The fact that it played host to crisps more than fruit is inconsequential.

Unless you're converting a box van, chances are good your walls have a slight curve to them. That's why I suggest using softwood pine beams that have a bit of bend in them. Pine is flexible yet strong and doesn't need pre-treating before you start, and it's also cheaper to buy than cedar or Douglas fir.

Picking wood for your van build isn't a one-size-fits-all type of affair, a phrase you will undoubtedly get sick of me saying as you go through this book. It's time to grab that tape measure and figure out what size beams you need for your van to avoid excess wastage.

**TIP**

As a reference point, I converted a Vauxhall Movano maxi-roof van, which is of a similar size and shape to a Mercedes-Benz Sprinter or a RAM ProMaster. I bought pine beams with measurements of $^{11}\!/_{16}$ inches thick × 1¾ inches wide × 94 inches long (18 millimeters × 44 millimeters × 2.4 meters).

Here's how to determine the size of beams you need:

1. **Measure the height of your van from your subfloor to your roof.**

   You might have done this already before you purchased it, but knowing how high your van is will give you an idea as to the length of beam you can buy, how many cuts you will need to make, and whether offcuts can be used in different areas. Thinking about wastage will help to keep costs down too.

2. **Measure the width of the metal ribs inside your van.**

This will determine the width of your pine beams. You want enough space for the beam to sit on the metal rib without overhanging excessively and enough room for drilling and screwing into the metal behind it. The wider the beam, the easier it will be when it comes to securing your chosen covering to hide your insulation, be it pallet wood, boards, or cladding.

3. **Consider the thickness of your proposed beam.**

The thickness of your beam added to the thickness of your cladding ultimately determines how far your walls eat into your living space. That might not seem like such a big deal, but every millimeter counts when you're living in a tiny house.

REMEMBER

When it comes to insulation and actually adding your choice of wall material, rockwool is much easier to tamp down into smaller spaces. Celotex boards have a fixed thickness, which will also determine how thick your pine beams need to be, so keep this in mind when you are wandering around your local hardware store. Don't get too bogged down with this just yet, though. I cover all the various types of insulation in Chapter 10.

To give you an idea of how many packs of beams I used in my van, I bought five packs of ten pine beams. Fifty beams might seem a little excessive, but considering you can use these beams for your floor and false wall, they soon get eaten up!

TIP

Before you move onto the next step in building the main internal structure inside your camper, you need to take some time to think about what insulation method you're going to use before you start affixing your wooden ribs to your van. For example, if you are going to use general-purpose insulation, you need to add it to the sides of your van before you fit the ribcage.

For my conversion, I used general-purpose insulation followed by glass mineral wool. If you opt for silver-backed insulation board like Kingspan or Celotex, then you won't necessarily need to use general-purpose insulation and you can skip right ahead to "Creating the Ribcage." If you want to bookmark this page and skip ahead to Chapter 10 to discover more about different types of insulation, then go ahead; I'll wait here for you until you're done.

# Adding General-Purpose Insulation

If you've ever seen camper conversions in process on the Internet that look like they have taken inspiration from the inside of a spaceship, then that's more than likely because of general-purpose insulation. Products like ThermaWrap (Europe) or Reflectix (U.S.) are easy to come by, cheap, and a great base layer to kickstart turning your metal box on wheels into a cozy home. General-purpose insulation is basically bubble wrap with silver foil on either side, and it's the first form of insulation you're going to add to your build.

But why do you need to use general-purpose insulation? What does it do?

Well, you know how when you're using tin foil in cooking you should put the shiny side on the *inside* to help keep the heat from escaping your little food parcel? Well, this super silver-backed insulation is great for reflecting heat particles looking to make a quick getaway out of your van walls back into your living space.

Thermal energy moves in one direction — hot to cold. If you want to get really fancy, this is the main point raised in the first statement of the second law of thermodynamics. We don't need to use big words here though; all you need to know is that ThermaWrap, Reflectix, or other brands of general-purpose insulation significantly reduce thermal energy created inside your van from drifting out into the colder temperatures outside your camper.

While it's pretty clever stuff, ThermaWrap isn't something you can rely on solely for all your insulation needs; you use it in conjunction with other materials.

## How much general-purpose insulation will you need?

If you haven't already, measure the height and width of your van to get the overall area of your living space. This will give you the exact amount of space that you need to cover with your general-purpose insulation.

I know I just said *exact amount,* but if I'm being honest, these things are never exact. There may be instances when you rip sheets of insulation or cut them wrong, and times when you don't account for the wheel arch or that space in the bulkhead where the tape just won't stick. Add an extra couple of yards/meters onto your calculation when it comes to working out how much general-purpose insulation to buy, or grab an extra roll to be on the safe side. If you do end up with extra, there's bound to be someone in your neighborhood or someone you meet on your travels who could put it to good use!

## Installing general-purpose insulation

Installing general-purpose insulation couldn't be simpler. Just look for a bare metal surface inside your van and stick foil to it — it's that easy!

Things you'll need:

>> General-purpose insulation (such as ThermaWrap or Reflectix)

>> Adhesive spray

>> Aluminum tape

>> Scissors

>> Safety equipment (gloves and mask)

Here's how to add general-purpose insulation to the inside of your van:

**1. Using scissors, cut a piece of general-purpose insulation to fit in a specific section of your van.**

You don't need to worry about cutting it completely accurately so that it slots in perfectly; you'll probably end up layering some sections over each other and cutting little slivers to fill in any gaps. Just make sure you seal any joins with tape in Step 4.

**2. Spray one side with adhesive spray and then press it lightly into place onto your chosen surface.**

WARNING

Stick on your mask and gloves for this bit as spray adhesive can be harmful if inhaled. If you can, spray any pieces out in the open and not in a confined space.

**3. Run your hands lightly over the side facing you to make sure that every part of the insulation is stuck down securely.**

**4. Cover any joins with aluminum tape.**

Aluminum tape is easy to get hold of from most hardware stores or online and helps to cover up joins between pieces of foil neatly and with a shiny surface.

TIP

If in doubt, just cover everything metal in general-purpose insulation. That includes the space above your cab, your wheel arches, and the inside of your van doors behind the door cards.

# Creating the Ribcage

Okay, now that you have your wood picked out and added any general-purpose insulation you might need, it's time to pick up those power tools and start building that ribcage.

It should go without saying at this point, but remember to take your time when using power tools, both for making sure your cuts are straight and accurate and to keep your body parts on your body where they belong. It's hard to attach wood back together after you cut it off, and even more so a finger, so take your time so I don't lay awake worrying about you at night!

If you skipped ahead and haven't done any planning as to where you want certain parts of your camper build to go — the kitchen, seats, storage, and so on — now is a good time to plan this out. Knowing what layout you want will help when figuring out whether you're going to add a door or a window hatch into your bulk-head wall and also for placing horizontal support beams for you to screw cupboards into if you decide to go for overhead storage.

## Using your van's metal skeleton

Here's how to install your pine wood ribcage in your van:

1. **Measure the height of each metal rib piece inside your van.**

   Notice I said *each metal rib piece* and not the entire height of the van. This is because some vans have separate ribs for wall and roof pieces that might be set back from one another. Hopefully, you can go straight up to your roof with one piece of pine, but don't worry if you can't. I discuss what to do in this scenario in a minute.

2. **Using a 4-millimeter wood drill bit the same thickness as your easydrive screws, make a minimum of four pilot holes up the length of your beam.**

   I highly recommend using easydrive screws when affixing your wooden beams to give you that helping hand when screwing into the metal of your van.

3. **Using your countersink drill bit, make a depression for your screw head to sit in so it sits flush with the wood.**

4. **Pushing the beam against the metal rib, use an easydrive screw to drill into the wooden beam.**

5. **Pushing the beam against the wood with one hand, drill an easydrive screw through your pilot hole and into the metal rib behind.**

   This is definitely easier if you can have someone else bending the beam while you drill into it. If you're converting a van on your own, call a friend and pull in a favor or two by getting them to help you.

   If you want to use all-purpose screws here, make a mark through the pilot hole on the metal rib of your van, remove the pine beam, and drill through the metal rib using a corresponding metal drill bit the same size as your wood drill bit.

**6.** **If you are planning on installing overhead cupboards in your kitchen area, add horizontal beams in a similar fashion to the horizontal ribs passing between your vertical beams (see Figure 6-1).**

This gives you a solid surface to screw brackets for cupboard or shelves. Use the rib positions when designing your cupboard as they will automatically give you a predetermined height for each unit.

FIGURE 6-1:
Adding wooden
beams to the
metal ribs on
your van wall.

TIP

There might be an instance where you need to bridge a gap or create an extra beam to attach onto, the latter being something I had to contend with having bought a van with a fiberglass roof and no metal rib above the back doors to attach a pine beam. These two scenarios are why you should always keep your offcuts handy. I ended up creating a wooden beam to attach my cladding onto by using three offcuts from the bedframe I was sleeping on at the time all cut to the same size with a piece of pine wood screwed into the top of them (see Figure 6-2). I then screwed each block into place using two easydrive screws through the metal lintel above the back doors to prevent them from pivoting, and that created a surface for me to screw my roof cladding into.

The point I'm essentially making here is that sometimes, with all the skill in the world and all my hindsight to aid you, you still have to get a little creative to overcome some problems, whether that's creating new wooden beams or inserting blocks of wood into slots in your metal ribcage in order to bridge the gap from your van walls to your van roof. All vans are different, and many require you to "work with them." As I say earlier, keep all your offcuts in a bucket; little pieces of cladding come in handy all the time, so don't throw anything away until you're definitely sure it can't be used.

**FIGURE 6-2:**
The roof beam I fashioned out of offcuts so that I had something to screw my roof cladding into. The flat vertical pieces were then used to screw cladding in to box off the back of the recess above the back doors.

## Drilling into your roof

It goes without saying that drilling into your roof can be risky business. One false move or a slip of your hand, and you've turned your van roof into a colander, which is only useful if you're considering having a shower indoors during the rainy season.

**WARNING**

Use as small a screw as possible when screwing into your roof beams. It needs to be big enough to pass through the thickness of your pine beam so it doesn't fall from your roof, but not too big that it passes through the roof itself. Having a metal mohawk sticking from your roof might seem cool if you're into '80s punk bands, but it's bound to attract unwanted guests . . . like lightning bolts!

Okay, now we've got that covered, let's check out how to make a false wall.

# Building a False Wall

Whether or not you build a false wall depends on the design of your living area and what you are planning on doing with the bulkhead area of your van. I used the bulkhead area to make my kitchen and place my wood burner, and later a comfortable seat to look out at the world while writing once I removed the wood burner and installed a diesel heater (more on that later).

Some vehicles incorporate the cab area of the van into the main body of their build, either keeping the space open or creating a cut through from the cab into the living space. Depending on whether or not you have a bulkhead wall blocking the cab from the back of your van, creating a wall in this area might be incredibly easy or require a little more thought.

The *bulkhead wall* is essentially a removable piece of metal bolted into place in your van. In a typical cargo van setup, it stops all the goods in the back from shunting forward into the cab, and prevents the driver from being squashed by a thousand boxes every time they brake at a set of lights.

You have three options available if you have a bulkhead wall in your van:

>> You can keep the bulkhead wall intact and screw beams directly into it for cladding/boarding.

>> You can remove the bulkhead wall and open up the entire cab space.

>> You can remove the bulkhead wall and build a false wall in its place, with the choice of implementing a door and/or window.

The bulkhead wall had already been removed from my van when I bought it, so I chose to go for option three (see Figure 6-3). I wanted to keep the cab separate and use it as another storage area when I wasn't driving, and I didn't want to have shoes and coats on show that made the living space look cluttered.

**FIGURE 6-3:**
My false wall halfway through construction complete with prep for installing the wood burner.

If you can't see the mess, it doesn't exist, right?

Building a false wall gives you the option to create an insulated wall as thin or as thick as you like while adding in a window, hatch, or door into the main cab area. The premise for all three is essentially the same: You need to mark out where you want your opening to be and build your false wall frame accordingly.

TIP

If you're thinking of building a door into your cab area, you will have to remove the double passenger seat and replace it with a single seat. This wasn't something I was too bothered about, and having both passenger seats available meant I remained optimistic about making friends on the road . . . and it's always good to be optimistic!

Adding a door or some kind of hatch is also a good safety feature if you want to drive off without having to leave your vehicle. Hopefully, you will never find yourself in this situation while out traveling, but there may well be a time where you don't feel safe and want to move off for your own peace of mind. I did push myself through the little hatch that I made on a couple of occasions and drove off when people were playing music incredibly loudly next to me at 3 a.m., so I'm speaking from experience here. If you are 100 percent against any kind of opening, then I'm not here to force you. Just mull it over throughout the rest of the chapter and don't dismiss it out of hand; it could come prove useful.

TIP

By making a false wall all the way to your roof, you can create a little cupboard space out of your bulkhead storage area — the shelf above your cab area that's accessible from the living area of your build.

TIP

I originally integrated something called cement board into my wall, which is a non-combustible board that is often used behind fireplaces. Sometimes known as HardieBacker or Durock, this board screwed into my false wall frame and sat flush with the cladding on the rest of the wall. The original plan was to use this for its actual purpose as a base for creating a tiled fireplace, but in the end, I liked the simple aesthetic of the grey board and left it as is. You can always add tiles directly to cement board to make it feel more like a fireplace and add an extra feature to your living space if you fancy getting out the grout and giving it a go.

## Creating your false wall frame against a bulkhead wall

Making a false wall frame might feel incredibly easy now that you've spent so much time screwing beams into ribcages. Use every metal rib you can when making a frame against your bulkhead wall. Place at least one extra horizontal wooden beam above the bulkhead shelf to help secure your wall as it builds up from your floor. This will also act as the anchor point for your bulkhead cupboard hinges.

Here's how to make your false wall against the bulkhead wall:

1. **Use a spirit level to make sure your bulkhead wall is straight.**

   If your vial is in a central position, then you have a straight surface to work with. For the purpose of this section, I assume your bulkhead wall provides a straight measurement when using your spirit level. If your bulkhead wall isn't straight, you may have to add a beam onto the floor at the base of the wall in order to get a straight measurement. Play around with your spirit level and use those offcuts as and when you need to.

2. **Measure and cut vertical beams to screw into your bulkhead wall, and mark out an area for a bulkhead shelf cupboard.**

   These beams won't all be the same size. Due to the curved nature of your van walls, your beams will get bigger toward the middle of your van. You will need around six beams in total running vertically up your bulkhead wall.

   TIP

   Use masking tape to label the beams 1 through 6 moving left to right so you know which beam goes where. You will need a horizontal beam as close to the top of your roof as possible spanning the width of your van in order to secure your vertical beams into place over the bulkhead storage area. Call this the roof beam.

   TIP

   If you opt to make a bulkhead storage cupboard, then leave a rectangular section of your bulkhead storage section free of pine beams, stopping just below the storage shelf itself. This will form the dimensions for your cupboard door, with the horizontal beam at the very top of your wall running across the width of your van acting as the perfect spot for your cupboard hinges to sit. If you plan to cover your false wall with smooth boards that you're going to paint over or otherwise decorate, making your cupboard door is as simple as measuring the open space and cutting out a piece of board to those exact measurements. If you plan to add cladding to your false wall, check out how to create this door in Chapter 10.

3. **Drill pilot holes into your wood using a wood drill bit the same thickness as your chosen screws and countersink.**

   You're doing the same thing here as when you attached pine beams to the metal ribbing of your van.

4. **Using easydrive screws, attach your beams to the bulkhead wall.**

   Remember to add pressure to your beam when screwing in so it doesn't shift while drilling.

Your bulkhead wall is now ready for adding cladding or boarding and any cement board if you are considering adding a log burner into your build. I touch on how to add cladding in Chapter 10, so just hold tight for now.

TIP

If you're adding insulation in-between your horizontal beams and are thinking about adding a log burner to your setup, just remember to leave the space behind your cement board insulation-free.

## Creating your false wall frame without a bulkhead wall

The premise for making your false wall without a bulkhead wall isn't all that different from creating the frame against one. In essence, you bypass the bulkhead wall completely and make your own wall by attaching pine beams to anchor points in your floor and a wooden beam screwed into the bulkhead shelf.

TIP

Use every metal rib you can when making a false wall. Above the bulkhead shelf you should find places where you can add extra wooden beam pieces to help secure your wall frame as it raises up from your floor.

REMEMBER

I can't stress enough how important it is that you take the time to make sure your wall is straight by using a spirit level.

Things you'll need:

>> Marker pen to mark points on your floor

>> Thick wooden beam ideally 3½ to 4-inches (90 to 100-millimeters) thick (this beam will act as an anchor point for your beams to screw into)

>> Array of multipurpose screws

Here's how to create your false wall frame:

1. **Resting a beam against the edge of your bulkhead shelf, tilt it either toward your cab or toward your back doors until your spirit level shows a straight measurement.**

   Mark this point on the floor with a marker pen or tape and repeat the process four or five times along the length of your bulkhead shelf until you can join your marks up into a straight line.

2. **Using a thick wooden beam, create an anchor piece that sits behind the straight line you drew on the floor.**

3. **Screw this piece into the metal base of the raised area under your seats to form a sturdy block to screw your beams into.**

   You may need to pack this out with offcuts behind in order to reach the line you have drawn on your floor, screwing blocks of the same size into the seat base first and then in turn screwing your thick wooden anchor piece into the offcuts. I used the metal base here as opposed to screwing into the floor just to make sure it has the sturdiest anchor point possible. If for some reason you can't screw into this metal base, then screw down into the wooden ladder frame you made for your insulation to sit in back in Chapter 5.

   If you are planning on making a doorway into your cab area, make sure your anchor beam is split into two pieces to give you a clear gap to pass through.

   TIP

4. **Screw a piece of wood into your bulkhead shelf, making sure the edge of your beam is flush with the edge of the shelf.**

   This provides an additional surface for you to screw your vertical beams into to secure them down.

   You also need a horizontal beam spanning the width of your van as close to the top of your roof as possible in order to secure your vertical beams into place over the bulkhead storage area. Call this the roof beam.

   TIP

5. **Measure and cut vertical beams to screw into your anchor beam on the floor, bulkhead shelf beam, and roof beam, using the same method of drilling pilot holes and countersinking before screwing.**

6. **Mark out an area for a bulkhead shelf cupboard.**

   Once again, due to the curved nature of your van walls, your beams will get bigger toward the middle of your van. You will need around eight beams in total running vertically up your bulkhead wall.

   Use masking tape to label the beams 1 through 8 moving left to right so you know which beam goes where.

   TIP

7. **Using the three horizontal beams that you used to make the bottom, middle, and top of your wall frame, secure beams 1 through 8 into place.**

   If you opt to make a bulkhead storage cupboard like I did (see Figure 6-4), remember to leave a rectangular section of your bulkhead storage section free of pine beams, stopping just below the storage shelf itself. This will form the dimensions of your cupboard door. The horizontal beam at the very top of your wall running across the width of your van (your roof beam) creates the perfect spot for your cupboard hinges to attach to. (I discuss making a door for this cupboard in Chapter 10.)

   TIP

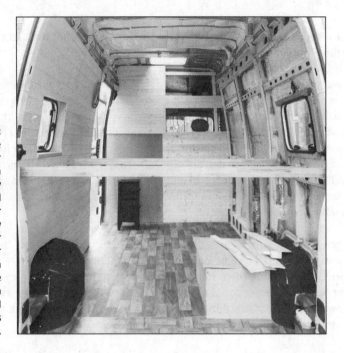

**FIGURE 6-4:**
This is my false wall under construction with space for my bulkhead cupboard door and window hatch, the latter of which was later covered by a canvas picture that swung open on hinges when I needed to access the cab.

**REMEMBER**

Before you clad your new false wall, take the opportunity to add insulation between your vertical beams. You can do this by boarding the side that faces into your cab with a medium-density fiberboard (MDF) to create a backboard and a surface for insulation to sit against. Simply clad over the top to keep the insulation in place.

And don't forget, if you're planning on adding insulation in-between your horizontal beams and are contemplating adding a log burner to your setup, leave the space behind your cement board insulation-free.

## Leaving space for a door or window hatch

Planning is everything when it comes to implementing a window or door into your false wall, and the good news is that it isn't a difficult process at all. Providing you leave enough width between two of your vertical beams for your door or window area, you can measure accordingly and clad up to those points, creating a clean-edged finish and leaving you free to add shutters and door curtains at your leisure. (Check out Chapter 10 for information about adding cladding.)

For a window hatch, create a rectangular frame by measuring, cutting, and screwing two smaller horizontal beams into the gap you have made for your window hatch into the cab, essentially framing your new window space.

For a doorway, you don't need to do anything else other than leave a gap in your vertical wall beams big enough for you to pass through.

TIP

Use a metal rod and a thick door curtain to separate your cab and living areas. Alternatively, use cladding or pallet wood to make a feature piece door that fits the gap. Measure your space, create a template with cardboard, and then build a door by attaching pieces of wood together and cutting to size, bracing the back by screwing offcuts of wood (beam or cladding) in a neat Z shape to help maintain structural integrity. You can also cut MDF to size for a smooth finish and create an insulation gap using pieces of pine beam around the inner edges and fill with insulation to help with soundproofing. This also works with cladding and pallet wood doors too.

When hanging your door, attach two hinges to your door and, holding them up against your left or right door beam (depending on which way you want it to open), draw around them to mark their position. Using a sharp chisel and a hammer, create a recess for the hinge to sit in, otherwise known as a *mortise,* and screw into place. Once done, you should have nice flush hinges and a door that opens out into your living area.

Door hinges usually come with a handy instruction leaflet. Keep this safe and follow the instructions if you get stuck.

TIP

Whenever the words "sharp chisel" are used, I have visions of someone losing a finger. Take your time when using a chisel and wear protective gloves if you're worried about losing that pinky.

REMEMBER

Chapter **7**

# Getting Some Air: Windows and Skylights

There is perhaps no greater feeling than lying in bed and watching the world from your van window, spotting animals going about their business or just feeling the breeze on your toes as you read a book and listen to the sounds of a trickling steam. On a more practical level, installing windows, skylights, and roof vents into your van provides a means of filling your tiny home with natural light and fresh air. Whether creating a draft to keep your camper cool or having a means of letting that pasta steam escape, keeping your home light and airy may leave you feeling much happier and help to reduce the build-up of cooking smells and dampness.

In this chapter, you discover how to measure and cut holes in your van as well as what equipment you need. You also find out how to install bonded windows and skylights. Don't panic; it's not as tricky as it may sound!

REMEMBER

For this chapter, I'm working on the premise that your chosen van has no holes or windows in the side walls. Some vans do come with windows pre-installed, so if you're one of the lucky few, head to the skylight section and use the time you've saved to have a chocolate bar.

# Getting the Right Tools

Let's get right into it. You're about to cut a big hole in your van. Take a deep breath and get ready, because once you make that first cut, there's no going back! Don't worry, though; I've made this section as straightforward as possible so you can get your windows installed in no time.

You probably already have most of the equipment you'll need for cutting your window holes. Here's a rundown.

## Drill

You've definitely used a drill before now when making pilot holes in wooden elements of your build for your screws to run into, and now you're going to use one to make holes for your jigsaw blade to enter and follow as you cut out the shape of your window.

**TIP**

Initially, once you've drawn the shape of your template onto the metal of your van, you're going to make a hole for your jigsaw blade to fit in so you can begin making your cut. It's a good idea to make a few holes at different stages along your template line — almost like a very simple dot-to-dot puzzle. This gives you chance to take a bit of a breather every now and again and means you don't have to cut the whole window in one go.

## Jigsaw

Just like when cutting the beams for your internal structure, it's important to have a sturdy and reliable jigsaw when cutting out the hole for your window or vent. As I mention in Chapter 6, the Makita cordless 18-volt jigsaw is a great choice as you don't have to worry about trailing extension cables or your wire pulling tight half-way around cutting your hole.

## Jigsaw blades

There's a strong chance you're going to go through a lot of jigsaw blades while cutting your window. Therefore, I suggest using a blade with as fine a tooth as possible; the aluminum blade from the Bosch jigsaw blade set provides a clean and neat cut and passes through the metal of your van wall very smoothly.

## Angle grinder

From the outside of your van, you should be able to see the areas where windows would have been installed on the production line had your vehicle started its life as a minibus. Some of these sections may have metal struts running up them on the inside of your van, and they need to be removed before you cut out the shape of your window using your jigsaw. Cutting the struts at both the top and the bottom with an angle grinder will be enough to remove them, leaving the space clear for you to make your window preparations.

**WARNING**

When using your angle grinder, make sure to just cut your strut and not cut through the side of your van. Take your time and don't rush.

## Masking tape

Masking tape is great for marking out the area you're going to cut. It's also useful for protecting the paintwork around your window hole and for reducing vibrations while you're cutting too.

## Tape

Pick up some strong tape to help keep your bonded windows in place while the window sealant dries.

## Mastic tape

This caravan join-sealing tape is great for when you need to pack out areas on your roof to make a level surface.

## Cardboard

Didn't get a template with your window? Don't worry; there's plenty of cardboard in the world that you can use to make your own. Simply place your window on top of a sheet of cardboard and draw around it with a pencil or fine marker, then carefully cut it out with a pair of scissors or a craft knife. If you've ordered any of your equipment from Amazon or other online retailers, you should have plenty of boxes on hand!

## Tape measure

How many times am I going to tell you to measure twice throughout this book? It's both the first and second rule of Van Conversion Club, which means that having a premium tape measure is a must-have item.

## Metal file

I don't mean a file-o-fax made from aluminum; I'm talking about a handheld file to smooth down any raw edges that you cut with your jigsaw before you install your window. There's no real science to buying a metal file; you can grab one with a straight front and a rounded back from any hardware store.

## Microfiber cloth or small brush

Have a microfiber cloth or a small brush on hand for rubbing over the edges of your cut to remove any metal filings before you use any rust-proofing paint or sealant.

## Bonding sealant and sealant gun

Bonding sealant is used to glue your bonded window to the metal of your van. Grab a strong glue like Dinitrol 500 or Masterbond 1 Hour Windscreen Bonding Adhesive. Don't worry about how much to use yet; I get into that in the step-by-step instructions later in this chapter. You'll also need some Sikaflex sealant for when you get onto installing your roof vent.

## Hammerite metal paint

Hammerite metal paint comes in lots of different color shades. Apply it straight to the raw metal edges of your new window cut to treat the metal and protect it from rusting.

## Rubber auto trimming (optional)

In certain builds, cutting through the metal of your van will leave an exposed double skin. If once you've cut your window you find a second lip that you could potentially catch things on, you can cover it with rubber auto trimming to finish it off.

## Safety equipment

Obviously when using power tools in an environment where sparks are involved, it's important to make sure you're wearing the correct safety equipment. Protect your eyes from stray sparks and metal filings by wearing safety goggles and keep those digits safe by wearing safety gloves. It's also a great idea to put ear defenders on too when using jigsaws and angle grinders; cutting through metal is loud!

# Looking at the Different Types of Camper Window

Having the right tools is only half of the battle; you also need to pick the right window for your camper. Let's take a look at a few of the different types of windows you can install in your camper and how they differ.

REMEMBER

If you don't feel comfortable installing your own camper windows after reading any of the examples that follow, there's no shame whatsoever in asking a professional to step in and do it for you. Understandably, this is a huge part of the installation process and can be quite daunting, so don't feel like you've failed if you don't want to take this on yourself. You certainly won't be the first person to have made that decision, and you won't be the last!

## Bonded windows

Most of the newer vans you see coming off production lines have bonded windows installed. They're not cheap to buy but do have one of the cleanest finishes and are straightforward to install. These windows take up most of the pre-marked out window area on the side of the van and come in specific sizes and styles to match the contours and shape of your chosen van. Bonded windows are stuck on using adhesive strips or types of glue and are the type of windows most professional van builders opt for.

## Rubber-mounted windows

Rubber-mounted windows are often easier to get hold of than bonded windows, and certain models come with sliding components to let air into your build. They're held in place by a rubber seal and locked into place with a separate fixing strip.

TIP

If you find an old minibus at a scrapyard, you might be able to take a sliding door with a rubber mounted window pre-installed, or cut out old windows with an angle grinder to use in your build, thus saving on costs.

## Hinged caravan/trailer windows

Likely you have seen these plastic-hinged windows on caravans over the years. While they don't look as cool as tinted, bonded windows or sliding models, hinged caravan windows are simple to install and don't glint in the sun, making them better for stealth camping. These windows are also pretty cheap to buy and utilize locking arms that prevent them from being cracked open. These windows are screwed or bolted into place from the outside of your camper.

TIP

If you're going to take windows from a discarded caravan or trailer that pinch against the caravan wall and install them on your van, just make sure the walls of the caravan are the same thickness as your van walls.

## Porthole

If you want to live on a narrowboat but don't have a canal nearby, then you can always add portholes into your build and pretend you're floating alongside swans and ducks. Portholes are more than just a quirky feature, however. If you install them securely, they can be a safer option that thieves can't smash and climb through. (Unless the thieves in your area have trained polecats to do their stealing for them, then I'm afraid you're completely out of luck.)

TIP

If you're going to install portholes in your van, make sure you've checked and double-checked the dimensions of your template before cutting a hole in your wall or door. Cutting a perfect circle is much harder than cutting a rectangle, so take your time and use a curved metal file to make sure those edges are rounded smoothly.

# Marking Out Windows

Whether you bought a window with a template or made a template yourself out of cardboard, you're going to need to tape it to the side of your van wall to transfer the shape of your window onto the bare metal.

When the time comes, marking out your windows is as simple as sticking your template up onto your wall with masking tape and drawing around it with a marker pen. When you're ready to start cutting, be sure to stay on the inside of your template line. Remove the pieces of tape holding your template up one at a time and, while using your free hand to hold the template in place, carefully join up any gaps between your lines where the tape blocked your pen's path.

## BEFORE YOU MAKE THAT FIRST CUT

Okay, it's almost time to start making cuts for your window. Before you power up that jigsaw, here's a recap of the information presented so far in case you've skipped ahead and some other handy tips. Take a deep breath; you've got this!

- **Measure twice, cut once.** There it is again, but once you've made that first cut, there's no going back. Welding sheets of metal back onto your van is much harder and more of a waste of time than is taking your time and confirming that the lines you've made by drawing around your template are accurate.

- **Make a stencil.** If you have some spare cardboard on hand (like the cardboard your window came in), make a stencil of your window and offer it up to the side of your van so you can see if it looks right before you cut.

- **Use your fine-toothed blade.** Cutting metal with a blade designed for cutting plastic piping isn't going to end well. For a cleaner cut and more control, use a blade with a finer tooth.

- **Get help from a friend when lifting glass.** There's no use crying over spilled milk, but a smashed window that should have been a solid pane in the side of your van is definitely something worth getting upset over. On a more serious note, you might end up slicing a finger off or cutting yourself if you don't handle glass correctly; those sheets can get heavy. Ask a friend to help you lift heavy panes or to help steady the glass while you put it into position.

- **Start with your sliding door before moving onto the other parts of your van.** Starting with the sliding door provides a safety blanket in the sense that, if you mess up, you can always purchase a new door or find a replacement in a scrap heap. Hopefully you won't make any mistakes, but knowing that there is a possible "get out of jail free card" available when you make your first cut might make the whole process feel a little less daunting.

# Installing Windows

Okay folks, it's time to make those cuts. Once again, the steps that follow outline how to install bonded windows in your van, just so we're on the same page. If you're literally on a different page, however, then you aren't even reading this sentence, so I guess I'll just get started.

1. **Determine where on your van you're going to cut and assess the area.**

   Take a look at the area you're going to cut and familiarize yourself with the space before you start making templates or grabbing your tools. Spend as long as you want mapping out what you're going to do so you can get it right the first time.

2. **Using your angle grinder, remove any struts that cover the window space.**

   If you have a strut in your window area, use your angle grinder to make a cut at the top and bottom. Remove this piece and put it outside your van so you don't trip and cut yourself on it.

**REMEMBER**

   Take care to only cut out the strut and not cut through the side of your van. That bit is coming soon enough!

3. **Place your template on the side of your van (inside) and draw around it with a marker pen.**

   Now that the space is clear, you're free to place your template flat on the side of your van. Stick it up using masking tape and draw around it.

4. **Drill a hole in each of the four corners of your template line, taking care to make sure they're on the inside of your line.**

   These holes are entry points for your jigsaw, giving you more room to move your blade when going around the curve of your template. They also allow you a little place to have a breather and to split your cut into smaller, more manageable chunks.

**WARNING**

   It is important these holes are on the inside of your template guideline and not outside. If they're outside of the line, then depending on the window choice you opt for, you might end up having a hole outside your window that will potentially let air, water, or prying fingers inside.

5. **Insert your jigsaw blade into one of the holes and begin to cut out the shape of your template.**

   Go steady here and remember that cutting your window hole out isn't a race. Take your time and keep a steady hand so that you don't deviate from your template line.

TIP

Place masking tape over the cut that you've made at regular intervals to prevent the waste piece of metal from vibrating too much, making the process of cutting your hole out much easier. This will also prevent the metal from falling inward on you after you've finished your cuts.

It is possible to cut your window from the outside of your van, but you are leaving yourself open to the possibility of damaging the paintwork. I always suggest cutting from inside, but do whatever feels most comfortable.

6. **Using gloves, carefully remove the piece of metal you have just cut out from your van wall.**

Your masking tape will keep the piece of metal in place for the time being, allowing you to remove it safely.

WARNING

This piece is going to be incredibly sharp, so make sure you're wearing protective gloves; otherwise you run a serious risk of cutting your hands.

7. **Tape a bin bag or some plastic sheeting underneath your hole on the floor to catch all your metal filings.**

Metal filings cause rust, so do a thorough cleanup afterward.

8. **Using your metal file, smooth the edges of your hole.**

Take your metal file that has a straight edge on one side and a rounded edge on the other. Run the straight edge over the flat edges of your cut and use the rounded edge to smooth out the corners. If your template is for a rectangular hole with 90-degree corners, you won't need to use your rounded edge.

TIP

You're not trying to change the overall shape of your hole, so go gently with your file.

9. **Wipe or brush off any filings around your hole, and then, using a paint-brush, add Hammerite metal paint to the raw edge you've just cut to treat it.**

You don't need to go crazy here; add just a nice layer to cover any bare metal and protect it for years to come. Leave it for the recommended four-hour period to properly dry before continuing.

10. **Using a glass wipe or isopropanol and a cloth, clean the inside edge of your glass.**

The inside edge of your bonded window piece is going to stick to the metal area around your window hole. To make sure your window adhesive sticks properly, it's a good idea to clean the window and the side of your van thoroughly. Make sure both are dry before adding your window sealant in the next stage.

**11.** Using your sealant and sealant gun, add a generous amount of adhesive around the hole you've created and offer your window up to the side of your van.

**WARNING**

These bonded window pieces can be big depending on the style and type of van you are converting, which means they can often be heavy and cumbersome. If you don't have a suction cup lifter to lift glass on your own, get a friend to help you lift it into place.

**12.** Use tape to keep your window in place while the sealant dries.

Place tape loosely around the edges of your bonded window before you lift the window into place and press it against the side of your van. While holding the window in place, lift and fasten each piece of tape against the body of your van to help secure the window while the sealant dries. The drying process is usually quite quick; with Masterbond 1 Hour Windscreen Bonding Adhesive, you'll only have an hour to wait!

**13.** Add rubber auto trimming to any exposed edges inside your van if you've had to cut through a double skin.

As I note earlier in this chapter, cutting through the side of your van might leave an exposed double skin — essentially a second edge that is now left exposed. If you find yourself in this situation, use rubber auto trimming to cover the edge of the metal and create a tidy finish. You can usually buy this trimming by the yard/meter and cut it to size.

**REMEMBER**

When you're finished cutting and sticking, set aside some time to thoroughly clean up all the metal filings you've created from making your hole. As I mention earlier, loose metal filings cause rust, and that's not something that is welcome in your new tiny home!

Here's looking at you, kid, through your brand-new camper windows! That's a massive step toward making your van feel open, light, and airy. I know it might have been a little tense at times, but it's all done now. Give yourself a massive compliment and take five minutes to do a wordsearch as a reward.

# Adding Skylights and Rooflight Vents

Putting windows in the side of your van is one thing, but cutting holes and installing skylights and rooflight vents in your roof — a place that is notorious for collecting water and where rain often hits the hardest — is taking things to the next level.

The temptation to crack on and get all cutting and window-fitting done and dusted is probably keeping you awake at night by now. I know how it feels once you get started with your build, but it's important to both take note of and work with the elements when you're going to make massive holes in your roof. Don't pick a day with a strong chance of rain, and don't try to install your window a couple of hours before sunset. This job needs doing properly and with plenty of time in case things go wrong.

**TIP**

Check the weather forecast and pick a couple of days that look as though they're going to be sunny. Start in the morning and give yourself a full day plus time overnight for any sealant to dry without getting wet from a downpour.

In this section, I discuss how to install two different types of skylight: a simple rooflight vent and a glass skylight. The initial process is fairly similar for both.

## Installing rooflight vents

Rooflight vents open to let light and air into your vehicle. They usually operate via a turn-wheel or winch that pushes open a plastic cover, letting in a cool breeze or the sounds of nature around your parking spot. Rooflight vents are essentially a simpler version of a roof fan vent system that don't require electricity. They're a great option if you're stealth camping or don't want a van with a large electrical setup.

Let's take a look at how to install a rooflight vent into your camper.

1. **Draw out the area you're going to cut on the outside of your van roof.**

   Your chosen vent should come with an instruction manual or a template that gives the exact dimensions you need for your hole. If not, you can either make your own template using cardboard or draw out a square directly onto your roof using a marking pen and a ruler.

**REMEMBER**

   You know what I'm going to say, but I still have to say it: Measure this square twice, three times, half a dozen times if you must. You need to be sure it's correct before you make any holes or cuts with power tools.

2. **Drill a hole in each of the four corners of your square large enough for your jigsaw blade to fit in, taking care to make sure they're on the inside of your line.**

   Just as with cutting a hole for a window, make a hole in each corner inside your template line for your jigsaw blade to fit and turn in.

3. **Insert your jigsaw blade into one of the holes and carefully cut out your vent hole.**

Slow and steady wins the race here. Follow your lines and concentrate on keeping them straight.

4. **Using your metal file, smooth the edges of your hole.**

TIP

Tape a bin bag or some plastic sheeting underneath your hole before you start filing to catch all the little pieces of metal you're about to send shooting everywhere.

5. **Wipe or brush off any filings around your hole, and then paint the raw edges with Hammerite metal paint to finish.**

6. **Use wooden beams to make a frame to sit underneath your rooflight vent.**

This is as simple as it sounds. Screw or glue four pieces of wooden beam into a square to stick to the metal around your wooden hole on the inside of your van. These beams don't want to be any thicker than the metal ribs of your van but can easily be around 2¼-inches (60-millimeters) wide.

7. **Stick the wooden frame onto the inside of your van roof with Sikaflex, clamp it in place, and leave to dry.**

Some rooflight vents will specify the maximum thickness of roof they can be installed in. You may find that they don't need a wooden frame to screw into, especially if they have a faceplate that holds everything together from inside the van. Double-check your model to see what would work best before gluing and clamping that frame.

8. **Check the space around your hole on the top of your van before adding your rooflight vent.**

Some vans have flat roof sections without any ribbing, while others have metal ribs that stick up from the roof and run down the length of the van. If this is the case, grab some mastic tape from Amazon or a caravan supplies shop and use it to level out the gaps between your roof ribs on top of your van before attaching your rooflight vent unit.

9. **Apply a layer of Sikaflex sealant around the edge of your hole before placing your vent onto the roof.**

Eventually you will screw the vent down into your roof, but there's no harm in adding some Sikaflex into the equation too. Plus, doing so has an added bonus that is revealed in the next section.

**10.** **Use self-tapping screws to screw down through the van roof into your wooden frame.**

Self-tapping screws don't require a pilot hole to be drilled first. Use your drill and the relevant adapter to screw them straight down through your roof into the wooden frame below.

You'll hear me mention this again in Chapter 12 when we come onto roof flashing, but screwing down through your Sikaflex sealant helps to seal up the hole you're making, ensuring that no water droplets can travel down your screw thread and sneak inside your camper van.

**11.** **Place lots of sealant around the outside of your vent to seal up the join between the unit and your roof.**

This doesn't need to be pretty; it doesn't necessarily need to be tidy at all, in fact. Not unless you're planning on spending time up on the roof of your van on a regular basis or have designs of filming wildlife from up there. Add a generous amount around the edge of your vent and use your finger to push in and smooth off as you go.

**12.** **Attach any finishing faceplates to the inside of your van either now or after you have installed your cladding, depending on how you are planning on finishing off the inside of your roof.**

Depending on the model that you choose, you may have a plastic faceplate to add onto the inside of your van. If you follow the cladding steps in Chapter 10, then you might want to attach this to your roof after you've finished cladding, screwing it into place over the top of your boards. Alternatively, you might choose to place boards with curved ends flush up to your faceplate so that it sits neatly in line with your new roof; the choice is up to you. Just make sure that any bug-mesh linings are securely in place, and you're good to go!

## Installing glass skylights

One of the parts I loved the most about building my van conversion was getting creative with a window taken from an old narrowboat and using it as a skylight. I bought a ¼-inch (6-millimeter) pane of glass with a metal frame from eBay and fixed it into my roof above the sink, giving me plenty of natural light coming into the van at the front of my living space and a nice view of the trees and blue skies above when washing the dishes.

While similar to installing a roof vent, the next set of instructions are going to be slightly more niche as I, along with my friend Andy, had to get a little creative on the fly to make this window work. Still, if you want to go down the route of having a glass skylight and a roof vent, a setup perfect for stealth campers who want to let in light and air without having side windows, then keep reading to check out how I installed this narrowboat window into my build!

This window unit came with a pane of glass and a metal frame, but no rubber insert. If you find yourself in a situation like this, you need to find something to make a seal between the window and the metal frame to create a waterproof seal. I took the inner tube from an old bicycle tire and clamped that between the metal frame. Sometimes it's about getting creative and using whatever you have to hand, a proper DIY van life hack!

Here's how to install a glass skylight like the narrowboat window I added to my build:

1. **Use your drill and a metal drill bit to make some pilot holes in your metal window frame.**

   My setup was comprised of a ¼-inch (6-millimeter) pane of glass and a metal frame that it sat in. Drill holes in each corner of the frame and another two or three along each side depending on how large your frame is. You'll use these to pass bolts through to bolt the unit into your roof.

   Pre-drilling holes in your frame means you already have a template to mark out where you need to drill on your roof. Just use your trusty marker pen to mark out the points where you need to drill.

   Make sure your rubber seal is clamped in place between the frame before drilling your holes. As I said before, I used the inner tube from a bicycle tire cut down to size, but any kind of rubber would do the trick.

   Don't drill through the glass. It will definitely crack and smash, and then it's game over.

2. **Create a template of your window pane using cardboard so you know how big the hole in your roof needs to be and attach it to your roof with masking tape.**

   We touched upon creating templates earlier when talking about cutting holes for windows in the side of your van. The premise is exactly the same; just draw around your pane of glass and apply this template to your roof.

   This hole needs be the same size as your pane of glass but smaller than the pane and frame combined. The frame will bolt through the metal roof of your van, but if the hole is too big, the whole thing will fall through. A natural skylight might be good if you live in a place where it never rains, but you might have a lot of birds dropping in for breakfast while you're trying to sleep.

3. **Draw around your template with a marker pen.**

4. **Drill holes for your jigsaw blade to fit into and cut out the shape of your glass pane.**

Once again, take your time here. If you can, place something padded in the van underneath where you are cutting in case the metal piece falls through the roof on your last cut. If it's possible to hold onto it while cutting, make sure you're wearing protective gloves as it will be incredibly sharp.

5. **Use your metal file to smooth the edges of your hole and then clean away any filings and treat with Hammerite metal paint.**

You likely have this process nailed down now after prepping your van walls for a window install. Just remember that you're not aiming to change the shape of you hole with your file, but rather to smooth the edges of your cut, so don't go at it like a bull in a china shop. Use steady strokes and don't apply too much pressure.

**REMEMBER**

Tape a bin bag or some plastic sheeting underneath your hole before you start filing to collect all the little pieces of metal you're about to send flying everywhere.

6. **Dry fit your skylight to see if you are happy with the hole you made in your roof.**

7. **If the hole is the right size, use a marker pen to mark the points in your frame that you're going to drill for your bolts.**

Who knew that marker pens were going to play such a big role in this build, eh?

If your skylight frame is sitting on raised ribbing up on your roof, grab some mastic tape to build up a level area for you to install it on.

8. **Drill holes in your roof for your bolts to pass through.**

Use the same thickness of metal drill bit as your chosen bolts. You don't want to pick bolts that are too long either; otherwise they'll end up causing you problems with your roof cladding and leave you hacking away at them with a coping saw.

9. **Squeeze a line of Sikaflex around the edges of your hole so that your frame has something extra to bond with.**

I know you're going to be bolting the frame to the roof, but having that extra adhesive sealant ensures a secure fix and provides extra weatherproofing. Raindrops have a habit of getting in everywhere, so sealant is your best friend in situations like these.

10. **Using nyloc nuts, secure each of your bolts in place.**

**TIP**

This is easier to do if you have someone inside the van screwing nuts onto bolts as you hold the bolt heads in place from the roof. Call in a favor from a family member or the mailperson when they next call round if you're struggling.

You could easily just screw this window frame into your van, but bolts are a much more secure method of ensuring something doesn't potentially fly off and hit another driver as you're trundling down the motorway, especially when that "something" in question is a big pane of glass. Nyloc nuts are much less likely to work themselves free than normal nuts too, giving you peace of mind when out and about on your adventures.

## 11. Add sealant everywhere, and don't be shy with it!

No one wants water droplets falling on their head while washing up. Seal every join with some waterproof sealant, and I mean every join.

In my build, I added sealant around the edge where the metal frame met the roof of the van, and over each of the bolt heads. I also added a tidy, thin line around the inner edge where the metal frame met the glass pane and smoothed it out with a wet finger to create a nice finish. Some might say that this is a bit extreme, but those people can spend a lifetime being dripped on as punishment for questioning my motives.

# Chapter **8**

# Getting to Grips with Electrics

**H**ere it is folks, the moment probably none of you have been looking forward to but an essential step, nonetheless. I am, of course, talking about delving into the world of camper van electrics. Joking aside — and I want you to trust me on this — getting to grips with the electrical equipment in your van is not really as bad as it seems. Sure, it can be a bit of a minefield when you don't know your MC-4 connectors from your midi fuses, but after this chapter, you'll have just the right amount of knowledge to both fit electrics in your camper and wow your friends at your next party.

Over the course of this chapter, you discover the joy of fuses, what switches do, and how to safely install electrics. You also pick up key information on fridges, solar panels, and the wizardry of the split charge relay. Then, in Chapter 9, you use all this information to put your electrical system together.

**WARNING**

I've been trying to keep this book light and breezy so far, but the truth of the matter is that electrical systems can be incredibly dangerous if not calculated, thought out, and put together properly. Mistakes in your electrical system could lead to serious harm to both you and your camper, so pay attention to all the symbols at the side of the pages and, as always, if you're not sure at any stage, consult an auto electrician for advice.

# Don't Perform Surgery Blindfolded: Install Electrics Before Insulation

Now, before you get too carried away sticking insulation into every nook and cranny or covering your walls in cladding, you need to take a deep breath and start thinking about wires. I know it's nowhere near as exciting as visualizing your finished van, but trust me, it's going to be a lot easier if you do it now.

I've seen some guides that advise adding the frame, installing cladding, and *then* going back in to feed electrical wires behind planks of wood and insulation. Imagine doing keyhole surgery blindfolded; that's exactly how fiddly and annoying that process would be, so do your brain a huge favor and install your electrics while you can see your bare walls and plan out those cable runs with ease.

TIP

Take the time now to plan out where your lights are going to go, where your plugs are going to go, and how much energy the devices you will be bringing along with you on the road will need to run. Tape out light connectors, mark out where your switches will go, and feed cable conduit through the metal frame of your van. Don't worry about setting it all up right away or making any of it live; we'll do that together as we move through this and the following chapter.

REMEMBER

Cable conduit isn't just there to give your wires a cozy little home to live in. It's there to prevent your wires from becoming damaged by the sharp metal edges of your van frame while you're driving around the world. Think of it as a protective shield against the vibrations of all those off-grid tracks you're about to explore once your van is built.

I've said it before, and I'll say it again: This is not a race. It doesn't matter if you've watched a video online about a couple who completed their camper conversion in seven days; I can guarantee you they made plenty of mistakes along the way that weren't filmed. Take your time, don't rush, and enjoy the process.

## Getting the Right Equipment

Before you calculate your energy consumption and become acquainted with all the basic electrical terms, it's time to start looking into the equipment you'll need to build your electrical system inside your van.

**WARNING**

I'll warn you now before you go on: This is the most expensive part of the build by far other than buying the van itself. But then again, it's also one of the most complex parts of your van build that gives you the chance to live comfortably off the grid without spending money on an electrical hookup or even an electricity bill!

## Solar panels

For those wanting to get away from the stresses and hassles of modern life and just head off grid (ahem, away from other people), then solar panels are an essential feature of your camper van conversion. I still can't get over the fact that for four and a half years I never paid a single electricity bill thanks to that big burning ball of energy sitting up in the sky. For those who don't know, solar panels soak up the sun's rays and turn them into energy that we can then use to power all our appliances. It's like plugging an iPhone directly into the sun, though I seriously wouldn't advise that; we all know what happened to Icarus, after all.

If you're planning on installing solar panels (which I strongly recommend), then you'll need a Maximum Power Point Tracking (MPPT) solar charge regulator and display to be able to keep tabs on your panels once they are installed.

An MPPT solar charge regulator takes all that free energy the sun gives off and turns it into charge to top your batteries back up. The display that comes with it lets you know lots of useful parameters too, such as how many volts the panels are taking in and how many amps are being generated. You can also set the type of battery you're using, the float charge, the boost charge, and other beneficial features to keep your electrical system running like clockwork.

**TECHNICAL STUFF**

An MPPT solar charge regulator is always rated in both volt and amp size. For example, you might see "75 15" on the front casing, meaning that the voltage is 75 and the amperage is 15. If it's not on the front of the unit itself, then you'll see these figures somewhere in the product title or description or in your manual. These figures are the maximum amount of voltage and current that the MPPT can convert into usable charging power.

When picking an MPPT for your solar panel, you need to choose a unit that can handle the maximum voltage and current output of your solar panel. In other words, the voltage and amperage figures of your MPPT need to be higher than that of your solar panel. Here's a quick example using a 175-watt solar panel with a maximum rating of 24 volts and 9 amperes (amps):

> » With one 175-watt panel on its own, a 75-volt and 15-amp MPPT will cover these figures perfectly. As I said earlier, the figures on your MPPT need to be bigger than that of your solar panel voltage and amperage.

>> With two 175-watt panels in parallel, you now have 350 watts of solar to deal with. As you discover later on, the amperage in a parallel setup always doubles, giving you 24 volts and 18 amps. This means that the MPPT in the first example won't suffice. You'll need a unit with a bigger amperage, such as an MPPT with 100 volts and 20 amps.

TIP

Don't cheap out on a solar regulator setup. This is one of the most important parts of your electrical setup, so it's worth putting the money in to buy a reliable one. Mine cost me £250 (about $300), which seems a lot for something I don't look at that often. Still, the alternative is panels that don't work properly, and no one wants that.

REMEMBER

If you're opting for a LiFePo$_4$ (lithium-iron phosphate) battery setup, then you'll need a solar regulator that works with lithium batteries. The Rover MPPT solar regulator series from Renogy includes a display in the main unit with parameters that can be changed over Bluetooth. When picking your regulator, look at the individual specifications to double-check that it's compatible with your total solar input wattage.

## Shore power and chargers

If you've ever been to a campsite or perhaps lived on a narrowboat in a marina, you will have no doubt come across the electric hookup pedestals dotted around between either the different park-up spaces or at the end of your mooring. These pedestals comprise of CEE sockets that you can use in conjunction with CEE plug cables and a CEE van inlet to charge your batteries or run users directly from the household voltage electricity supply provided by your campsite.

If you're using these electric hookup points to bring power into your van, you'll need a battery charger unit such as the Victron Blue Smart Charger series.

REMEMBER

Make sure you pick a battery charger that is suitable for your chosen battery style and amp hour (Ah) capacity size.

## Batteries

Batteries are the beating heart of your 12-volt electrical system inside your camper. They're the power hub for your living space and allow everything from your lights to your diesel heater to run with the push of a button or the flick of a switch.

## SPLIT CHARGE RELAY

What if I told you that it was possible to charge up your batteries every time you drove? Well, you can, and you don't have to get a degree from Hogwarts to make it happen. All you need to secure a slice of the magical action is something called a *split charge relay*. While I always advise having solar panels installed to keep batteries topped up at all times, a split charge relay unit is great to give your batteries a boost when driving a long distance or in cloudy countries like the U.K.

A split charge relay is a little voltage-sensitive box that hooks up to both your starter battery and your leisure batteries. When the voltage of your starter battery hits 13.7 volts or goes higher (when your engine is on), current will flow from your starter battery down to your leisure batteries. When your engine shuts off and the voltage returns back to 12.8 volts or below, the split charge relay disconnects. You don't even have to be moving to charge up your batteries. So long as the engine is on, the split charge relay will be doing its job.

Solar power is undoubtedly the way forward, and it's great when there's sun to be harvested. Still, there isn't always enough sunlight to fill your batteries back up again, so having a secret weapon tucked away seriously helps and gives you that extra peace of mind.

Like most things in life, you have several options when it comes to batteries depending on how much money you want to spend. The most commonly used models are wet batteries (otherwise known as lead-acid batteries), though I tell you all about the different battery types in the following sections and give you my verdict as to which one might be best for you.

## Lead-acid

Lead-acid batteries are named thusly because they work via lead plates that sit in a box of sulfuric acid. For science buffs, the sulfuric acid is the electrolyte, which means a liquid that conducts positive ions. Lead and lead oxide on the submerged plates react with the electrolyte and form lead sulfate, which generates power. When the batteries are charged, the lead sulfate is converted back into its original components.

The plates inside lead-acid batteries hold around 2.1 volts each. There are six plates in each battery, and they can very easily become damaged through corrosion due to the sulfation process.

Lead-acid batteries take longer to charge and don't work very well in cold temperatures, but they are undoubtedly a cheap and cheerful option for day trips.

## AGM

AGM batteries aren't filled with as much liquid as lead-acid units. AGM stands for *absorbed glass mat,* and these batteries work by allowing the electrolyte to flow right through the absorbed fiberglass mat. (See? That's something else fiberglass can be used for!) Having less corrosive liquid sloshing around in the back of your van is a huge plus. And, as AGM batteries only use the minimum amount of electrolyte needed, you won't have to run for the hills if you crack or break one.

## Gel

Twelve-volt gel batteries do away with the liquid electrolyte all together. Instead, they use a gel electrolyte (go figure), which holds lead plates, allowing electrons to flit between them with ease. Put simply, gel batteries are like the upgraded versions of lead-acid batteries — lead acid 2.0, if you will. They don't leak, users can take advantage of slower discharge rates, and they cope much better in both colder and warmer climates.

## LiFePO$_4$

And finally, we come to the grandmasters of the battery world, LiFePO$_4$ batteries, otherwise known as lithium-iron phosphate batteries. Lithium power is used in pretty much all our modern devices, from handheld games consoles to mobile phones. In LiFePO$_4$ batteries, lithium ions pass through an organic electrolyte and attach themselves to a negative electrode to store charge for us to use. When the batteries are charging, the ions attach themselves to a positive lithium-iron phosphate cathode.

LiFePO$_4$ batteries can hold charge for up to 365 days (or a year to most folks) without losing a single drop of charge. They're real workhorses too, allowing for deep discharge and use in sub-zero temperatures!

## Author's verdict

I don't think it would take a rocket scientist to figure out that I much prefer LiFePO$_4$ batteries. When I first moved into a van, I bought two lead-acid batteries and wondered why I had to sit in the cab with the engine on while eating my pasta to charge them up through winter. Later, I installed some LiFePO$_4$ batteries from Battle Born Batteries and they changed everything. I had more power more of the time and no fluctuation with bad weather. Sure, LiFePO$_4$ batteries cost more, but they're more than worth the extra expense, especially for full-time vanlifers.

# Inverters

If you're planning on spending a lot of time inside your camper or going on some long trips, then having the right inverter will help you use household items such as food processors, monitors, games consoles, laptops, drone chargers, and many more useful gadgets and tech. As with batteries and solar panels, there are many different brands of inverters and different power ratings too. While I can only advise on which brand to buy, I *can* help you understand what power rating would best suit your camping needs.

## How does an inverter work?

An inverter takes 12 volts and magically manipulates it into your country's standard voltage. That's all you need to know on that. Essentially, if you want to plug in something that you would have plugged into your house no matter what country you live in while off-grid, you'll need an inverter.

Here in the U.K., a 12-volt current comes in one end and 240 volts comes out the other. In the U.S., it goes in at 12 volts and converts it to 120 volts. It's then a case of either plugging directly into the inverter or feeding a plug and wire up to additional sockets and wiring them up.

## What size is right for me?

Inverters all come with a power rating. Some are 300 watts, while some go all the way up to 2000 watts and beyond. The key to figuring out which size inverter is right for you is probably the simplest of all the calculations we've done so far because we're basically just adding numbers together.

For example, if you have a 400-watt food mixer, a 500-watt inverter will be able to cope with this just fine. However, if there's a chance you might run a 400-watt food mixer while playing your Nintendo Switch through a monitor at the same time, you need to make sure your inverter can cope with both items at once. Otherwise, you'll run the risk of overloading your inverter and everything turning off at once.

**REMEMBER**

It's also important to remember that higher-powered tools like jigsaws or sanders require double the amount of power to kickstart. It'll only need it for a split second, but it's required, nonetheless. This short increase in power is called *peak power*. For example, if you're plugging in a 750-watt jigsaw, it will require an inverter with 1500-watts peak power to run. Don't worry too much about this as it will tell you on the inverter box what the peak power limit is, but it's just something to keep in mind when scouting for the right piece of kit.

In my first camper, I went for a 1000-watt sine wave inverter with 2000-watts peak power, mainly because I knew I was going to be charging up camera equipment and running power tools from time to time.

REMEMBER

Bear in mind that if you choose to buy a larger inverter, you need to make sure you have a battery bank system that can handle the amount of power drawn.

## Twelve-volt refrigerator

If ever there was a time for a klaxon that shouted "hindsight alert!" at incredible volumes, then now is that time. I thought I had found a massive life hack when I made my first camper, a flaw in the system that other people just hadn't discovered. I thought I could just use a normal tabletop refrigerator in my van rather than spending $550 (about £460) on a 12-volt one. I had an inverter, I had batteries, I had everything sorted . . . . How wrong was I!

### MODIFIED SINE WAVE VERSUS PURE SINE WAVE

For many of us, expensive purchases like DSLR cameras or MacBooks aren't something we can make regularly. We've saved up for these items, and now we want to look after them. Well, it's no good looking after the exterior of your devices if you're not giving them any TLC on the inside.

Cheaper inverters tend to use *modified sine waves*. On a graph, they would look more like solid block lines forming stone henge shapes, the kind of thing you might see Mario jumping on and off of on his adventures. Modified sine waves are clunkier and intermittent; they're like a swimmer without any grace, just splashing around and making a bit of a mess.

*Pure sine waves,* however, are cleaner and more kind to the delicate batteries in our expensive gear. On a graph, these signals look more like curving waves; you can tell just by looking at them that they're going to be better for those electrical innards.

You've probably guessed that pure sine wave inverters are in fact more expensive. Still, remember what my cousin Kev said back in Chapter 3? "If you buy cheap, you buy twice." Skimping out on a cheaper inverter might mean you have to purchase new batteries for all of your gear too.

I won't be the first one to think that I had cheated the camper van electric gods, but hopefully I can stop you from making this same mistake. You see, the truth is that a household tabletop fridge draws way too much power. They gobble up more amps than Pac-Man on a dot-munching rampage. Plus, there's the added strain of having your inverter on all the time to consider too. It's too much, and 12-volt fridge manufacturers know this all too well.

These refrigerators don't come cheap. And you know what? I wouldn't even suggest getting one secondhand. My 12-volt Waeco CRX-50 fridge lasted four years of constant use before it broke. The good people at Waeco fixed it for me, and it's still going strong today. My point being that they last a heck of a long time when bought new and are definitely worth the money.

## How does a 12-volt fridge work?

Have you ever heard a fridge whirring away? I bet you have, but I bet you couldn't tell me how many times it's come on today or how long it's been on. Most fridges run on a compressor; that's the humming noise you hear every now and again when it's quiet at night. Compressor units kick in when the internal temperature inside the fridge itself goes above a certain point. The compressor pumps fluid, which rises and cools, helping to reduce the temperature inside the fridge. Once cooled, the compressor shuts off and waits for the temperature to rise again before coming back on.

Twelve-volt compressor fridges work in exactly the same way as household compressor fridges. The only difference is that they hook up to your batteries and are earthed to the metal of your van rather than being plugged in to the socket next to the washer.

Because these fridges only draw amps when the compressor is running — and a small number of amps at that — they don't drain your batteries. Plus, the more food you have in them, the easier it is for the unit to maintain its cold temperature, thus requiring the compressor to turn on less. With the dial in the recommended halfway position, my compressor came on for around 2 minutes every 20 minutes. It only drew 0.5 amps from the batteries, which was less than the front four spotlights together.

Don't forget to include your fridge wattage and amp draw in your energy calculations when choosing your battery size.

# Looking at Essential Safety Devices

You know how when you try to turn the toaster and put the kettle on at the same time and all the lights go out? Well, that's because a switch has tripped in your fuse box. Fuses are the first line of defense for our whole electrical circuit and protect your wires from heating up or burning when too much current flows due to a component failure or wire damage.

And if you thought that example about the toaster and kettle above was very specific, that's because it always seems to happen in every house I walk into. I think all that solar energy has turned me into the world's most useless super villain: "The Fiendish Fuse." I'm not sure it will stick, are you?

## Fuses and fuses boxes

A blade fuse box is a key component in your camper electrical build. Plugging into the solar regulator along with wires from your batteries and solar panels, it houses the blade fuses for your lights (both internal and external mounted lights) as well as any USB charging points you decide to install.

Fuses act as breakers in circuits, which also means that your circuits won't work if a fuse is missing or broken. Don't worry, I get into simple circuits in a minute, so you know what's what. First, let's look at the different types of fuses you'll be using in your camper build and their individual functions.

### Blade fuses

I can't look at these fuses without thinking about the prisoner transport ships from the film *Tron*. Still, that could be just because I'm a massive nerd and am often thinking about another planet, but it's a good way of remembering what the blade fuses look like.

If you're not a nerd, then blade fuses are really small, quite fiddly, and look like a robot's tooth. They're commonly used in car electrics; just take a look in your engine area and you'll find them powering all the different components of your van from the windshield wipers to the radio.

These little teeth-shaped fuses go from 1 amp all the way up to 40 amps. For something that doesn't produce much current such as a 4-watt bulb, you'll only need a small fuse like a 3-amp blade fuse. They're all color-coded and come with a little number printed onto the top, so you won't need to swot up on all the different colors before you start.

Blade fuses are splash-proof too, hence them being the fuse of choice for the marine fuse box I recommend you use in your build. They also work in inline fuse holders, the type that you might solder into place in your positive fridge wire before it hits your batteries.

## Midi fuses

Continuing the spaceship theme, midi fuses look a little like 2D TIE Fighters. They also come color-coded and boast little numbers on them and sit in inline midi fuse holders via little circular holes in their metal wings. Just bolt them in and you're good to go.

Whereas blade fuses are lower rated and used for smaller electrical appliances, midi fuses come in higher ratings and tend to span from 40 amps to 100 amps. These higher ratings are useful for placing in your positive wire run from your batteries. Don't worry about this for now; you'll calculate fuse sizes soon enough.

## Plug fuses

Plug fuses are the fuses you'll find in the main plug of household electrical appliances. You'll find these in the U.K. but not in Europe or the U.S., and they usually cost around £1.50 ($1.80) for three.

# Residual current devices and miniature circuit breakers

If you're bringing a household voltage electric supply into your camper using the previously mentioned CEE sockets and inlets, then you'll need to include residual current devices (RCDs) and miniature circuit breakers (MCBs) to respectively protect yourself from being electrocuted if devices malfunction and wires burn up when the current flow exceeds safe levels due to components or wires running through your van short circuiting.

**REMEMBER**

RCDs protect you from electrocution if devices malfunction. MCBs trip when your wires or any device short circuits. You need both next to each other in this order from your inlet when using shore power. Don't worry, you figure out how to install these in Chapter 9.

**WARNING**

Twelve-volt electrics are all earthed to the metal side of your van. I know it seems weird, but that's just how it works, and I get to that soon. Earthing wires to the side of your van is a safe practice, and 12 volts aren't anywhere near enough electricity to cause you any harm if something did go wrong.

Twelve-volt and household electric voltage both have their dangers for very different reasons. 120- to 240-volt household electric voltages can electrocute you in a potentially fatal way whereas 12 volts are not going to shock you. Due to the high current in a 12-volt system, however, the chances of an electrical fire are far greater.

In the unlikely event that something does go wrong with your household electric voltage setup, your whole van may become a giant electrical conductor that you won't be able to touch. See why I take electrical safety so seriously? With that in mind, here are some extra features that you should definitely add into your wiring diagram when the time comes (later in this chapter).

## Isolator switches

As I mention earlier, fuses are one of the main lines of defense if an electrical current decides to get a little unruly. Still, if you hear a pop or see a spark, your first point of call should be to flick an isolator switch and cut your circuit. Remember that scary electrical metal conductor scenario I told you about a second ago? Well, an isolator switch would cut the power between your batteries and the rest of your appliances, thus stopping everything from working.

An isolator switch works like a drawbridge; once installed within your circuit, current will only flow if the bridge is down. If you turn your isolator switch key and raise the bridge, the current has nowhere to go.

REMEMBER

Isolator switches, and any switches for that matter, look like see-saws on a wiring diagram. I used one directly after my batteries and had it as a "bridging point" for every appliance from the solar regulator to the inverter so that I could cut the power to everything should a problem arise.

TIP

Put this isolator switch somewhere that is easy to access so that you don't have to root around under boxes or crawl behind a drawer in an emergency. Mine sat in an easy-to-reach spot in the toilet cupboard that could be reached within seconds.

## RCD/GFCI plugs

Most inverters these days come with all sorts of built-in protection features such as overload, short-circuit, and overheat protection. Still, adding an RCD or a GFCI plug into the mix is a good idea for that extra peace of mind. RCD stands for *residual current device*. This is the name that you'll see most often in the U.K. GFCI stands for *ground fault circuit interrupter* and is the most common U.S. equivalent.

These plugs are clever little units that continually monitor the power supply feeding through to an electrical appliance. If there's a problem such as an earth fault or an unwanted surge, they'll cut the power within 40 milliseconds. I don't even know what something that fast would look like . . . a cheetah on fast-forward, perhaps?

I used two of these RCD units in my camper, one for each of the plug outlets on my inverter. For the sake of $30 (£25), it's 100 percent worth it.

# Understanding Watts, Volts, and Amps

Before you go any further, it would be helpful to understand some key terms in not just the world of camper van electrics, but also in terms of all electrics in general. If you're going to successfully determine the wattage of a food processor to see if your inverter can power it, or if you need to figure out how many amp hours you need from your batteries, you first need a handle on the basics. And believe me, easing you into this chapter gently is exactly what the doctor ordered.

## Power, voltage, and current

To give a very simplified explanation, power (P) provided by electricity is the product of two components: voltage (V) and current (I). You see those letters in parentheses? Those are the symbols that are used to signify quantities in electrical calculations.

To put that into perspective, $P = V \times I$. If you look at the triangle shown in Figure 8-1, you can also derive that $V = P \div I$ and that $I = P \div V$. Clever stuff, huh?

**FIGURE 8-1:**
The relationship between power, voltage, and current.

When it comes to *measuring* power, voltage, and current, we use watts (W), volts (V), and amps (A), respectively. For example:

P = 60 W means power equals 60 watts.

V = 12 V means voltage equals 12 volts.

I = 5 A means current equals 5 amps.

Let's link those together. Using the formula $P = V \times I$ in an example calculation, we can say that 60 W = 12 V $\times$ 5 A.

I advise taking a little look at the definitions of watts, volts, and amps that follow. But, if you already know your stuff and feel confident with these terms, head on to the next section.

# Watts

What is a watt? Well, *watts* are the units that measure power — in other words, the rate at which energy is both generated and consumed. These units represent energy per unit time. To be precise (which you know I love to be), 1 watt is the equivalent of 1 joule per second.

So if you have a light bulb with a power rating of 60 watts, commonly displayed as 60 W, over the course of one hour that bulb will pull 60 watt hours, which is normally displayed as 60 Wh.

The formula here is W $\times$ t = Wh.

Here's another example: If a food processor has a power rating of 450 W, over the course of two hours it will use 900 watt hours.

REMEMBER

The unit "watt" is used to display the amount of power that will be used when immediately turning on an appliance. A "watt hour" is the amount of energy used over a given period of time, which could be anything from three seconds to multiple days.

REMEMBER

The time, or "t" in the formula earlier is measured as time in hours. This means that if you are dealing with durations of time that are not whole hours, such as 30 minutes, then you need to divide the duration by 60 to get the time as a decimal number. For example, 30 minutes $\div$ 60 = 0.5 hours. This is half an hour written as a decimal number. For a more complex example, 1 hour and 35 minutes, or 95 minutes, can be worked out using the following calculation: 95 minutes $\div$ 60 = 1.58 hours.

TIP

You'll more than likely need to round off these numbers to the nearest hundredth decimal value. So if a number comes out as 1.5833333, you'll just use 1.58. If a number comes out as 0.816666, then you would round off to 0.82, which coincidentally is the decimal value for 49 minutes!

## Volts

A *volt* is essentially a unit of electric potential difference. In scientific terms, it's the size of the force that fires electrons through any given circuit. You'll often see voltage referred to by an uppercase "V."

You're going to deal with two different voltage systems in your camper van conversion: 12-volt auto electrics and the same household voltage that you have in your home country.

For reference, here are a few examples from around the world:

>> 100 V in Japan

>> 120 V in the U.S. and Canada

>> 220 V in China

>> 220–240 V in Mainland Europe (typical standardized voltage = 230 V)

>> 240 V in the U.K., New Zealand, and Australia

## Amps

*Amps,* shown in electrical diagrams by an uppercase "A," is short for *amperes.* They're the official measurement for electrical current in any circuit.

All you need to remember about amps is that the bigger the current — in other words, the more amps there are — the more electricity is flowing. Simple, right?

In the same way we'd use a watt or a watt hour when measuring power that is needed to run an appliance or to find how much power has been used over a given period of time, we can use amps to express how much current is needed to run an appliance, and "amp hours," commonly referred to as Ah, to measure the amount of current used to run an appliance for a given period of time.

**REMEMBER**

The unit "amp" is used to display the amount of power that will be used when immediately turning on an appliance. An "amp hour" is the amount of current used over a given period of time, which could be anything from three seconds to multiple days.

# Determining Your Energy Needs

Before you go ahead and start surfing the Internet for "the best camper van batteries," it's important to know why you're going to be using certain products and what their role is in your electrical setup. Each component serves a different function that can handily be organized into three categories as shown in Figure 8-2.

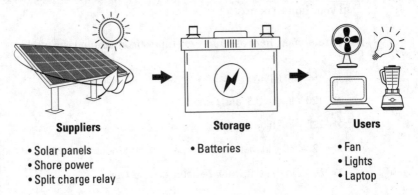

**Suppliers**
- Solar panels
- Shore power
- Split charge relay

**Storage**
- Batteries

**Users**
- Fan
- Lights
- Laptop

FIGURE 8-2:
Three categories
of electrical
components.

*Suppliers* are the components that provide a source of electricity. Solar panels convert the sun's rays into electrical power, shore power provides an electrical feed straight from an outlet (such as an electrical hookup pedestal at a campsite), and a split charge relay supplies electricity from the starter battery in your engine while the engine is turned on.

*Storage* is the means of storing the energy created by the suppliers. In this case, that's going to be a leisure battery, and you've seen the most-used types earlier in this chapter.

Suppliers and storage are variables that change depending on the last category: *users*. Users are items that literally use the electricity that your suppliers create and that your storage stores! These items can be anything from a USB fan to a food processor, or a 12-volt fridge or a heater. The number of items you use, the way you are using them, and their individual power ratings will all determine how big or how many batteries you need, which in turn will have an effect on how many or how big your solar panels are.

Now that you've seen what the energy suppliers, storage, and users are, I'm going to mix things up a little and go back through them in reverse order. Users are the items that will dictate how much storage and supply you need, so it's important to calculate the energy needs for the items you'll be using every day first.

# Users

Depending on where you live and your lifestyle, the number of items you take with you in your van or use on a regular basis will vary. For example, if you work from your van and need to charge a laptop or run an extra monitor, then you will use more electricity than someone who spends most of their time outside. Likewise, if you live in a colder country, then the chances are you'll be running a heater a lot more than someone who lives in a warmer climate.

TIP

On average, you have ten times more hours of direct sunlight in the summer months than you do in the winter months. This needs to be taken into account when designing the supply and storage elements of your electrical system.

With that in mind, if you're expecting that you will be using a lot of electricity in the summer months but very little in the winter months, then your solar panels will cover most of your everyday usage, meaning your storage capacity is replenished regularly and does not need to be as large.

On the other hand, if you're expecting that you will be using a lot of electricity in the winter months where there isn't as much direct sunlight but very little in the summer months, then your solar panels will do very little to fill your storage. This means you will need alternative ways of replenishing your storage, such as shore power or a split charge relay, and a larger storage capacity to last you longer without charging up.

REMEMBER

To summarize, in times or areas with less sun, it's good to have more batteries to store electricity and multiple ways to charge them. In areas with lots of sun, you can get away with fewer batteries as your solar will keep them recharged on a regular basis.

Using the calculation shown earlier (W × t = Wh), fill in Table 8-1 with the appliances you will use in your van, listing their ratings and the duration of time you expect to use them during both the summer and the winter to discover how many watt hours you'll need.

REMEMBER

Remember that summer usage dictates your solar supply needs, while winter usage dictates your battery storage needs. In other words, if you want to live in a van all year round, you need to make sure you're properly equipped.

## Storage and supply

It's good practice to keep your leisure batteries above 50 percent charge to keep them healthy. Over time, constant discharging can lead to plates curling up and touching (which can lead to instant short circuiting inside the battery), or just generally decrease the overall lifespan of your batteries. Using the calculations that follow and with some choice tips, you're going to do everything possible to ensure that this never happens.

**TABLE 8-1** **Expected Summer and Winter Electricity Usage**

| Appliance | Rating (W) | Time Summer (hr) | Time Winter (hr) | Usage Summer (Wh) | Usage Winter (Wh) |
|---|---|---|---|---|---|
| LED lights (2) | 5 | 2 | 6 | 10 | 30 |
| USB charger | 12.5 | 1 | 3 | 12.5 | 37.5 |
| Fan | 12 | 4 | 0.25 | 48 | 3 |
| Heater | 30 | 0 | 4 | 0 | 120 |
| Laptop (via inverter) | 100 | 2 | 2 | 200 | 200 |
| Fridge/cooler | 15 | 24 | 0 | 360 | 0 |
| **Total Expected Usage** | | | | **630.5** | **390.5** |

Just because you have solar panels on your roof doesn't mean they're always going to work at their full potential whenever it is light outside. Luckily for us, some people who are way more qualified than me at measuring solar energy have given us an easy method of determining how much power your solar panels will generate at specific times of the year in different countries across the globe.

**REMEMBER**

Peak sun hours is the total amount of sunlight your panels will be exposed to over a full day converted down into hours of maximum sunlight.

**TECHNICAL STUFF**

Here's a great way to understand peak sun hours. Imagine you come across eight bottles of water in one day, each with different amounts of water in them. If you collect them all up and add all the water together, you end up with two full bottles of water rather than eight partially filled ones. The total amount at the end of the day is two full bottles. The same thing happens with the sun; take each bottle as an hour of sunlight where a certain amount of energy is given as the sun arcs across the sky. There is less solar energy in the morning, more in the afternoon when temperatures are at their highest, and then less as the sun descends toward the horizon in the evening. The amount of energy given over these eight hours is added up, just like the water in the bottles, and is measured in peak sun hours. So five peak sun hours is all the solar energy in one day added up into a block on a graph that is much easier for us to read and use in calculations.

**TIP**

By searching for your local "peak sun hours" or "average solar radiation" in your area, you can use a simple calculation to discover how much energy your solar panels will bring in, and in turn what size panel or panels you need for your van.

For the following calculations, let's take a trip to snowy Alaska to figure out how much energy your solar panels will be pulling in in the height of summer, and then again in December, possibly everyone's favorite winter month. I've taken old measurements here that, though accurate, should only be used as an example, so double-check the current readings in Alaska if you've just moved there on whim after buying this book. So that's:

>> 5 peak sun hours for the summer measurement

>> 0.2 peak sun hours for the winter measurement

**REMEMBER**

Battery capacity is measured in amp hours, commonly referred to as Ah. To find out how many Ah you need for your setup, you need to convert your watt hour total usage into amp hours. Don't worry, you've already made acquaintances with the type of formulas you'll be using. Think of this as like seeing an aunt at Christmas who you haven't spent much time with . . . shame on you.

Remember the triangle shown earlier in Figure 8-1 for understanding watts, volts, and amps? Well, you can use the same $P = V \times I$ formula to determine how many amp hours you'll need. Simply replace the values with watt hours (Wh) and amp hours (Ah) to find the total amount of energy consumed (see Figure 8-3).

**FIGURE 8-3:**
The relationship between watt hours, voltage, and amp hours.

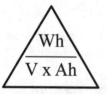

**TIP**

It doesn't matter how you use this formula, as long as you are using watts and amps or watt hours and amp hours. Don't combine the triangles and have a watt or an amp hour in the same one; otherwise the world might implode, and no one wants that!

## Calculating the size of your battery bank

Next, let's determine the size of the battery bank you need. Remember the summer and winter watt hour usage calculations from Table 8-1? I'm now going to take those two figures and use them to make sure we have a battery bank that can cope with them both. For reference, those calculations were:

>> Summer daily usage = 630.5 Wh

>> Winter daily usage = 390.5 Wh

You already know that battery capacity is measured in amp hours (Ah) and that watt hours (Wh) can be converted into them by using the handy triangle shown in Figure 8-3. Let's take that winter daily usage measurement first, as we need to make sure that you have enough battery capacity to cover that usage in times with minimum peak sun hours. Using the formula, Wh ÷ V = Ah:

390.5 Wh ÷ 12 V = 32.54 Ah daily usage

Keeping in mind the 50 percent discharge rule for a battery, a 65-Ah battery not hooked up to any solar panel or charger would get you through one day of using your winter item setup. Clearly, having to charge up a battery every single day at a campsite is not the reason you bought this book or a Mercedes-Benz Sprinter van. The whole idea of van life is to be in the middle of nowhere feeling more relaxed than a puppy getting a head massage, right?

Well, now that you know how many amp hours you need for one day of off-grid usage in the winter where there might not be any sun to charge your batteries back up, you can multiply that number by the number of days you want to be off-grid for any given period of time.

Suppose you want to be off-grid for four days. 65 Ah × 4 = 260 Ah, meaning a 300-Ah battery would more than suffice for your off-grid exploring needs. See, all this calculating isn't as scary as you first thought, is it?

Now, let's discover whether this battery bank size will work for your summer usage too by calculating the size of your solar panel setup.

## Calculating the size of your solar panels

Let's jump right in with that summer daily usage calculation again. Remember, it was 630.5 Wh, and we know that the Alaskan summer is going to provide us with an average of five peak sun hours of energy over the course of one day.

**TECHNICAL STUFF**

A solar panel is always rated in watt peak (Wp or W), which is often referred to on websites or in stores as the "maximum power" a panel can produce.

Taking a 100-Wp panel (or maximum power: 100 W) for example, on an Alaskan summer's day with five peak sun hours, this panel will produce:

100 Wp × 5 hours = 500 Wh of generated electricity

Taking our summer usage of 630.5 Wh, you now need to source a solar panel that covers this usage amount while giving you a little breathing room should there be an overcast day or perhaps at the beginning or tail end of the summer months.

You might, if for instance you work on the road and have a deadline approaching, use more power in the summer, which also needs to be taken into account.

With that in mind, you'll need a solar panel that can surpass your summer daily usage in less peak sun hours. So instead of generating 630.5 Wh over a period of five peak sun hours, you're going to aim to generate 700 Wh over a period of four peak sun hours.

700 Wh ÷ 4 = 175 Wp solar panel

Let's put everything together to look at your current electricity setup. Table 8-2 includes two columns for winter and summer electricity usage. In each case, I used our sample figures to show the amp hour usage for both seasons, the amount of time in days you can spend off-grid without charging your battery bank (the battery buffer), and the watt hours generated by your solar panels converted into amp hours so that you can see how much your batteries will be filling back up again per day with that sweet, sweet free power from the sky.

TABLE 8-2

### Expected Solar Energy Generated by Season

| | Winter Usage | Summer Usage |
|---|---|---|
| | 32.54 Ah | 52.54 Ah |
| Battery buffer (300 Ah) | 4 days | 3 days |
| Solar energy generated per day (175 Wp) | 2.92 Ah | 58.33 Ah |

Check out the bottom row of Table 8-2. In the summer, your batteries are being topped back up to full again every day by your solar panels, even though you're using a lot of electricity to power your items. Take a look at the winter figure, however. With 0.2 peak sun hours in the Alaskan winter, your solar panels aren't going to be doing much battery filling at all. That's where shore power and the magical wizardry of the split charge relay come into play.

## Using shore power or split charge relay

You cannot use shore power to power your batteries directly; you must hook your CEE van inlet to a 12-volt battery charger. Spending a little more money on a smart battery charger that you can leave in situ 24/7, especially one with a Bluetooth connection that allows you to monitor charging progress via an app, will take all the hassle out of manually hooking up your batteries and monitoring their progress with a multimeter and head torch in the middle of the night.

Battery chargers come in various sizes and power ratings. The general rule of thumb is to use a charger that with an amperage that is 10 percent of your total amp hour storage capacity of your battery bank. For example, a 150-Ah battery requires a 15-amp charger, and a 300-Ah battery requires a 30-amp charger.

I talk a little more about choosing a CEE van inlet and the associated cables in the next section, as well as give you more information on how to install inlets and battery chargers in Chapter 9.

REMEMBER

While your split charge relay is useful for charging your battery bank on the go, it's not a charging method that can be measured or used to make calculations with. This is because the main variable — the amount of time it is going to be operational — will be different every day. The amount of electricity your split charge relay creates on a ten-minute drive or while running for ten minutes will be significantly less than the amount it creates on a three-hour drive or while the engine is ticking over for three hours.

WARNING

I also don't recommend keeping your engine on for three hours while sitting in your van as it's going to be incredibly noisy, not to mention how annoying it would be for people living in houses or sleeping in other vans nearby. Also, the fumes from your exhaust will build up very quickly which *could* lead to a build-up of carbon monoxide. Always make sure you have multiple carbon monoxide monitors in your living space to keep yourself safe.

# Fuse Sizes and Wire Gauges

The next step in calculating your electrical needs is to determine which size fuses you need and the correct lengths of wire to use when wiring up your different components.

## Number of amps per user

When it comes to running specific items, or "users," through your fuse box, it is best to group them together in order to not have too many users on a single fuse. For example, if you have six lights in your van and three switches, it's best to split these into three groups of two lights, with each group given its own fuse and its own connection in the fuse box. This enables you to use less thick wires, thereby saving your hard-earned cash, and it also makes your setup much safer by tailoring fuses to specific items.

To find the right fuse, you need to know the right number of amps per grouped user. Let's look at two examples: two downlights on one switch, and one USB charging port, the kind you would use to charge up your Kindle, smartphone, or iPad, on another. So that's:

Two lights with a total power rating of 5 W:

5 W ÷ 12 V = 0.42 A

One USB charging port with a maximum power rating of 25 W:

25 W ÷ 12 V = 2.08 A

Now you know how many amps two lights are going to draw and the maximum number of amps a USB charging port will draw.

## Fuse sizes

The fuse size *always* needs to bigger than the number of amps a user is drawing, but not so big that its rating ends up being bigger than the wire it is protecting. Let's look at those two examples again:

>> Two lights draw 0.42 A.

>> One USB charging port draws 2.08 A.

With two lights, you can safely use a 1-amp fuse. For the USB charging port, you can use a 3-amp fuse.

REMEMBER

The wires you use need to be able to handle the amp of the fuse, not the amp of the user. In other words, the fuse rating needs to be greater than the draw, and the maximum wire current rating (the amps passing through it) needs to be greater than that of the fuse. This is to prevent the wire from burning out before the fuse does.

## Wire gauges

Picking the right wires can be like looking at heaps and heaps of spaghetti at a pasta-making festival. Luckily, I've been there before and waded through the cable quagmire and can offer a few wire-picking tips to spare you the headache.

TIP

To determine the wire gauge you need two things: the amps running through the wire and the length of the wire itself. With these two variables, you can look up the wire gauge you need in a chart. You can use any generic chart or the chart that the manufacturer of the wire you have chosen to use has supplied. Keep in mind that the length used by these charts may differ depending on how they refer to wire length. Some may tell you to use the total distance from the supplier to the user, so from your batteries to your fuse box, for example, while others may ask you to use the length of your negative wire added to the length of your positive wire ("the round-trip length") to determine the correct wire gauge.

In the U.S., this chart is called an AWG chart (shown in Table 8-3), while European and U.K. users should look out for a metric chart (shown in Table 8-4).

**TABLE 8-3**     ## AWG Wiring Gauges

| Round-Trip Length of Conductor (Feet) | | | | | | | | | |
|---|---|---|---|---|---|---|---|---|---|
| Current (Amps) | 10 | 20 | 30 | 40 | 60 | 80 | 100 | 120 | 140 |
| | | | | *Minimum Wire Size (AWG)* | | | | | |
| 1 | 16 | 16 | 16 | 16 | 16 | 14 | 14 | 14 | 12 |
| 2 | 16 | 16 | 16 | 14 | 14 | 12 | 10 | 10 | 8 |
| 5 | 16 | 14 | 12 | 10 | 10 | 8 | 6 | 6 | 6 |
| 10 | 14 | 10 | 10 | 8 | 6 | 6 | 4 | 4 | 2 |
| 15 | 12 | 10 | 8 | 6 | 6 | 4 | 2 | 2 | 1 |
| 20 | 10 | 8 | 6 | 6 | 4 | 2 | 2 | 1 | 0 |
| 25 | 10 | 6 | 6 | 4 | 2 | 2 | 1 | 0 | 2/0 |
| 30 | 10 | 6 | 4 | 4 | 2 | 1 | 0 | 2/0 | 3/0 |
| 40 | 8 | 6 | 4 | 2 | 1 | 0 | 2/0 | 3/0 | 4/0 |
| 50 | 6 | 4 | 2 | 2 | 0 | 2/0 | 3/0 | 4/0 | |
| 60 | 6 | 4 | 2 | 1 | 2/0 | 3/0 | 4/0 | | |
| 70 | 6 | 2 | 1 | 0 | 3/0 | 4/0 | | | |
| 80 | 6 | 2 | 1 | 0 | 3/0 | 4/0 | | | |
| 90 | 4 | 2 | 0 | 2/0 | 4/0 | | | | |
| 100 | 4 | 2 | 0 | 2/0 | 4/0 | | | | |

Let's take our lights as an example. If the round-trip length of the wires combined have a total length of 30 feet and the size of the fuse we are using is 1 amp, then the AWG chart in Table 8-3 shows us that the gauge of wire we need to use is 16 AWG.

Now let's take our USB charging port, with a round-trip wire length of 15 feet and a 3-amp fuse. Looking at the AWG chart, we see that there isn't a choice for 15 feet, nor a 3-amp choice. In this case, go to nearest higher rating and length and use the measurement provided. On this occasion, the chart tells us that measurement is 14 AWG.

In the metric chart shown in Table 8-4, you can see that the equivalent metric measurement of 10 meters of wire with a 1-amp fuse tells us we need a wire gauge of 0.75 mm². For the USB charging port with 5 meters of wire and a 3-amp fuse (use the 4.5-amp rating as it's the nearest highest rating), the wire gauge is 1.5 mm².

**TABLE 8-4**  ## Metric Wiring Gauges

| Cable Diameter (mm) | Cable Section (mm) | L(+) + L(−) total 5 meters | L(+) + L(−) total 10 meters | L(+) + L(−) total 15 meters | L(+) + L(−) total 20 meters |
|---|---|---|---|---|---|
| 0.98 | 0.75 | 2.3 | 1.1 | 0.8 | 0.6 |
| 1.38 | 1.5 | 4.5 | 2.3 | 1.5 | 1.1 |
| 1.78 | 2.5 | 7.5 | 3.8 | 2.5 | 1.9 |
| 2.26 | 4 | 12 | 6 | 4 | 3 |
| 2.76 | 6 | 18 | 9 | 6 | 5 |
| 3.57 | 10 | 30 | 15 | 10 | 8 |
| 4.51 | 16 | 48 | 24 | 16 | 12 |
| 5.64 | 25 | 75 | 38 | 25 | 19 |
| 6.68 | 35 | 105 | 53 | 35 | 26 |
| 7.98 | 50 | 150 | 75 | 50 | 38 |
| 9.44 | 70 | 210 | 105 | 70 | 53 |
| 11.00 | 95 | 285 | 143 | 95 | 71 |
| 12.36 | 120 | 360 | 180 | 120 | 90 |

**REMEMBER**

Multiple charts and conversion tables give different readings, so feel free to use a few until you find a result you feel comfortable with.

# A Beginner's Guide to Circuits

You'll use two types of circuits in your camper van build: series circuits and parallel circuits.

## Series circuits

*Series circuits* can best be described as a loop. Imagine a square of wire with a battery at the very top. Series circuits start and end at the power source and have all the components sitting alongside each other in the same loop. This creates something called *resistance* as a sort of byproduct. Resistance is a force that counteracts the flow of current. The more components the current passes through, the more resistance is created.

To make it easier to understand, check out the diagram shown in Figure 8-4. Of the four lights in the series circuit, the one at the top right will be brightest, and the one on the top left (on the return back to the power source) will be dimmer than the rest. There's also the added problem that if one part of the circuit fails, the whole circuit will fail, preventing any of the bulbs from turning on.

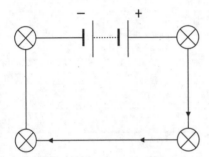

**FIGURE 8-4:** Diagram of a series circuit with four lights.

## Parallel circuits

*Parallel circuits* work differently to series circuits. Instead of a loop, a parallel circuit looks more like a ladder. Rather than each component sitting on the same circle, the components sit on the part of the ladder that would be the rung or foothold.

In this type of circuit, each component receives the same amount of electricity as the last, not a weakened current that has passed through multiple components. This has the added bonus that if one of the component rungs breaks or fails, the other lights on the other rungs will continue to work as if nothing happened. There is also far less resistance produced using this method, which is why it's the main circuit we're going to use for the majority of the electrical work in the next chapter. Check out the diagram shown in Figure 8-5 for reference.

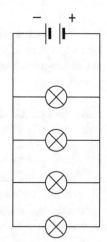

**FIGURE 8-5:**
Diagram of a
parallel circuit
with four lights.

# Earthing

You might have noticed me mentioning "earthing" electrical wires (also called *grounding*) to the side of your van a few times throughout this chapter. Once again, I know it sounds incredibly odd, but that's just how 12-volt automotive electrics work and it's perfectly safe.

Here in the U.K., we have three-prong plugs for our 240-volt appliances that house three wires: live, neutral, and earth. If anything goes wrong and there's a surge of power, one of the places this power goes is to the earth. (In other words, it becomes grounded and disappears.) The same happens with plug sockets in the U.S. — the neutral wire marries up to an earth wire at the service panel. This wire is sometimes referred to as the ground wire.

But what happens when you don't have a service panel in your house on wheels? The metal of the van and the chassis act as your earthing points to complete your 12-volt system in this case, and earthing your wires couldn't be simpler.

I want you to remember two things from here on out:

>> Red wires are positive.

>> Black wires are negative.

You should only ever be grounding black wires to earth in a 12-volt system. Keep that in mind, and you won't go wrong.

**WARNING**

This method of grounding is only for 12-volt electrics. I can't stress this enough. Please do not earth your 120-volt or 240-volt electrics to the side of your van.

**TIP**

One of the easiest places to earth your negative wires is the wheel arch frame inside your van. It's easily accessible from the back of the van and has space either side to move your hands when bolting crimped connectors. Don't worry about what a crimped connector is yet; that's coming soon.

When earthing wires to the metal of your van, make sure to rub off any paint with sandpaper so that you can see the bare metal and then give it a good wipe over. This will provide a much more stable and reliable earthing point.

**REMEMBER**

When drawing wires that are being earthed on your wiring diagram, they are represented by three lines that get incrementally smaller. Imagine a traffic cone, or a loud hailer or bullhorn, and you'll get the general idea. You should have this sign coming from pretty much all the main components of your electrical system: batteries, fuse box, fridge, diesel heater, and so on.

The only exception to the rule is your lights. These will be earthed within the fuse box itself, but that will all be revealed shortly.

## MEASURING WITH A MULTIMETER

Now seems as good a time as any to introduce a little tool that has proved invaluable to me over the years: the multimeter. It doesn't matter where in the world you live, you should be able to buy a multimeter from Amazon, eBay, or your local hardware store with ease, and they're invaluable gadgets when it comes to keeping tabs on your electrical setup.

Sometimes known as a multitester and referred to as a volt-ohm-milliammeter by about three people in a laboratory somewhere, a multimeter measures voltage, current, and resistance in an electrical circuit.

For reference:

- Volts = V for volts

- Current = A for amps

- Resistance = Ω for ohms

If you need to figure out how much voltage is running through your circuit or if any voltage is being lost, how many amps are being drawn, or the level of resistance anywhere in your camper electric system, then a multimeter can provide you with accurate reading. Every now and again, I would also pass the pins over my battery terminals to check how much charge they had straight from the source rather than relying on the MPPT solar controller. A multimeter is certainly a useful tool to have stored away in your bulkhead or in the back of your van.

# Drawing a Wiring Diagram

Sitting down to draw a wiring diagram might not be at the top of your list of things to do, especially if all you can think about is heading out into the wilderness on your first adventure. Still, having a reference point to look back on when trying to find faults or fix problems once your van is completed is incredibly helpful, so take the time to make yours now so that you know exactly where everything is going to go when we start putting everything together in the next chapter. A sample wiring diagram for a converted camper van is shown in Figure 8-6, and Table 8-5 lists the symbols you'll need to use when making your diagram.

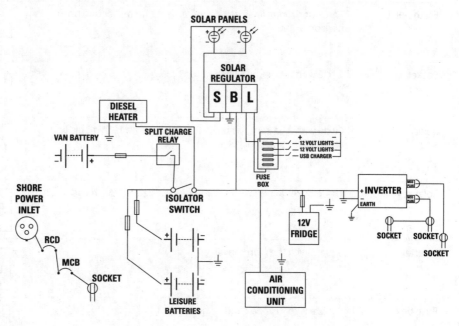

**FIGURE 8-6:** A sample wiring diagram.

| TABLE 8-5 | **Wiring Diagram Symbols** | |
|---|---|---|
| Battery | Four black vertical lines, the positive larger than the negative, with horizontal lines feeding away from them | |
| Inline fuse | Box outline with a line passing through it | |
| Switch | One line with a 45° bend in it like a drawbridge, with another smaller horizontal line under it | |
| Isolator switch | Two small circles with a line as a bridge, sometimes encapsulated inside a circle | |
| Circuit breakers | Two dots with a curved line (use this for all your circuit breakers with the unit written underneath) | |
| Earth point | Three horizontal lines getting incrementally smaller and one horizontal line | |
| Socket | Circle with two vertical lines | |
| Solar | Circle with a battery symbol in it including + and − symbols and arrows denoting sunlight | |
| Solar regulator | Three boxes joined with solar, batteries, lights (SBL) in each | |
| Inverter | Square with the word "Inverter" | |
| Fuse box | Square with fuse box and inline fuses | |

# Chapter 9

# Putting Your Electrical System Together

Now that you have gathered all the electrical equipment you need as outlined in the previous chapter, it's finally time to discover how to put it all together. If you looked at the table of contents for this book, you already know that this is a bit of a hefty chapter. Don't let that put you off, though; there *are* a lot of steps to cover, but I laid everything out in easy-to-follow steps that I hope make the process super simple to follow.

From crimping wires to soldering lamp holders and installing 12-volt refrigerators, you delve into the world of camper van electrics throughout the course of this chapter and discover how to turn your van into a self-sufficient tiny home on wheels. Plus, when you finish, you'll have new skills to wow people with at parties. This book is the gift that keeps on giving!

**REMEMBER** If you're itching to install air-conditioning or a heating source in your camper before you crack on with getting your electrical system sorted, then head over to Chapter 12 and soak up some tasty information. Find a cool bookmark and mark your place so you can come straight back here once you're done!

# Laying Everything Out

As a chef may do before starting a recipe, before you crimp that first wire or fire up your soldering iron, it's a great idea to lay out all the parts you're going to use for each step of the process. Not only does this make it easier for you to visualize what is going where and how much wire you'll need to cut for each segment, but it's also a great way to discover whether you're missing any parts you need.

**TIP**

For example, if you forgot to purchase a midi fuse holder or a length of cable, just hold off and wait until everything has arrived. I know it might be tempting, but there's really no point in starting a job this intricate if you don't have all the parts on hand.

# Wiring Techniques and Tips

It's time to start installing all that wire you bought after reading the previous chapter. There are a lot of different instructions throughout this chapter, so the best advice I can give you is to take your time, label up wires as often as you can, and keep taking regular breaks to give your brain a rest. In this section, you hone your wiring skills, learning how to earth, crimp, and other basic wiring skills you'll need to get the electrics in your tiny home set up and running.

## Earthing your electrics

I know I've probably said this a hundred times throughout the course of this book, but there's a very good reason for it, and that's because it's incredibly important: Once more, 12-volt automotive electrics use the side of the van as an earthing point. That means the negative terminals for your batteries, solar charge regulator, inverter, split charge relay, fridge, diesel heater, and any other component of your 12-volt system with a negative terminal will need to be connected to the side of your van via a ring crimp connector, a bolt, and a nut. Therefore, it's a good idea to position your batteries so that the negative terminals are closest to your wheel arch to avoid having lots of snaking cables. The wheel arch is a strong load-bearing area of your van too, so it's a good place to add excess weight.

Here's a quick guide on how to prepare this area to properly earth your electrics:

1. **Using a metal drill bit, drill a hole in the curved metal rim above your wheel arch on the inside of your van.**

   It doesn't matter where in the wheel arch you make this hole or whether you use the left or right-hand side of your van, and the chances are you will need to make a couple of holes to cope with all the connectors you are going to use (see Figure 9-1). Pick a drill bit the same size as a nut and bolt you have spare. The reason why will become apparent all too soon.

TIP

   Once again, this hole must be drilled on the inside of your van. You're using the metal rim that runs over your wheel arch as shown in Figure 9-1; you don't need to drill into the side wall of your van. From now on, I'll just call this the wheel arch.

**FIGURE 9-1:**
Here's a hole I prepared for earthing my leisure batteries with the paint already sanded back.

2. **Using some sandpaper, sand off the paint around your hole until you can see a shiny metal surface.**

   Connection is key when working with electrics, and you won't get a proper earthing if you don't have metal touching metal. You want to sand off the paint to expose the area of wheel arch back to the bare metal.

3. **Clean away any residue and make sure the area is dry.**

   Again, any particles of dust or paint could interfere with your connection, so make sure the area is spotless before you begin connecting terminals.

4. **Insert a nut and bolt into the hole ready for you to add your ring crimp connectors.**

   I'm giving you the gift of hindsight here. Put the bolt in so that the screw thread is pointing into the van toward you, allowing you to affix the nut on easily. I can't tell you how awkward it is if you're messing around with a nut that you can't see . . . something I didn't make the mistake of doing a second time.

## Hooking up battery terminal clip connectors

Battery terminals serve as the connection point between your battery and your electrics. There are two main different types of battery terminals: bolt and post.

» **Bolt terminals** consist of a square peg with a round hole for a bolt to pass through. Using the same method explained for how to bolt wires to your wheel arch, these terminals allow you to bolt a crimped connector to the battery terminal for a secure connection.

» **Post terminals** allow for the use of battery clip connectors, which are little colored clasps that clamp down onto each terminal (see Figure 9-2). I prefer using post terminals, as it's much easier to unclip them in an emergency, cutting all electrical supply from your batteries.

Post terminals are much more common in the countries like the U.K.; however, most battery companies provide a small bolt conversion system to turn any battery terminal into a post terminal should you want to go with the clip connector option.

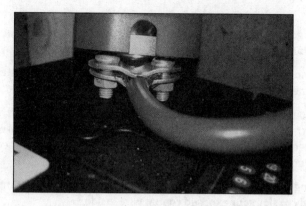

**FIGURE 9-2:**
One of my
red-colored
positive battery
clip connectors
attached to the
positive terminal
on my leisure
battery.

Hooking up a battery clip connector involves only a few steps. Here's how to do it:

1. **With a craft knife or some scissors, carefully strip back a few centimeters of the outer casing of your wire to expose the copper wires inside.**

   These copper wires are the bits you'll need to connect with your chosen connector.

2. **Loosen the screws in the clip connector and insert the end of your wire into the slot, and then tighten the screws back up again.**

   I'm going to level with you; this can get pretty fiddly, and it may take you a couple of times of trying before your connection finally holds. Tighten those screws as much as you can by hand and then get an adjustable wrench to finish them off.

## Crimping a wire

Crimping connectors come in a variety of shapes and sizes, though you're mainly going to use ring crimp connectors throughout this book. If you need a good way to remember what these look like, think miniature Quidditch goal rings or the little hooks you use to "hook a duck" at the fairground.

Adding crimping connectors to wires is relatively simple and doesn't require a soldering iron. Here's how to add a connector onto the end of your exposed wire:

1. **With a craft knife or some scissors, carefully strip back a few centimeters of the outer casing of your wire to expose the copper wires inside.**

   When cutting back your wire, make sure to leave around an inch of copper wire. Leave too little and you'll find it really hard to make a solid connection.

This goes without saying, but be careful when using a knife or blade to cut back the outer casing of your wire. Cut slowly and away from your body.

2. **Remove any rubber sleeves that come attached to your ring crimp connectors.**

   Seriously, these things are incredibly pointless and make it much harder to attach your wires into the crimping connector. Don't worry, you'll wrap all joins in electrical tape anyway to ensure all connections are safe and secure, so you just don't need these little sleeves.

3. **Using a pair of pliers, open out the chamber of your ring crimp connector ready to slot your exposed copper wire inside.**

   It's good that crimping connectors come in large packs, as this bit is incredibly fiddly. There is no real right or wrong way to open up this little metal chamber, but I found that using either the tip of my pliers or the wire cutting part in the middle provided the easiest solution for opening up the connector. Essentially, you want to open this section up so that you can fit as much of your copper wire inside as possible.

4. **Insert your exposed wire into the connector, making sure you insert all the copper strands to make a strong connection once you clamp the ring crimp connector shut again.**

5. **Using a crimping tool or the gripping tip of your pliers, firmly squeeze the folded parts of your ring crimp connector back down around your wire so that it's nice and snug.**

   This might take a few goes and you might throw your connector onto the ground in a huff, but keep persevering. Take your time and don't worry if you make a few mistakes.

Once the wire is in, give it a gentle tug. If it flies straight out, then you haven't used enough elbow grease. Try again and squeeze like you mean it!

6. **Wrap the join of the connector and your wire with electrical tape or a piece of heat shrink tubing.**

   Go over the join three or four times with electrical tape to make sure it's all nicely insulated or use some heat shrink tubing. The last thing you want is a stray copper wire snaking free and connecting with something metal.

When using heat shrink tubing, use a hairdryer to heat up the piece of tubing until it shrinks down and sits snugly over the join.

Don't put any tape on the ring terminal part of your crimp connector. You will need a clean connection there, so keep your taping nice and neat.

## Mapping out the isolator switch

The isolator switch isn't just an important safety element in your circuit; this switch will be a prevalent part of your electrical connections from here on out. As this connector acts as a bridge between your batteries and the rest of your appliances, these two terminals will play host to multiple ring crimp connectors.

Not all isolator switches are the same, so double-check the diameter of your battery terminals before adding the relevant crimp connector onto the wire that will be connected to it. If in doubt, go bigger.

Looking at the back of your isolator switch, your batteries need to be connected up to the left terminal. Everything else, bar the split charge relay, which I touch upon soon, needs to connect to the right side. This is so that when the switch is open (disconnected), no power can flow from your batteries to your appliances.

# Installing Batteries

Now that you have seen how to crimp and set up battery connectors, it's time to get those batteries installed. Remember how I spoke about series and parallel circuits in the last chapter? As a recap, series circuits can best be described as having multiple components along a ring or circle, whereas parallel circuits resemble a ladder, with each component sitting on a different rung.

When it comes to wiring up the leisure batteries that are going to power your electrical system, wiring in a series (as part of the same circle) increases the overall voltage, whereas wiring in parallel keeps the voltage the same and increases the overall battery capacity.

For the purposes of this book, we're going to wire up the batteries in parallel. This means that with two 100 Ah batteries, we create a total battery capacity of 200 amp hours while keeping the voltage the same, avoiding any overloading of our 12-volt appliances.

Things you'll need:

>> Appropriate gauge wire: red and black

>> 6 ring crimp terminals

>> 4 battery clip connectors (2 bearing a positive [+] symbol, 2 bearing a negative [–] symbol)

>> 2 midi fuse holders

>> 2 midi fuses (see the calculations you made back in Chapter 8)

>> 1 isolator switch

>> Electrical tape (red for positive wires, black for negative wires) or heat shrink tubing

To connect your batteries in parallel, follow these steps:

1. **Position your batteries, midi fuse holders, and isolator switch in your circuit.**

   Once everything is positioned, mark out how much wire you will need to reach from:

   - The positive battery terminal to the left terminal of your midi fuse holder. This is Wire A.

   - The right terminal of your midi fuse holder to the left bolt on your isolator switch (looking from the back). This is Wire B.

   - The negative battery terminal to the bolt in the side of your wheel arch. This is Wire C.

2. **With a craft knife or some scissors, carefully cut your wire lengths and strip back a few centimeters of the outer casing of your wire on either end to expose the copper wires inside.**

   These are the bits you'll need to connect with your chosen connector.

   Always cut a slightly longer length of wire than you need just in case you make a mistake. You'll thank me for this when you do.

TIP

3. **Connect Wire A into your positive post terminal clip and add a ring crimp connector to the other side.**

   This is the first part of your connection, leading from your positive terminal to the left terminal inside your midi fuse holder. Loosely secure with the midi fuse holder bolt to keep it in place for now. Insulate all connections with red electrical tape and repeat for the second leisure battery.

**4.** **Add a ring crimp connector to each end of Wire B.**

This is the wire that will connect the right terminal of your midi fuse holder to your isolator switch. Use the screw of the midi fuse holder to hold this in place for now. Insulate all connections with red electrical tape and repeat for the second midi fuse holder.

This connection won't be live until you add a midi fuse into the holder. If you remember from the previous chapter, these look like little 2D TIE Fighters with holes in their wings. These holes slot over the terminals in the midi fuse connector, followed by your ring crimp connectors and the included screws to create a tight connection.

**5.** **Connect Wire C into your negative post terminal clip and add a ring crimp connector to the other side.**

This negative clip connector sits on the negative terminal of your battery. The crimped end will attach to the bolt in your wheel arch when you're ready to connect everything up. Now, you should have two leisure batteries all with battery clips and wires connected as shown in Figure 9-3.

That's everything you need to worry about for the time being. Now, let's get those solar panels wired up!

**FIGURE 9-3:**
The power hub of my camper: two LiFePo$_4$ batteries hooked up to midi fuse holders and an isolator switch.

# Wiring Up Solar Panels

In a few hours, you will be 100 percent more self-sufficient than you were before reading this sentence. Yes, your journey to harnessing the sun's rays for free electricity starts right here. From this moment on, your life will never be the same again . . . probably.

TIP

One thing I want you to think about before you go into drilling holes or even touching solar panels is cable conduit, which is tubing designed to enclose wires. Plan your solar panel wires journey from your solar panels down to your electric box and line the route with cable conduit for the wires to run through.

These wires carry a lot of volts, and the last thing you want is for a wire to snag and make a live connection with the side of your van. Yes, I know it sounds like I'm being overcautious again, but I've covered enough conversions in my time as a journalist to know that it pays to be careful when it comes to your electric setup.

TIP

Solar panel fixing, or mounting, kits can be bought on eBay or Amazon and make installing your solar panels an absolute breeze. These kits comprise of four corner pieces and a cable entry box. You'll need one kit per solar panel. Follow the instructions that follow to discover how to use them.

## Installing the panels

You are about to install two heavy items on the roof of your van, which means you need to make sure they are locked down tighter than Fort Knox. Still, as always, I describe the next steps in a way that I understand best: simple, to the point, and with zero fuss.

Things you'll need:

>> Solar panels

>> Solar panel fixing (mounting) kit and cable entry box for each solar panel

>> Drill

>> 6-millimeter ( $^{15}/_{64}$ -inch) metal drill bit

>> M6 bolts (get plenty)

>> M6 nyloc nuts (again, get plenty)

# Attaching the panels to your roof

Follow these steps to attach the panels to your roof:

1. **Attach your fixing kit to the frame of your solar panel(s).**

   **a.** Holding your corner fixing kit to the corner of your solar panel, drill a hole through the plastic of the fixing piece and the metal frame of your solar panel.

   **b.** Thread an M6 bolt through the hole and tighten with an M6 nyloc nut.

   **c.** Repeat this process on both edges of the corner fixing kit and replicate for the remaining pieces on each panel.

TIP

   Use M6 nyloc bolts to clamp the fixing kit and solar panel securely. Nyloc bolts have nylon inserts that create friction on the bolt thread, greatly reducing the chance of your nut loosening over time as you head off-road while traveling.

2. **Using a marker pen, measure and mark out three points on the base section on each part of your fixing kit.**

   If you're not getting this already, I'm incredibly persnickety when it comes to measuring and the finer details. Ensuring that all your holes are in the same position on each corner fixing piece means that you have the option of swapping the position of your solar panels at a later date should you need to.

TIP

   Create a template using a piece of cardboard and mark these points onto each piece of your fixing kit. This way, you don't need to measure each one separately.

3. **Carefully drill through your markers in the flat base of each corner bracket using a 6-millimeter drill bit.**

   Drill carefully; if you make a mistake, you'll ruin all that hard measuring work with your template, so take your time and don't rush.

4. **Position your solar panels on your van roof.**

5. **Using a marker, create a mark to highlight each hole in the base of your fixing kit.**

   If nothing else, you should now be incredibly skilled at making dots with a marker pen.

6. **Carefully drill down through each of your hole markers into the roof of your van using a 6-millimeter drill bit.**

   I know that I'm going to sound like Captain Cautious yet again, but just like Mad Eye Moody, I want you to maintain constant vigilance when drilling holes in your vehicle, especially ones that might let rain flow into your insulation. Take your time and drill carefully. Going at this like a bull in a china shop will only ever end in tears.

**7.** **Bolt your solar panels to the roof of your van through your fixing kit.**

As you can see in Figure 9-4, I added a precautionary layer of sealant around each of my fixing plates to stop rain from getting underneath and down through the bolt holes.

**8.** **Using M6 bolts and M6 nyloc nuts, affix the fixing kit baseplates to the roof of your van.**

**WARNING**

I cannot stress how important it is to make sure that these fixing kits are securely tightened to the roof of your van. The last thing you want is a solar panel flying off your roof as you drive down the motorway. Make sure to go over every bolt twice with your wrench.

**TIP**

Use two nyloc bolts to make sure you have a secure connection. If you bought a pack of them, then the others are only going to sit in your toolbox doing nothing. You might as well put them to good use! Alternatively, you can use Dekasyl MS-5 to glue these baseplates onto your roof securely.

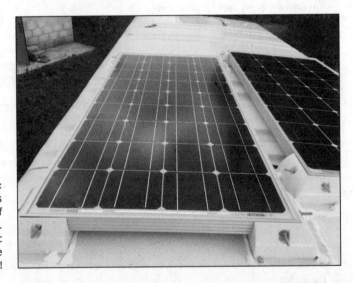

**FIGURE 9-4:**
Two solar panels bolted to the roof of my van. Goodbye electric bills, hello free energy!

So now that your panels are fixed onto your roof, it's time to get those all-important solar cables down into the main body of your van. Once again, there's a handy solution available to buy from the Internet: a cable housing kit complete with cable glands. This might have come with your solar panel fixing kit, but they're easy to pick up if it didn't. You're going to fix this box to your roof now and feed your wires through it into the living area of your van.

Solar panels come with solar wire already attached, usually around 16 feet (5 meters), which is plenty enough to make it down into the body of your van from your roof. This is a good thing, as you'll cut some off to create the feed into your solar charge regulator. These wires come with connectors attached, but you'll need to snip these off in order to feed them through your cable glands into your van. Put them to one side; you'll use more of these connectors once you get to hooking everything up, and you never know when they might come in handy!

## Bringing solar panel wires into your van

Cable entry boxes are the Gandalfs of the solar panel world; once affixed, the only thing that shall pass into your van is your solar cables, keeping the wind and rain outside where they belong.

Here's how to attach your cable entry point onto the roof of your van and get those cables down into your electrical area where they belong.

1. **Place your cable entry point box on the roof of your van and draw around it with a marker pen.**

   By now, you should be an absolute wizard with a marker pen. Drawing around your box gives you a reference point as to where you will fix it down and also the space that you have to drill holes for your cables to enter your van.

2. **Using a drill, make two holes within the confines of your marker outline.**

   This shouldn't prove too difficult; just make sure that each hole is well away from the edge of your box to be on the safe side.

3. **Use some sandpaper to smooth down the edges of your hole, and then use some electrical tape to line the gap.**

   This will prevent any cable snags. Always wedge a little bit of cable conduit in there.

4. **Separate the positive and negative wires from both solar panels and feed them into separate cable glands.**

   These wires come with connectors attached, so if you haven't already, snip these off in order to feed them through your cable glands and into your van.

   Before you go any further, use some masking tape to mark up your positive and negative wires. This bit is incredibly important, so take the time to get this right. Use a red addition sign (+) for positive and a black negative sign (–) for the negative wires. If you don't put both positive wires down through one hole and both negative through the other, it will end up being much harder to wire them up in the next stage.

5. **With the cable glands attached into your cable entry box, use a strong glue such as Gorilla Glue or Dekasyl MS-5 to secure it to the top of your van.**

These cable entry boxes don't have a space to screw them down onto the top of your van. The solution: Gorilla Glue or Dekasyl MS-5. Simply apply glue to one surface and hold down in place with some strong tape. Leave for 24 hours and then use some Sikaflex sealant around the edges of the box for good measure.

## Adding new connectors onto your solar cable

Cutting those connectors off of the solar panel wires in the previous steps was a necessary evil in order to weatherproof the entry hole into your van. Now, you'll need to reattach some new MC-4 connectors to them. (Can you see now why I was so adamant that you labelled those wires before you put them back through into your van?)

There are two types of MC-4 connectors: male and female. As you might have guessed, these correlate to your positive and negative wires.

» **Male MC-4** connectors are used for the positive wires from your solar panels. These connectors have a little red ring on them, a great way to remember that they connect up to positive wires.

» **Female MC-4** connectors are used for the negative wires from your solar panels. These are slightly longer in length than the male connectors and are more rectangular in shape.

Inside each MC-4 is a silver contact. I want you to treat these silver contacts in exactly the same manner as the ring crimp connectors I spoke about earlier in this chapter in "Crimping a wire."

MC-4 connectors come in packs of two: one male and one female. You need three packs for the following section, so buy these now before you carry on.

Here's how to hook up solar wire to the silver contacts inside MC-4 connectors:

1. **With a craft knife or some scissors, carefully strip back a few centimeters of the outer casing of your wire to expose the solar wire inside.**

When cutting back your wire, make sure to leave around an inch of solar wire. Leave too little and you'll find it really hard to make a solid connection.

2. **Remove the cap from the MC-4 connector and thread it onto your wire.**

   You won't need it right now, but I can guarantee that you'll get everything connected up and then have to remove it all to put the cap on, just like I did.

3. **Using a pair of pliers, open up the chamber of your silver contact ready to slot your exposed solar wire inside.**

   Just like the ring crimp connectors, you'll get a good result by using either the tip of your pliers or the wire cutting part in the middle. Essentially, you want to open this section up so that you can fit all your exposed solar wire inside as possible.

4. **Insert your exposed wire into the silver contact.**

   Just like the ring crimp connectors, make sure to put all the exposed wire into the contact to ensure a strong connection.

5. **Using a crimping tool or the gripping tip of your pliers, firmly squeeze the folded parts of your silver contact back down around your wire so that it's nice and snug.**

   Once the wire is in, give it a gentle tug. It should sit snugly and not pop out. Try again and clamp the connector tighter if it does.

TIP

6. **With the silver contact fixed onto the end of your wire (positive or negative), thread through the corresponding male or female connector.**

   Push this wire in until you hear a click. That's the magic sound that lets you know you've slotted it into place.

7. **Screw the cap onto the end of your connector, locking your wire in place.**

   I told you it would be handy to place that connector cap on the wire at the beginning.

8. **Screw it into place and stand back while you admire your handiwork.**

Now that you've got your male and female connectors hooked up, it's time to figure out how to connect them together and convert four wires down into two.

For this next section you need something called an MC-4 T-branch connector, and you'll need one male and one female. Simply connect your MC-4 connectors to the corresponding male and female connectors. You can't get this wrong; there's only one way they can connect up so there's no chance of making mistakes.

Okay, I want you to hold here a second while we take a look at different inputs on the solar charge regulator. Maybe have a coffee and a biscuit too. Gotta keep those energy levels up.

# Setting up your solar charge regulator

The solar charge regulator is the hub that controls all power created by the sun's rays. In layman's terms, it's kind of a big deal. There are three sets of inputs on your regulator (a positive and negative for each) signified by three different symbols:

>> A **solar panel symbol** for the positive and negative feed from your solar panel wires

>> A **battery symbol** for the positive and negative feed from your batteries

>> A **light symbol** (which looks a little like a crystal on some models) for the positive and negative feed from your fuse box

**WARNING**

Your battery wires need to go into your Maximum Power Point Tracking (MPPT) solar charge regulator *before* your solar panel wires to tell the regulator whether you're running a 12-volt or 24-volt system.

**REMEMBER**

Until your isolator switch is in the closed position and midi fuses are added into their respective position, no power will get from your batteries to the other components of your circuit. Only flip this switch once your batteries are earthed to the side of the van.

## Wiring up your batteries to your solar charge regulator

It's time to pay some attention to the empty bolt on your isolator switch. As you're looking at it from the back, that's the one on the right side.

Things you'll need:

>> A length of red gauge wire with a ring crimp connector on one end only. This needs to be long enough to reach from your isolator switch to your solar charge regulator.

>> A length of black gauge wire with a ring crimp connector on one end only. This needs to be long enough to reach from your solar charge regulator to your earthing point on the side of your wheel arch.

To wire up your batteries to your solar charge regulator, follow these steps:

**1.** **Bolt the ring crimp connector on the positive wire to the empty bolt on your isolator switch.**

2. **Screw the bolt on by hand and tighten it with a wrench for a secure connection.**

TIP

You haven't put fuses in your midi fuse holders yet, so there won't be an active connection. Still, it's good practice to keep your isolator switch in the open position when messing around with electrics so you know you're not working while electricity is flowing.

TIP

The isolator switch key is removable when the switch is in an open position, so take it out and stick it in your pocket for extra peace of mind.

3. **Unscrew the screw clamp under the + sign beneath your battery symbol, insert the bare end of your red wire, and tighten.**

Follow the same method you used for inserting your solar wire into your regulator once again.

4. **Unscrew the screw clamp under the – sign beneath your battery symbol, insert the bare end of your black wire, and tighten.**

Remember to be careful while unscrewing those screws so you don't lose them.

5. **Add the ring crimp connector on the other end of your black wire onto your earthing bolt in your wheel arch.**

Once bolted tightly, your solar charge regulator will be earthed and ready to go.

Now it's time to get those fuses in place and bolt your earth wires to the side of your wheel arch.

## Making your connection live

Things you'll need:

>> 2 midi fuses (see Chapter 8 to calculate the appropriate fuse size for your setup)

>> The isolator switch key from your pocket

To make your connection live, follow these steps:

1. **Insert your midi fuses into the midi fuse holders.**

2. **Place the ring terminals from the wires feeding to and from your fuse holders over the bolts, then add your midi fuse holder.**

3. **Screw the nuts included with your fuse holder back onto the bolts, securing everything down.**

4. **Take the ring crimp connector ends of your two negative battery wires and the negative wire from your solar charge regulator and securely bolt them to the side of your van.**

   Take care to make sure the bolt thread is sticking out into the van for ease. Tighten with your fingers and finish off with a wrench for a tight connection.

5. **Insert your isolator switch key and turn into the close position.**

   You should now see lights on your solar charge regulator, which means that power is flowing through your circuit. Take a break and have a cup of tea — you've earned it.

REMEMBER

Once in the closed position, your key will be fixed in place and can't be pulled out.

TIP

Use a multimeter to check for any breaks in your circuit if you can't see any lights on your solar charge regulator.

Now, let's finish hooking up those solar panel wires.

REMEMBER

Turn your isolator switch and remove the key to make sure no electricity is running to your MPPT while you work on it.

## Wiring up your solar panels to your solar charge regulator

At this stage, you should have the following connected:

>> Two positive wires with male MC-4 connectors attached

>> Two negative wires with female MC-4 connectors attached

>> A male MC-4 T-branch connector attached to each of the positive connectors

>> A female MC-4 T-branch connector attached to each of the negative connectors

REMEMBER

You really can't connect your T-branch connectors wrong. As long as you're plugging male connectors into female ports and female into male, then you've done it right.

Now that you have four wires leading into two T–branch connectors, the next job is to complete the connection into your solar charge regulator.

Things you'll need:

➤ 1 MC-4 male connector

➤ 1 MC-4 female connector

➤ Small lengths of solar wire to reach from your T-branch connectors to your solar charge regulator

Here's how to finish your solar panel cable run and insert them into your solar charge regulator:

**1.** **Take two lengths of solar wire offcut, and with a craft knife or some scissors, carefully strip back a few centimeters of the outer casing of your wire on each end.**

By stripping back some of the outer casing, you expose the solar wire inside ready for MC-4 connectors.

**TIP**

Take a moment to use some masking tape and label one length of wire with a red + symbol and one wire with a black – symbol.

**WARNING**

This might sound confusing, but you now need to use your male connector for the negative wire, and your female connector for the positive wire in order to bring your feed home into your solar charge regulator. This will make sense when looking at the bottom of your T-branch connectors. In essence, as long as you have wire with a piece of masking tape bearing the same symbol above and below each segment of "the connector junction," then you're winning.

**2.** **Follow the earlier steps in "Adding new connectors onto your solar cable" for adding a silver contact and an MC-4 connector, male and female, onto one end of each wire.**

You should now have two pieces of wire: a positive length with a female connector on one end, the and a negative length with a male connector on one end. Leave the other ends bare; these are the exposed ends that will slot into your solar charge regulator.

**3.** **Using a screwdriver, unscrew the screw clamps beneath the + and – symbols directly below the solar panel symbol on your solar charge regulator.**

These screws act as clamps that will lock your wires in place. They do the same job as the little chambers on your ring crimp connectors but are a heck of a lot easier to manage.

Unscrew these screws enough to get your wire in but no further. They're little and easily lost, so make sure you don't pull them all the way out.

4. **Connect your MC-4 connectors to the T-branch connectors.**

   This feels like making a Power Rangers Megazord as a kid . . . a niche reference that will only apply to the "mega nerds" out there.

5. **Insert the bare ends of your solar wire into the appropriate slots and tighten them back up.**

   Just to be clear, that's the positive wire into the slot with the + symbol, and the negative wire in the slot with the – symbol.

And there you go! You've now hooked your solar panels up to your solar charge regulator.

## Hooking up your solar charge monitor

Some solar charge regulators like the Renogy Rover MPPT solar charge regulator come with a screen built in. Some, however, require an additional monitor to be able to change parameters, or perhaps you might prefer to have a monitor in an easy-to-reach place rather than delving down into your electric cupboard every time.

So what does this little monitor do then? Well, it allows for parameters related to your solar panels and battery feed to be changed — such as your battery capacity and type and float charge settings — to further customize your electrical setup. The main things you will use this solar charge monitor for is to see how many volts your panels are drawing in, how many amps this is being converted to, and how many amps specific 12-volt appliances are pulling from your batteries.

Most solar charge monitors are powered via an ethernet cable that comes with the monitor itself. This port isn't hard to miss; you'll have seen this type of port on computer towers for most of your life. Once connected, affix to any point you want using the provided screws.

## Connecting your solar charge regulator to your fuse box

It's time to fill the last two slots on your solar charge regulator: the + and – ports for your lights. In your circuit setup, these wires are connecting up to the fuse box that houses the fuses for all your lights and the terminal points for your light wires. Here's how to get that fuse box hooked up and into the mix.

Things you'll need:

» A length of red wire with a ring crimp connector on one end only. This needs to be long enough to reach from your fuse box to the positive port on your solar charge regulator.

» A length of black wire with a ring crimp connector on one end only. This needs to be long enough to reach from your fuse box to the negative port on your solar charge regulator.

Let's first take a look at the fuse box diagram shown in Figure 9-5. As you can see, there are multiple bolts and screws — so many, in fact, that it looks like something you might find lurking around inside Inspector Gadget.

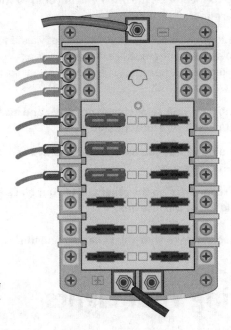

**FIGURE 9-5:**
A rough sketch of a typical camper van fuse box.

For starters, let's talk about the three main bolts: the single bolt at the top and the two at the bottom. The one at the very top is the negative earthing point for the entire fuse box. This is the bolt that will feed into the — port on your solar charge regulator.

For this particular fuse box, power goes in at the bottom and is earthed at the top. The two bolts at the bottom are for bringing current into your fuse box. Now, if you draw an imaginary line up from between these two bolts to the top of the fuse box, you'll automatically split the face into two separate banks: a positive feed bolt for each bank. For the purposes of this section, we'll concentrate on the bottom-left bolt and the left bank of odd-numbered fuse slots.

TIP

If your fuse box doesn't look like the one shown in Figure 9-5, then use a multi-meter to determine the positive and negative bolt positions and act accordingly.

Here's how to connect your solar charge regulator to your fuse box:

1. **Turn your isolator switch into the open position, removing the key.**

   Removing the key isn't a necessary step, but I like a visible reminder that the circuit is open.

2. **Unscrew the + symbol on your solar charge regulator and insert the exposed end of your red wire into the slot.**

   A good tip is to twist the end of the wire into a point to help get it into the slot.

3. **Bolt the ring crimp connector on the other end of your red wire to the bottom-left bolt terminal.**

   This brings power into your left back from your batteries via the solar charge regulator. It will also allow for the amperage draw when using your lights and other appliances linked to your fuse box to be shown on your solar charge monitor.

4. **Unscrew the – symbol on your solar charge regulator and insert the exposed end of your black wire into the slot.**

5. **Twist the end in the same way you did with the positive wire and be careful with that little screw.**

6. **Bolt the ring crimp connector on the other end of your black wire to the bolt terminal at the top of the fuse box.**

Now your fuse box is hooked up to your solar charge regulator!

## Wiring and Soldering Your Lights

Now that your fuse box is up and running, it's time to start planning where your lights are going to go. This is another reason why it's important to leave cladding until *after* you've sorted all your electrics out.

WARNING

This bit is going to require a lot of patience and some nimble fingers. If you're reading this section at 3 p.m. and thinking about starting with your wires, then do yourself a favor and read the rest of the chapter with a cup of coffee and leave the practical element until the morning. There's no point in rushing, so make sure to give yourself plenty of time.

TIP

Spend lots of time planning where your lights are going for this next section. Use pen and paper to make a separate wiring diagram showing the location of lights and switches, then use masking tape to mark out the physical locations inside your build.

I used so much wire in this section that I had to use black wire with red tape dotted on it here and there in the place of positive red wire. Of course, the innards of black and red wire are exactly the same; it's more a visible reference when wiring up components. The moral of this story, and yet another hindsight alert, is to make sure you have enough of the appropriate gauge wire in both colors before starting so you don't get yourself confused.

TIP

When it comes to picking light switches, you don't need to just opt for the standard panel switches that you might find inside a house. The beauty of building your own conversion is that you can use whatever style switch you want, from missile launch-style switches to miniature push-button switches in discreet places. I opted for the missile launch flip switches in my camper as they made me feel like I was a James Bond movie villain. And more important, they were only $1.80 (£1.50) each.

Things you'll need:

» A length of red wire. This wire needs to be long enough to pass through your switch and to the position of the last lamp in your circuit for each cable run.

» A length of black wire. This wire needs to be long enough to run from the last lamp in your circuit back to the fuse box for each cable run.

» Soldering iron or WAGO lever connectors

» Solder

» Spotlight lamp holders

» Wire stripper tool

» Safety goggles, gloves, and mask

REMEMBER

All your lights don't need to be on one switch. You can have as many switches as you want in your build and as many lights on each switch as you require. For the purposes of this section, I'm going to imagine that you have two switches with two lights on each switch. That means you'll use two fuse slots down the left side of your fuse box.

Follow these steps to hook up your lights in your van:

1. **Run a length of red wire from your fuse box to the position of your first switch.**

2. **Make a little loop around your finger, and then pass along all the points where you have marked for your light bulbs, finishing at the position of the last bulb.**

   The little loop around your finger is so that you have a little extra length to play around with when it comes to splitting your wire, adding crimping connectors, and attaching them to your switch.

   Depending on where your switch is, you might have to run your wire up one wall, along the roof, and down the side of the other wall. It doesn't matter where this switch is just make sure your wire runs past it for now.

TIP

   Tape your wire up with pieces of masking tape as you go so that it's secured out of the way and doesn't drop on your head.

3. **Using wire cutters, split your wire at the center of your loop, strip back the casing of both ends, and add ring crimp connectors to each exposed end.**

   The size and style of crimp connector will depend on the size of the switch you are using. Buy your switch first and then purchase the correct size and style connector to go with it.

4. **Attach the crimp connector on the length of wire leading from your fuse box to the bottom or left terminal on your switch, and then attach the other connector to the second terminal on your switch and tighten both for a secure connection.**

   You should have a good idea about how switches work now after all the times you've turned your isolator switch on and off. Essentially, a light switch breaks the current flow to your lights by cutting the feed through your positive wire, thus turning your lights on and off. It's basically a miniature version of your isolator switch and does a similar job.

5. **With your red wire in place, follow the run back in the opposite direction with your black wire, starting at the position of the last lamp in your circuit and ending back at the fuse box.**

   Your black wire doesn't need to go anywhere near your light switch. Once it has passed through the position of all your lamps, feed it down toward your fuse box.

6. **Add ring crimp connectors to the bare ends of your red positive and black negative wires located near your fuse box.**

   For a refresher on how to add these connectors, follow the steps outlined earlier in "Crimping a wire."

**7.** **Attach your positive and negative wires to the fuse box.**

There are lots of screws here, but once you know what's what, everything becomes a lot simpler. The screws next to the blade fuse ports are for positive inputs. That's where you attach your red positive wires. The bank of six screws sitting close together at the top of the fuse box are for earthing your connections, so that's where you'll attach the crimp connectors from your black wires.

TIP

It doesn't matter which positive and negative port you use; they don't have to be corresponding. So long as there's a fuse next to your positive wire and your negative wire is earthed on the left bank, you'll have a working circuit.

**8.** **Repeat the process for any other lights and switches in your build.**

As I said earlier, I'm working on the assumption that you have one switch controlling two lights at the front of the living area, and one switch operating two in the back. You can have as many lights as you want on these switches, but just remember that more lights mean more amps drawn.

WARNING

Keep all fuses out of your fuse box for now and make sure your main isolator switch key is still in your pocket to ensure no electricity is running through your circuit.

You should now be in a position where you have red wires passing through your switches to the proposed position of all your lights and black wires passing parallel to them. The next step is to use wire strippers to expose sections of copper wire for soldering on lamp holders/sockets.

## A BRIEF NOTE ON BULBS

I used downlighting spotlights in my van and never changed the bulbs once in five years. Not only do they last forever, but they don't pull lots of energy. A 4-watt LED bulb can produce the brightness of a 30-watt bulb, brightening any tiny space with ease.

Before you think about inserting bulbs, however, you'll need to solder in lamp holders into your wire trail. A lamp holder is essentially a little connector with two wires coming off it. There is no positive or negative wire to worry about here; so long as you solder one to the red wire trail on your ceiling and the other to the black wire trail, you'll be fine.

Lamp holders can be picked up from Amazon, eBay, or your local hardware store relatively cheaply. Get a pack of ten; mistakes may happen, so be prepared.

## A BRIEF NOTE ON WAGO LEVER CONNECTORS

If you don't feel confident using a soldering iron, then you can always switch out soldered joins for WAGO lever connectors. These are little boxes with multiple compartments that you can use to connect segments of wire together that you have cut and stripped. Essentially, every time I mention soldering one of the lamp holder wires onto your red or black wire trail, you can use a three-compartment WAGO lever connector to connect the split segment of wire (the wire heading toward the lamp holder in the first box, and the wire heading out away from the lamp holder in the third box), and one wire from the lamp holder in the middle box. You can do the same on the opposing black length of wire too.

## Connecting lamp holders/sockets

**WARNING**

In a second, you're going to be using a red–hot soldering iron and solder above your head while looking up at the work you are carrying out. That means that there is a small yet potential risk of solder falling onto your face. If this hits your eyes, it *will* blind you, so please wear safety goggles. Soldering irons are hot, and hot solder also makes fumes too, so wear your gloves and mask to complete the safety set.

Soldering fumes all also hazardous, so make sure you wear a mask, work in a properly ventilated area, or use a table extraction fan to remove the fumes from your work area.

Here's how to connect your lamp holders into your red and black wire trail:

1. **Remove lengths of casing on both your red and black wires in the areas where you will be installing your lamp holders using a wire stripper tool.**

   A wire stripper tool will remove a specific length of cable without damaging the copper wire inside. You can use a knife, but the chance of you actually cutting through the wire is incredibly high. Play it safe and use the correct tool.

2. **Wrap each end of the lamp connector around the exposed sections on your red and black wire.**

   Wrap it around a couple of times so that it stays in place without holding.

3. **Heat up your soldering iron.**

4. **Using your soldering iron, apply solder to the wound wires to create a secure connection.**

5. **With your roll of solder in one hand, hold a piece of solder to the join between the two wires.**

6. **Apply the soldering iron to the point you want to fuse together and let solder flow around it.**

   This practice of heating the metal wire and the solder so that solder flows into all the individual copper strands is the most efficient way of creating a strong connection that will last the test of time.

7. **Keep feeding solder into the equation until you're happy that you have a chrome-colored join that covers both wires.**

   Don't skimp out with the solder on this section but keep things tidy. You don't need to make any big blobs or wrap the join in an inch of solder.

8. **Once the solder is cold, wrap it in electrical tape or heat shrink tubing to cover the join.**

9. **Repeat the process for any other lamp holders.**

   Once you've done one, the whole process will feel much simpler. You might feel like you want to speed up a little, but just take your time and keep your eyes on the prize.

## Adding blade fuses

Remember the little prisoner transport ships from *Tron* I spoke about in the previous chapter? Well, it's time to start implementing them into your electrical setup.

Now that you've got wires coming to and from your fuse box, you'll need to add some blade fuses into the slots next to where your red positive wires are secured. Your lights won't work unless you have a fuse finishing off your circuit, just like power won't pass through your isolator switch unless the key is in the closed position.

As there isn't a lot of current required to power LED bulbs, you'll only need a small-rated fuse. A purple 3-amp rated blade fuse will do just fine. They might be small, but they'll still act as a source of protection should anything go wrong with a bulb.

TIP

When something goes wrong with an appliance, nine times out of ten it's just a fuse that needs changing. With that in mind, it's important to position your fuse box somewhere that you can access easily to make this easy check for yourself.

# Connecting Your Inverter

Let's leave 12-volt talk behind now and get onto some real power, shall we? No matter your region, an inverter connects to your 12-volt system and provides you with the same electrical power that you might use inside a house, hotel, or café. It gives you the ability to plug any external appliance in, like a food processor, laptop charger, projector, basically any item with a cord and plug.

Connecting an inverter into your setup is actually pretty straightforward. It doesn't need to go via your solar charge regulator or even your fuse box, making the whole process much easier. In most cases, inverters come with all the necessary cables you'll need to insert them into your electrical system. You should find:

» A positive red cable with ring connector ends attached

» A negative black cable with ring connector ends attached

» An earth wire (usually green and yellow)

Here's how to install your inverter, and a helpful (and slightly dusty) picture of mine once installed is shown in Figure 9-6.

**FIGURE 9-6:** My inverter fully installed and accessible from inside my toilet cupboard. I raised it up to let air underneath and plugged two RCD plugs into the front.

**WARNING**

Make sure your isolator switch is in the open position and the key is safely in your pocket before continuing.

1. **Familiarize yourself with your inverter terminals.**

   Just like batteries, inverters have a positive and a negative terminal that need connecting to your system. Luckily, the positive terminal is usually colored red, and the negative terminal is colored black.

2. **Connect your red wire to your positive terminal and your black wire to your negative terminal.**

   As inverters come as a kit, your wires will already be crimped and ready to go. These connectors attach in a similar way to the smaller terminals in your fuse box. Use a crosshead screwdriver and make a tight connection.

3. **Connect the second end of your red wire to the right terminal on your isolator switch (looking from the back).**

   Just as a reminder, this is the one that your batteries are *not* attached to.

4. **Bolt the second end of your black wire and earth wire to the side of the van.**

   Bolt this to your wheel arch in a similar fashion to the other negative wires from your leisure batteries. You'll most likely have a smaller earth wire too as inverters deal with higher voltages. Earth this to the wheel arch in the same way.

TIP

   If this earth wire comes with a flimsy crocodile clip on the end, replace it with a ring crimp connector and bolt it on securely. A crocodile clip has the integrity of a chocolate teapot, so sort that out right away.

One thing I discovered when doing my own van conversion is that inverters don't like being part of your solar charge relay and fuse box setup. Think of it as being like an exclusive party for one — the antisocial element of your electrical setup. It's not necessary to include your inverter in line with these components, but double-check your inverter manual to see if you can if that's something that you're keen on doing.

# Installing Plug Sockets and USB Ports

Adding an inverter into the mix means that you can finally start to think about installing plug sockets. Part of this section needs to be done now before your cladding goes up, and the other half will only be able to be completed once you're nearly completed with your walls.

For the time being, you need to be working in an area that's cladding-free, as you'll need to snake cable conduit around your van to those areas where you're thinking about installing plug sockets. Don't worry if you've never wired up a plug before. Here's a step-by-step guide for you to sink your teeth into.

Things you'll need:

>> Plugs (two-pin or three-pin depending on your region)

>> Plug wire

>> 1 13-amp fuse (U.K. plugs only)

>> Cable conduit

REMEMBER

The U.K. is the only country to put fuses in the plugs themselves rather than just relying on the consumer unit or fuse box for protection. I don't want to say that we do things better over in the U.K., but you know I'm thinking it.

Plug wire is a little like the British game of "Pass the Parcel." Unwrap one wire and you'll find more wrapped wires inside, three to be exact:

>> In the U.S., these wires are live (black), neutral (white), and earth (green).

>> In the U.K., these wires are live (blue), neutral (brown), and earth (mixture of yellow and green).

>> In the E.U., these wires are live (brown), neutral (blue), and earth (mixture of yellow and green).

In each case, you'll need to follow the same principle for stripping back wire. Here's what to do:

**1. Remove some of the outer plug wire, exposing the individual wires underneath.**

This wire is quite thick as it acts as an insulator for the other three wires inside too. Use a craft knife to cut this wire but be careful not to nick the wires underneath.

**2. Use a wire stripper to remove an inch of casing off the three wires inside, exposing the copper strands within.**

It's these exposed wires that need to be clamped into place in the designated areas inside your plug.

**3. Open up your plug by unscrewing the screws and wire up accordingly based on your style plug.**

Take your time and make sure you get this right. It can be fiddly, so don't worry if you feel the need to check those connections half a dozen times. It's better to be safe than sorry.

**4.** **If your plug needs a fuse, add one in at this point.**

Not all plugs have the space for a fuse, but if you're reading this book in the U.K., then you'll need to slot a 13-amp fuse into place to make your plug work. You can pick these up relatively cheaply from hardware stores or from eBay, and it's always handy to have a few lying around.

**5.** **Attach your cable grip and screw the outer casing back together.**

The only purpose of the cable grip is to keep the cable in place and prevent it from moving around. Still, if your plug comes with one, it's useful for keeping everything in place where it belongs.

Why did I just explain how to wire up a plug? Well, these plugs are going to sit in the sockets on your inverter, and the wires are going to feed to plug sockets up on your walls in your living, sleeping, or kitchen area. It doesn't matter if you only have two main sockets on your inverter either. I show you how to connect multiple plugs up to one wire as we move through these next steps.

Things you'll need:

» Plug

» Plug wire

» Cable conduit

» Plug socket set (facing and back box)

To install your plug sockets, follow these steps:

**1.** **Mark the points in your van where you want to install your plug sockets.**

**TIP**

You can have plug sockets at pretty much any area in your build, but it makes most sense to put them on the same wall so that you aren't using excessive amounts of plug cable and cable conduit. Having plugs on the wall that stands adjacent to your electrical system is a great bet.

**2.** **Feed cable conduit through the metal ribbing of your van as a cable track for your plug wire to run through.**

Hopefully you should still have some cable conduit leftover from feeding your solar wires into your van. The wires inside your plug wire are already insulated to a certain degree by the outer casing, but as always, it's better to be safe than sorry.

**WARNING**

If these wires become snagged and make contact with your metal van wall, you will immediately turn your home on wheels into one giant live wire. For the sake of some extra cable conduit, it's definitely worth giving you that extra peace of mind every time you turn on your inverter.

3. **Make a small cut in your conduit to allow for making a loop on the outside of it.**

   Use electrical tape to smooth off the edges of the opening.

4. **Measure how much wire you need to get from your inverter to your plug sockets.**

TIP

   If you're planning on putting two sockets on one cable, then measure all the way to the last socket and make a little loop at the position of the first socket to give you enough wire to play with. When it comes to wiring up your plug sockets, you'll use the same method you used to wire up your plug earlier.

For the remaining part of this section, you'll either need cladding in place or some way of securing your plug sockets until they can sit within the wooden frame of your living area. You're going to be making your sockets lie flat with your cladding, which means the back boxes will sit behind the wood. Back boxes come in all different sizes, so if your set doesn't come with one, measure the space behind your cladding and pick up the appropriate size from eBay, Amazon, or your local hardware store. Like the cable conduit, they keep all the wires feeding into your plug socket away from insulation and the highly conductive metal wall of your vehicle.

Before we continue, let's take stock of where we are. At this point, you should at least have one plug with a wire attached to the end, snaking through cable conduit to the location (or locations) of your plug sockets. Now we need to look at how to connect said wire up to the back of each socket. The process is a little different depending on whether you're wiring up to one socket or wiring up two in a row. Let's check out those different options now.

TIP

You can use any style of plug socket here, from the simple plastic one-switch options to chrome plated plugs with USB ports built into them. The wiring process is exactly the same for both.

## Wiring up to one socket (single or double)

Here's how to wire up to the back of a single plug socket with either one or two ports on it:

1. **Expose the wires in the bare end of your plug cable using the same method you carried out for wiring your plug.**

   Once again, exact caution when snipping into those wires so that you don't make any unwanted snags in the process.

**2.** **Insert each of the three exposed wires into the corresponding slots on the back of the plug socket.**

*For U.S. readers:*

- Earth (ground) wire clamps behind the green screw at the bottom of the socket.

- Neutral wire clamps to the silver screws.

- Live wire clamps to the brass screws.

*For U.K. readers:*

- Earth goes to the E port.

- Neutral goes to the N port.

- Live goes to the L port.

*For readers in mainland Europe:*

- Earth screws into the bottom of the socket.

- Neutral goes to one side of the socket (left or right).

- Live goes to the opposite side of neutral.

Now you know how to wire up a plug socket! Still, what do you do if you want to connect two plugs on one length of cable?

# Wiring up two sockets from one length of plug wire

**WARNING**

Make sure once again that all electricity supply to the inverter is cut off. Double-check that the isolator switch is in the open position with the key in your pocket and remove plugs from the inverter sockets to be on the safe side. Then, follow these steps to wire up two sockets on one length of plug wire:

**1.** **Cut the loop of wire that you made at the point of your first socket when you installed your plug sockets earlier.**

You should now have a length of wire leading from your inverter that now ends at your first socket, and a second length of plug wire with two bare ends that you've just created thanks to your incision.

**2.** **Remove the outer casing on the new segments and expose the individual wires as before.**

Repeat the tried and tested process, taking care with the copper wires.

3. **Double up the live wire going into the back of your socket.**

In essence, instead of putting one live wire into the L socket on the back of your U.K. plug, you will insert both live wires into the L socket and screw together securely. The same applies for E.U. readers with their chosen live port.

For U.S. readers, the live wire on the inverter plug socket length of cable goes to the first brass screw, and the live wire from the new strand screws into the second brass screw.

4. **Double up the neutral and earth wires.**

Follow the same process you followed for the live wire. For U.K. readers, that means placing two neutral wires in the N slot, and two earth wires in the E slot. The same applies for E.U. readers with their chosen neutral port (opposite the live) and the earth wire.

For U.S. readers, follow the same process as the live wire for your neutral wire. The neutral wire on the inverter plug socket length of cable goes to the first silver screw, and the neutral wire from the new strand screws into the second silver screw. Double up with both earth/ground wires on the earth/ground screw.

5. **Taking the bare end of the remaining length of wire, connect up the remaining plug socket by following the earlier instructions for wiring up one socket.**

Wiring up the second plug is simple now that you've got all fiddly while slotting wires together and navigating multiple screws. Hook up the last socket using the same method explained previously in the one socket section, and you're good to go!

Remember the RCD/GFCI units I spoke about in Chapter 8? Well, this is where those units come into play. Instead of plugging your newly wired plugs directly into your inverter, slot an RCD/GFCI unit in between to make your electrical system even safer. This RCD/GFCI plug is an external plug that is different from the RCD/MCB setup you use in your shore power setup.

## Fitting a plug socket with a back box in cladding

As I mention at the start of this section, some parts of this instruction can only be completed after your cladding is fully installed. One of those parts is fitting your back box and faceplate together on either side of your cladding to create a low-profile plug socket — one that doesn't stick out into your living space.

After your cladding is in place, follow these steps to attach your plug socket and back box:

1. **Cut out a hole in a piece of cladding big enough for the main part of your plug socket to fit through.**

   Just make the hole big enough for the main bulk of the plug socket to fit through. The edges of your faceplate want to rest up against your wood and not pass through it.

2. **Place the back box behind your cladding.**

3. **Drill pilot holes using a wood drill bit the same size as your back box screw, and screw your plug socket faceplate into the back box, nipping the cladding between the two.**

Now you have a plug socket that has protection at the back and a nice sleek finish at the front!

## Installing a USB socket (12-volt powered)

Of course, there may be times when you might not want to have to turn your inverter on to charge things, especially when just charging devices such as smartphones or tablets. That's where USB sockets come in handy. There are so many different camper van USB packs sold online that you can pick up for next to no money. Hooking them up is easy too, thanks to your trusty fuse box.

**TIP**

USB plug sockets aren't the most attractive looking gadgets in the world, especially if they come with big plastic faceplates. One idea is to find a nice piece of wood and make a mount for both the USB socket and the switch, creating a feature piece out of something that might otherwise have been a bit of an eyesore.

Things you'll need:

>> USB socket kit with wires

>> Ring crimp connectors

Follow these steps to wire up your USB socket and switch to your fuse box:

1. **Install your USB socket and switch in your chosen surface.**

   This can be with or without a homemade mount. Use a hole saw (the size will vary depending on the size of your unit) to create a space in your chosen surface, install, and secure tightly.

2. **Attach one piece of the included red wire from the positive terminal on the back of your USB socket to the top terminal on your switch.**

Just like with your light switch, your positive feed needs to pass through your switch so that you can cut the electricity flow when the socket is not in use.

3. **Attach the second piece of included red wire to the empty slot on your switch and bolt it in place using one of the screws on the left bank of your fuse box.**

**TIP**

There is a strong possibility that you will need to remove the existing connector on the wire provided in the kit. Either way, you'll need to add a ring crimp connector onto the end of the wire before you can attach it to your fuse box.

4. **Attach the included black wire to the negative terminal on your USB socket and bolt in place to any of the screws in the top cluster on your fuse box.**

This is the same place you bolted your negative wires from your lights. Once again, it doesn't matter which screw you use; all that matters is that the negative connection is earthed.

5. **Place a blade fuse in the slot next to where the positive wire from your USB socket is positioned.**

USB sockets don't need much power to run. See Chapter 8 to determine the correct size fuse to use here.

And there you have it! A working USB socket ready and waiting to charge up your phone or tablet.

# Wiring Up a Shore Power Inlet

If you're thinking of hooking up to a power supply at a campsite or charging your batteries up via an electrical outlet, then you'll need a shore power inlet. Here's how to get one safely installed in your camper.

Things you'll need:

>> Drill

>> Jigsaw

>> Measuring tape

>> Marker

>> Sikaflex

- » CEE van shore power inlet
- » RCD (residual current device)
- » MCB (miniature circuit breaker)
- » 3-core plug wire (preferably 2.5 mm²/14 AWG)
- » Household plug socket

Follow these steps to wire up a shore power inlet:

1. **Measure and cut a hole in the side of your van to fit your CEE inlet.**

2. **Screw and glue into place using Sikaflex, adding extra around the edges to seal, and then leave to dry for 24 hours.**

    Take time cutting your hole and make sure to wear all the same safety gear that you've been sporting throughout the previous sections of this book.

3. **Strip the outer casing of your length of plug wire at one end, revealing the three wires inside, and carefully remove a little bit of this outer casing to expose the copper wires inside.**

4. **Wire up your CEE inlet by connecting the earth wire to the biggest prong at the bottom, and the live and neutral wires respectively to the smaller prongs at the top.**

5. **Strip a larger portion of the outer casing on the other end of your plug wire to reveal the three wires inside (for now, leave them in their respective casings).**

6. **Cut the live and neutral wires shorter while leaving the earth wire longer and intact.**

    This earth wire is going to bypass your RCD and MCB but connect up to your socket at the end of this run. You should now have one long earth wire and a short live and neutral wire. Just tuck the long earth wire out of the way and ignore it for the time being.

7. **Feed your live and neutral wires into the respective L and N ports on the RCD.**

8. **Using the segments of live and neutral wire that you snipped away previously, connect up the bottom L and N ports on your RCD to the L and N wire inputs on the MCB.**

9. **Using the remaining segments of live and neutral wire that you snipped away, connect your L and N output ports on the MCB to a single plug socket that you can mount anywhere in your van.**

10. Take the earth wire that has thus far bypassed your RCD and MCB and connect this to the plug as well, thus completing your shore power setup.

Now, you can plug your devices straight into this plug or keep a battery charger plugged in to this socket and hook it up to your batteries to use your existing electrical system in the same way as you normally do when off grid. If you want this shore power feed to work with multiple plug sockets, follow the instructions for wiring up multiple sockets in one wire run earlier.

**WARNING**

Do not connect the wires from your CEE inlet to the same socket you have connected up to your inverter. Keep all those loops and components separate.

# Wiring Up Your Split Charge Relay

It's all well and good when the sun has got his hat on. (Hip hip hooray!) But what do you do when the sun's hiding behind a cloud, and you just can't get enough sunlight to charge up your batteries through your solar panels?

The answer: You reach for your split charge relay.

The main use of a split charge relay is to top your batteries back up while you're driving. To recap what a split charge relay does for those who may have skipped the previous chapter, a split charge relay is a little voltage-sensitive box that hooks up to both your starter battery and your leisure batteries.

When the voltage of your starter battery hits 13.7 volts or goes higher (such as when your engine is on), current flows from your starter battery down to your leisure batteries. When your engine shuts off and the voltage returns back to 12.8 volts or lower, the split charge relay disconnects. You don't even have to be moving to charge up your batteries. So long as the engine is on, the split charge relay will be doing its job.

This clever little box helped me out a bunch back when I used lead-acid batteries in my camper. There were times in the winter when the sun didn't make an appearance at all, and I had to sit with my engine on in order to top my batteries back up again. It's not ideal by any stretch of the imagination, but it's there if you need it.

TECHNICAL STUFF

Once I installed LiFePo$_4$ batteries in my camper, I had to remove my split charge relay because the voltage of the lithium batteries was continuously higher than the starter battery. This meant that my lithium leisure batteries were keeping the split charge relay turned onto starter battery charging mode all the time, draining my leisure batteries when there was no real need.

Things you'll need:

» A length of red positive wire to make it from your starter battery to your split charge relay

» Split charge relay unit

» Ring crimp terminals

» Midi fuse holder

Make sure your isolator switch is in the open position, then follow these steps to install your split charge relay:

1. **Lay out all your components.**

   Okay, so that sounds like a bit of a boring first instruction, but it's necessary. It'll also be a little bit fiddly, so make sure you have plenty of time to dedicate to this section.

2. **Remove the back plate from your split charge relay and take a look at the terminals inside.**

   You will see two bolt terminals: one with a red dot, and one with a white dot. You'll also see a thin black wire; this is your negative wire that will need to be earthed to the wheel arch as with the other negative wires.

TIP

   Use this opportunity to decide where you want to place your split charge relay in your electricity box/cupboard. Screw your back plate onto the wall as a reference point.

3. **Feed a length of wire from the proposed location of your split charge relay to your starter battery.**

   This is the bit that might be a little fiddly. In essence, you need to take a length of wire on as secure a route as possible into the cab of your van, and then into the engine bay.

   If you're using your van through all four seasons, then the chances are you are going to be stepping in and out of both the cab and living area in all sorts of weather. With that in mind, it's important that you try to keep your cable out of sight, secured behind cupboards, chairs, and even under plastic step trimming in the cab area.

If you peer into the passenger footwell in your van, you should see an existing cable run feeding into the engine area. You'll need to feed your length of positive red wire through this gap and into the engine bay under the hood. Not all cable runs are the same, and it may be that you have to make a little incision in some foam or covering in order to get your cable through. If this is the case, take your time and cut carefully.

Use as much cable conduit as you can for this section, especially in the cab area where you're likely to be storing coats, tents, and boots, and climbing in and out on a regular basis. It all helps to protect the cable leading to your starter battery from snags and tears.

Make sure your cable runs all the way to the positive terminal on your starter battery but make a loop in between the cable gland entry point and the positive terminal. You'll snip the wire and add in a fuse in a second, so give yourself some extra wire to work with.

Keep your fuse out for the time being as you're still going to work with ring crimp connectors on the remaining pieces of wire.

4. **Snip the loop in your wire to create two bare ends.**

5. **Add ring crimp connectors and wire them up using the same method used in Steps 3 and 4 of "Crimping a wire" earlier in this chapter.**

As a quick recap, add ring crimp connectors to the ends of the wire, place them over the bolts, and screw the caps back on to hold the ring connectors in place. You'll need a fuse in this section too. (Refer to Chapter 8 to calculate the correct fuse you'll need.)

You should now have a length of wire with a midi fuse holder attached.

6. **Add a ring crimp connector to the exposed end of your wire and connect it up to the positive terminal of your starter battery.**

Make sure your engine is turned off while doing this. You may also experience a few sparks when connecting your split charge relay wire, so wear goggles and gloves to avoid getting a shock. A shock from 12-volt electrics certainly won't cause you lasting harm, but it still isn't pleasant.

7. **Return to the split charge relay in your electric box/cupboard.**

8. **Add a ring crimp connector to the other end of your long length of wire and connect it to the bolt with the red dot on the back of it.**

This is the terminal that takes the feed from your starter battery. Tighten the nut with your fingers and finish it off with a wrench for a tight connection.

9. **Use more red wire to connect the remaining bolt on the back of the split charge relay to the left terminal on the back of your main isolator switch.**

**10.** Take an appropriate length of red positive wire, expose the ends, and add ring crimp connectors to it.

**11.** Secure one end to the empty bolt on the back of the split charge relay (the one with the white dot on it) and connect the other to the left bolt on the back of your isolator switch.

**REMEMBER**

Looking from the back, you need to connect this second split charge relay wire to the bolt that the battery feed is coming from, *not* the bolt on the right side of the switch that your other appliances are attached to.

**12.** Earth the black wire to the side of your van to create the connection, then add an appropriate fuse into the midi fuse holder in the engine bay.

**13.** Add a crimp connector to the black wire and bolt it to your wheel arch.

**14.** Slot the fuse into the holder under the hood, and you're good to go!

**TIP**

As long as everything has been connected up correctly, you should see the voltage change on your solar charge monitor when your engine is turned on. If this doesn't happen, use a multimeter to determine whether any part of your connection isn't correct.

# Installing Your 12-volt Fridge

As I said in the previous chapter, I thought I was being incredibly clever by install-ing a normal tabletop refrigerator into my conversion. Cheating the electrical system, as it were. I soon found out that this fridge was drawing too much power when the fuses in my split charge relay kept blowing out. This is why it's so important to use those fuses, folks!

It took a lot of talking to myself and flinching while looking at my bank balance before I took the plunge and bought the Waeco CRX-50 refrigerator. This fridge has a compressor that can actually be removed and placed in a location alongside the fridge, making it easier to fit into smaller spaces while still allowing for air to flow around the compressor.

Hooking up a 12-volt fridge isn't as hard as you might have first thought, espe-cially now that you've done more crimping than you ever thought possible and soldered wires dangling above your head. Before you crank up that soldering iron, however, you'll need to work out what gauge wire you need to hook up your fridge. The wire gauge needed changes depending on how far away you have your fridge from your batteries.

Always double-check your fridge manual or use the appropriate wiring chart when determining the correct gauge of wire.

I've said this so many times now that I'm hoping you will have already done it, but just make sure that your isolator switch is in the closed position.

Things you'll need:

>> Red wire for positive feed (refer to the fridge manual to calculate the correct gauge)

>> Black negative wire (refer to the fridge manual to calculate the correct gauge)

>> Inline blade fuse holder

>> 1 blade fuse (refer to Chapter 8 to calculate the correct amp fuse)

>> Ring crimp connectors

>> Soldering iron and solder

>> Safety goggles, gloves, and mask

To install your 12-volt fridge, follow these steps:

1. **Locate the positive and negative wires on the back of your fridge.**

   Unfortunately, most 12-volt fridges don't just have long wires that you can just hook up to your batteries. You'll have to do a little soldering, though this gives you the chance to stick a fuse in the mix too, so it's not all bad.

   The positive and negative wires leading from your fridge should already have metal ends on them, making them easier to solder to your new lengths of wire.

2. **Using the tried and tested method honed throughout this chapter, strip both ends of your positive and negative lengths of wire and expose the copper wire inside.**

   I promise you won't have to do much more of this soon. You are approaching the final furlong!

3. **Take the exposed coper strands of your positive length of wire leading from your electric box and wrap them around the metal end of the positive wire on the back of your fridge.**

4. **Wrap the strands around the metallic wire ends just as you did with the lamp holders in "Connecting lamp holders/sockets" earlier in this chapter.**

   It will make soldering them on much easier.

5. **Put on your safety equipment and heat up your soldering iron.**

6. **With your soldering iron in one hand and solder in the other, press your soldering iron onto the join and feed solder onto the position where the two wires are wrapped.**

   Keep feeding solder into the equation until you have a nice chrome wrapped join, just like you had with your lamp holders.

7. **Repeat this process with your length of black negative wire, taking care to create a solid join with your solder.**

   Just do exactly what you did in the previous section, taking your time to avoid spilling any solder in the process. Cover with electrical tape or heat shrink tubing once cool.

8. **Split your length of red positive wire somewhere close to your fridge and then solder in an inline blade fuse holder.**

   You're going to use a blade fuse holder here instead of a midi fuse holder as blade fuses come in smaller ratings. The holders are also splash proof too, and there is always a small chance that you might have leakage around your fridge, so better to be safe than sorry.

   Blade fuse holders either come with two lengths of positive wire with pre-trimmed and exposed ends attached to them or a loop of positive wire that needs splitting manually. Either way, sorting out those ends shouldn't be a problem for a seasoned professional like you now.

9. **With your safety equipment in place once again and using the same soldering method just used to attach your wires to your fridge, create a strong join between the two lengths of positive wire and your blade fuse holder.**

   Once your fridge has been wired up to your batteries, you'll fit a 15-amp blade fuse into this holder.

10. **Attach ring crimp connectors to the bare ends of your positive and negative wire leading down from your fridge to your batteries.**

    You've now done this so many times that you should be able to do it with your eyes closed. I would advise against that, however, just to be clear.

11. **Looking from the back of your isolator switch, place your positive wire on the right bolt with the other appliances.**

    The manual that came with your fridge will most likely tell you to place your fridge as close as possible to your battery supply. In my cautious opinion, the right side of your isolator switch is close enough. That still allows you to cut off the electricity supply to your fridge should you need to in an emergency.

**12.** Bolt your negative wire to the earthing point on your wheel arch to complete the circuit.

TIP

If you find that your bolt is getting a little full now, then there's no reason why you can't make multiple earthing points along your wheel arch. Just make sure that you know what appliance is going where and add the extra bolts into your wiring diagram in case you need to refer back later.

Take a deep breath and pat yourself on the back; you have finally finished the main bulk of your electrical system! I discuss heating and cooling appliances in later chapters, but for now, kick back and take a little snooze. You've earned it!

Parked up beside the ocean in beautiful Sardinia.

Traveling is a tough job, but someone's got to do it!

Some of the greatest audiences I've ever played to have been sheep and confused cows.

Who said van life meals have to be boring?

Route planning with my co-captain.

It's amazing what you can fit in a camper van!

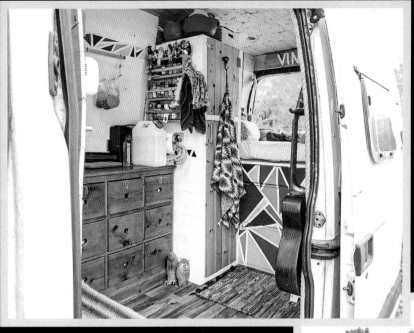

Life inside a tiny traveling home.

Looking out at Hallstätter See, Austria.

My first trip to California with Four Wheel Campers and experiencing life living in a truck camper.

A view into the main living space and kitchen of my van, and the seat that I worked from while traveling.

The view the opposite way. That's the whole tour; it doesn't take long when you live in a van!

Parking in the hills on the French border of
Lake Geneva, one of the quietest park-ups
I've ever stayed in.

A cold night in the southern
foothills of the Gotthard Pass,
Switzerland.

Calling an Italian monastery home for the night.

Off-roading with Four Wheel Campers in Truckee, California.

Camping out in the Sierra Nevada Mountains, Spain.

Essential items for life on the road, all packed
in using skills I learned from playing Tetris.

Red sky at night, van life delight!

Home is where you park it.

# Chapter **10**

# Adding Insulation and Cladding

Y ou first looked at adding insulation in Chapter 5 when you added it to your subfloor, and then again in Chapter 6 when you created your internal struc-ture, but now it's time to take things up a notch. After all, one warm floor does not a cozy camper make, and you'll need to pick the right materials to turn your van into a comfortable place to stay no matter the weather outside.

Over the course of this chapter, you find out all about the different types of insu-lation and discover which is best for your build, as well as how to install it. But that's not all. Think of this chapter as a two-for-one: By the end, you'll have a cladded van complete with fully fitted downlights. Finally, no more reading your favorite book by candlelight!

**REMEMBER**

If you're keen to install air-conditioning or a heating source such as woodburning stove before completing your insulation or cladding, then head over to Chapter 12 and find out how to implement them into your build. Don't worry, I'll still be here when you come back.

# Investigating the Types of Insulation

Before you dive straight into purchasing insulation and adding it to your conversion, it's important to know a little bit about the different types of insulation available. Let's take a quick look at what's on offer to give you a better idea as to which type would work best in your build.

## General-purpose insulation

| Pros | Cons |
| --- | --- |
| Great base layer for your van walls | Not suitable on its own |
| Reflects heat from the outside of the van | Doesn't provide any sound insulation |
| Easy to apply | |
| Great option for twinning with softer materials | |

I touch on general-purpose insulation in Chapter 6, but it only seems right to give it a spot in the limelight for a little bit. After all, general-purpose insulation is an incredibly integral part of the insulation process and something you see quite a bit of.

But what is general-purpose insulation, and what does it do?

Well, if you skipped Chapter 6 because you were so excited about making a toasty traveling house, then I guess I can let you off just this once. ThermaWrap, Reflectix, and other brands of general-purpose insulation are essentially sheets of bubble wrap lined with silver foil on both sides. It's super simple to attach to your van walls using spray adhesive and aluminum tape.

**TIP**

Aluminum tape is easy to come by from hardware stores or online. As well as providing a tidy finish, it ensures that heat is reflected back into the van at all the joining points between your pieces of ThermaWrap or Reflectix.

General-purpose insulation isn't a sole means of insulating your camper van; it acts as a preliminary layer before your main insulation method and should be applied to all metal panels inside your living space. That includes behind the door cards in your sliding and rear doors too! As a base layer, it reflects heat particles that are trying their best to escape out of the side of your van.

As I mention in Chapter 6, general-purpose insulation helps to stop thermal energy moving from hot areas to cold ones, something I picked up from geeking out on the laws of thermodynamics. Essentially, all brands of general-purpose insulation help to keep that heat you've made where it belongs, and not thawing the snow around your van tires.

TIP

General-purpose insulation also prevents softer insulation materials such as rockwool and sheep's wool from being directly in contact with the cold van wall. If you don't have this initial layer, then you can quickly get a build-up of condensation and have a lot of soggy insulation on your hands.

REMEMBER

General-purpose insulation isn't a breathable layer, but it does act as a waterproof barrier to prevent the build-up of condensation and prevents dampness. And, as I note in the handy table earlier, it's not advisable or recommended as a sole insulation method. It's a thin material that doesn't offer any sound proofing qualities either. Always use it in conjunction with other materials.

## Glass mineral wool

| Pros | Cons |
| --- | --- |
| Easy to pack into tight spaces | Itchy when handled with bare hands |
| Great insulating material and easy to cut/tear | Must twin with a waterproof layer to avoid condensation |
| Provides sound insulation | |
| Available in varying sizes | |
| Inexpensive and readily available | |

Glass mineral wool is often used as loft insulation all across the globe and can be bought from most hardware stores. Not only is it a great insulating method that's easy to pack into tight spaces, but it's what I used in my own van conversion. It's also what my mum has up in her loft, and her house is warmer than the inside of a RAB jacket! In the U.K., you can pick it up from B&Q under the brand name Eko Roll in large rolls, or Eco Roll in the U.S. from various retailers.

TIP

One of the best things about glass mineral wool is that you can tear strips off and just tamp it down into every nook and cranny of your van. And the best bit is that you don't need to worry about getting the right thickness of insulation board or slab; if you need more, just rip more off and pack it in.

TIP

Using glass mineral wool is a great way to create a tightly packed insulation layer behind your cladded or boarded walls. Prepare yourself to be adding glass mineral wool to your walls for a while, however, as you'll continually find areas where this stuff can be threaded and thumbed into. Still, it's one of the easiest methods of insulation going and can be done while listening to a podcast or audiobook!

## TO EACH THEIR OWN

I realize that some of you might be reading this right now and scoffing at my choice of insulation, and that's fine — we're all entitled to our opinions, after all. I've read posts from people on forums who say that glass mineral wool is rubbish when it comes to condensation, but I checked my insulation in a couple of areas on a fairly regular basis and found it to be as dry as the day I installed it. That's from living everywhere from wet and windy England to mountain villages in sunny Italy!

**WARNING**

Like fiberglass, glass mineral wool can make your hands and arms itch. Likewise, it can give you an itchy throat if you don't wear a mask. Be sure to stick on protective gloves and a mask when you're using it.

## Kingspan/Celotex

| Pros | Cons |
|---|---|
| Blocks come in different sizes and can be cut to fit into the gaps between your metal ribcage | Expensive |
| Easy and quick to install and tape together | Highly flammable |
| Requires the use of expanding foam to fill in any gaps | Not environmentally friendly |
| Provides a flat surface for putting under floorboards | |

Kingspan and Celotex are two brands of insulation board that are perhaps the most commonly used in van conversions. I touch on using insulation board when it came to insulating your floor in Chapter 5, and hopefully your toes are thanking you for making a good purchase already.

These blocks of insulation can be cut into segments easily with a craft knife and come lined with silver foil to further help with keeping that heat inside where it belongs. The boards come in different widths and are flat so they will sit under floor panels or cladding neatly. Joining them together is simple too: Just use spray adhesive to fix them down and fix the joins using aluminum tape or expanding foam.

**WARNING**

Use expanding foam very carefully as it's ridiculously hard to get off your skin and out of your hair. Always use the gloves provided, put on an old long-sleeved T-shirt, and tie your hair back. If you shave your head like me, then stick on an old hat; no one wants to be scrubbing their scalp with a scouring pad the next morning!

Insulation boards like these aren't the cheapest of options when it comes to insulating your van. That being said, installing them is much quicker than using torn pieces of glass mineral wool.

Another downside is that you might need to double up or use slices of foam board if the gap between your van wall and your cladding isn't the same thickness as your Kingspan or Celotex board. It's much easier to fill gaps using softer materials than it is rigid ones, so if you're set on the idea of using insulation boards, then make sure you measure twice!

If you're looking for an environmentally friendly option, then Kingspan or Celotex aren't it. These things are incredibly flammable too, so don't be lighting any candles until you've covered over them with your chosen cladding.

**TIP**

While I'm on the subject of fires, I purchased some fireproofing wood spray for my cladding and treated it once installed. I know that sounds odd and probably isn't something that many of you knew existed; wood burns rather famously, after all. Still, as the majority of my tiny house was in fact also made of wood, this spray seemed like a sensible idea.

Fireproofing wood spray works by manipulating the molecules deep inside the wood, thus making cladding less susceptible to bursting into flames should a spark fly from the fire or a piece of coal escape and roll across the floor. The bottle only cost about $30 (£25), which is much cheaper than having to buy a new camper van because your old one caught fire. Look for a spray that won't discolor wood and comes with up-to-date safety regulation information in the product description.

## Sheep's wool

| Pros | Cons |
|---|---|
| Environmentally friendly | Can be a bit smelly |
| Great insulating material and easy to cut or tear | Expensive |
| Provides sound insulation | |
| Easy to pack down into tight spaces | |

There's a reason you don't see sheep eating grass while togged up in a hat and scarf. Wool is a lovely insulating material; that's why we buy woolen jumpers and socks to keep our toes toasty, after all. Sheep's wool can also be used to keep your van conversion nice and warm just like it can our hands and heads during the winter months. It's a great insulating material and very environmentally friendly too!

If you're friends with a farmer or know of one nearby, you might be able to get some wool straight from the source rather than buying it from a shop, which will undoubtedly end up being cheaper for you.

Like glass mineral wool, you can twin sheep's wool with general-purpose insulation and tamp the soft wool down into all the tight and hard-to-reach spaces in your build. Plus, sheep's wool is easy to get hold of in any country where there are sheep, which happens to be pretty much everywhere.

So what are the cons of sheep's wool?

Well, as I mention earlier, sheep's wool is more expensive than glass mineral wool if bought through a shop. It also contains lanolin, which, while preventing the absorption of water and stopping critters from calling wool home in any usage, can smell a little bit at first. This smell will fade over time, however, so don't panic about your camper smelling like a farmyard forever if you're intent on using sheep's wool in your build.

## Spray foam

| Pros | Cons |
| --- | --- |
| Cover all walls quickly and easily | Expensive |
| No need to cut or tear; sprays on and expands to fit into gaps | Can be messy to both install and clean up |
| Provides sound insulation | Highly flammable |
| Great solution for bigger builds | |

I still remember the first time I saw a video of somebody spray foam insulation into their van. Imagine getting the world's biggest expanding foam can and just going to town on the inside of your van; that's basically what this method entails, except it uses a much bigger spraying system.

And, as you might imagine if you were to *actually buy* the world's biggest expanding foam can, it would be incredibly expensive. This is not a cheap option if you're looking to build a van on a budget, but it is one of the most thorough.

With spray foam insulation, there's no worrying about painstakingly filling every little gap with glass mineral wool or joining pieces of insulation board together with tape. This literally fills every available gap with expanding foam, giving you a fully insulated van in no time.

The great thing about spray foam is that it's dense. That means there's very little room for hot air particles to find a way through to the outside of your van, and because it makes such a thick wall, it's great for providing extra soundproofing. I'm not talking about a vacuum that completely blocks out traffic noises or a room where you can play Chris De Burgh's greatest hits full blast without anyone hearing (I'm not judging here), but it will help you sleep better if you're parked by a roadside for a couple of nights.

WARNING

This spray foam insulation expands in the same way the stuff you squirt out of your expanding foam can does. That means that once installed, you'll need to trim it all down to size to fit behind your cladding or wall panels using a knife or saw. It can be very messy and there will definitely be a temptation to hack away at it like Crocodile Dundee exploring the Australian bush. Just take your time and don't cut off more than you need.

TIP

As I hint at throughout this section, spray foam insulation can make a mess and easily get out of hand if you don't know what you're doing. While it's possible to do yourself, I advise getting a professional in to do the bulk of the work, leaving you to carve your living quarters like Michelangelo going to town on a piece of marble.

## Recyclable materials

| Pros | Cons |
| --- | --- |
| Completely environmentally friendly | Hard to come by |
| Re-use materials rather than buying new | Hard to install |
| A cheaper option | |

This last insulation option is one that I haven't come across that often while documenting van conversions, but it is another great option for anyone wanting to build an eco-friendly camper van. Recyclable material is also really cheap too, though you may find it tough to get hold of in large enough quantities to insulate your van.

Some of you might be thinking that "recyclable materials" means just crunching down your old orange juice cartons and those socks with a hole in them behind your cladding, but sadly it's a little more complicated than that. This insulation method *does* involve taking old materials and items such as newspapers, denim, and old books (please don't use this one!) and turning them into a type of mulch, which is then sprayed behind your walls in a similar way to spray foam insulation.

TIP

You have to build your walls before adding this insulation as it takes a little time to solidify.

The main problem with this method of insulating, however, is that it's not as readily available. You can easily hop onto Amazon to order some glass mineral wool, but you can't log on to buy 1,000 copies of *Fifty Shades of Grey* pre-mulched down into sprayable liquid for behind your walls.

# Choosing the Best Insulation

Unfortunately, asking what type if insulation is best is a little like asking "What do you think about the ending of *Game of Thrones*?" Everyone has their own opinion, and there's no right or wrong answer when it comes to picking an insulation method for your new van.

If you think about your carbon footprint as much as you think about what your next meal might be (as we all should . . . the carbon footprint, not the food), then you might prefer to spend a while sourcing insulation made out of recyclable materials.

Personally, building a self-sustainable tiny home that used the sun for power and wasn't wasteful with water felt like a good step for me, so I went with general-purpose insulation and glass mineral wool, mainly because glass mineral wool is so readily available and because it is easy to add more or take extra away in places. I know this book isn't titled *How to Build Seb's Exact Camper Van For Dummies*, but I never had any problems with my insulation setup, so if in doubt, go with my option.

TIP

Coincidentally, I outline the steps how to insulate with glass mineral wool later in this chapter, so if you want to make the insulation process as simple as possible, read on!

# Deciding How to Add Insulation

When it comes to installing the main bulk of your insulation, you have three ways to tackle it:

>> Build part of your interior wall and add soft insulation such as glass mineral wool or sheep's wool incrementally as you go.

>> Install insulation boards like Celotex or Kingspan and then build your interior walls.

>> Cut spray foam to the right thickness and then build your interior wall.

As I went with glass mineral wool and cladding for my van's walls, I outline the steps for the first option in the sections that follow.

# Knowing How Much Insulation to Use

Ever heard the phrase, "The tape measure is mightier than the sword and the pen combined"? I'd be worried if you had, as I just made it up on the spot, which means either you're lying, or you've somehow traveled back in time to when I was writing this chapter.

Measuring your van is the best way to figure out how much insulation you're going to need to kit it out with. If you're going with my general-purpose insulation and glass mineral wool method, then knowing your van's dimensions will help you buy the right amount and not have tons of excess insulation to deal with once you've finished your conversion.

**TIP**

Measure the height and width of your van to get the overall area of your living space. This will tell you how much insulation you need to purchase according to how many yards/meters squared it tells you your chosen product will cover. As I mention back in Chapter 6, it's always best to err on the side of caution when purchasing insulation. Double-check the returns policy of the shop or website you buy it from and whether you can return an unopened roll or box and get your money back.

# Installing Cladding and Adding Insulation

Now, in the interest of remaining impartial, I'm going to make it known that you don't have to use cladding in your camper. Just because I think it looks awesome doesn't mean that everyone in the world shares the same opinion. I know lots of people who have used painted boards or boards that they have then carpeted. Again, there's no right or wrong option for your van's walls; it's all down to personal preference.

Cladding is simple to put up and mostly requires just affixing straight pieces to your ribcage beams. The only cutting you'll need to do is a little bit of resizing and a few fiddly bits when it comes to fitting pieces around your sliding door and door handle.

# Picking the right cladding

I mention in Chapter 6 about taking into account the thickness of your beam and your cladding or boards when it comes to planning how much space you'll end up with in your living room. Don't worry if you can't remember me saying that; I just skipped back to check, and I definitely did. Every millimeter counts in a tiny home, so you're going to want to pick cladding that's strong but still quite thin.

For reference, I used smooth spruce tongue-and-groove cladding that measured $\frac{3}{10}$-inch thick × $3\frac{11}{16}$-inches wide × 94-inches long (7.5 millimeters × 95 millimeters × 2.4 meters). I started off with ten packs of 12 boards.

**TIP**

There's a very real chance that some of these boards are going to be unsuitable for use, so you might end up with some duds that you can use as scrap pieces. Once you've measured your van, you should have an idea as to how many packs you'll need to purchase, but bear in mind that if you're purchasing in bulk, you might not be able to take part of your order back for a refund.

# Getting the right tools

Luckily, you've likely already bought the tools you'll need to cut and attach your cladding, and you may even still have them set up in your garage or workspace. Unless your workspace was the front street like mine was, then chances are they're either soaking wet or have been stolen . . . or both.

Things you'll need:

>> Drill

>> Drill bit set

>> Countersink drill bit

>> Bronze or gold cladding screws

## TONGUE AND GROOVE

I know "tongue and groove" sounds like something that might happen when you meet other "likeminded singles" at a club night, but it's much less complicated than all that. Cladding is often referred to as *tongue and groove* as it has a groove on the bottom and a tongue on the top. The tongue at the top fits into the groove on the bottom of the next piece, sliding into place and creating a nice finish.

» Electric screwdriver (optional)

» Jigsaw

» Cladding jigsaw blade

» Tape measure

» Pencil

» Safety equipment (gloves and mask)

Here's how to add cladding and insulation to your van walls:

1.  **Starting on one side of your van, place a piece of cladding at the bottom of your wall and fit it flush up against your ribcage beam.**

2.  **Use a 3-millimeter wood drill bit to drill a hole through your cladding into your wooden beam.**

    The general idea here is that you're going to clad one wall, then the roof, and then come back down the other wall of your van. You will need to cut some pieces to the right size and shape to fit around your wheel arch, but if you're planning on building a static bed, then chances are good these edges will be hidden from view, so don't worry too much about making them spot on.

**WARNING**

    I know that you're probably sick of me constantly telling you to be careful when using a jigsaw, but motorized saw blades tend to slice through fingers pretty easily, so just keep your digits out of the way when making cuts, okay?

**REMEMBER**

    Take your time when cutting cladding boards. If your edge isn't flush and you're putting it up against a piece that is, then the results will be incredibly obvious, and there's no way to hide them. Trust me, it's much better to cut a new piece than to think "that will do," especially when you're going to be spending all your time in a tiny space and looking at any potential mistakes every single day.

3.  **Grab your countersink drill bit and create a small depression around your drilled hole to allow the screw head to sit flush with the surface of your cladding.**

    If you push too hard here, you'll end up making a massive crater or an odd-shaped depression that's bigger on one side. This will be annoying and make you wince every time you walk past it . . . trust me.

4. **Using an electric screwdriver or the screwdriver bit for your drill, screw your cladding into place.**

TIP

The electric screwdriver is an optional piece of kit, but I find it's much easier to have a separate tool with a screw bit pre-loaded rather than having to continually take bits in and out of one drill. In an ideal world, it would be best to have two drills on the go: one with your drill bit inserted and the other with your countersink bit inserted, and then an electric screwdriver. The amount of time I wasted trying to find bits that I had put down that had then rolled out of the van or fallen behind insulation doesn't bear thinking about.

5. **Once your first cladding piece has been attached, slide the groove of the next piece of cladding over the tongue of the existing piece, thus starting your sturdy wall.**

TIP

You might need to loosen the screws on your previous piece slightly to get your next piece of cladding on securely.

This is another one from "Seb's hindsight vault" — don't force a piece of cladding on if it won't go. That particular piece might have a large splinter that is causing a blockage in the groove part underneath, or it might just be that the groove isn't big enough or hasn't been cut right. Again, sometimes not all the boards are suitable, so just take your time and don't go heavy-handed when slotting boards together.

TIP

Also make sure that every time you put up a new piece of cladding it's the right way round. There's nothing more annoying than getting seven or eight boards up and realizing that the second piece is on back to front.

If you're using wood, I always think it's a good idea to use screws that will blend in with your cladding, or at least not stick out like a sore thumb. Bronze or gold screws don't stand out as much in cladding boards, especially once you've treated them with teak oil and you choose a darker shade. Bronze cladding screws come in boxes of about 200 from your local hardware store, and you will use a whole heap of them through your building process. Grab a couple of boxes so you don't have to break off midway through the job.

6. **Once you have attached four or five boards to your ribcage, put down the power tools and grab your glass mineral wool insulation, put on your gloves and mask, and start ripping off pieces to fit into the gap you've created between your cladding and your general purpose insulation layer.**

REMEMBER

Don't forget to put your gloves and mask on for this next bit as glass mineral wool can be itchy.

This step can be quite therapeutic and doesn't take a lot of thought, basically two of the factors I like the most about a job. Just start ripping off pieces and tamping them down into the space, making a thick wall of insulation.

If you get to a point where you're about ten boards up and you can't reach to push insulation down, use a piece of spare timber from one of your beam cuts as a kind of extendable arm — a little like a budget version of Inspector Gadget.

7. **Repeat the previous steps up one wall, across your roof, and then down the other side, insulating as you go.**

Make sure the tongues on your cladding pieces are facing up on both walls. That way, the groove pattern will be the same on each side of your living space. You can either affix them to your ribcage from the ground upward on each side or go up one wall and down the other if you're aiming to create a curved roof.

Make your life easier and only clad up to the point where your first set of lights are going to be. That way, you won't have to struggle removing whole pieces to cut holes in after you've finished cladding. Once your lights are installed, you can add insulation around them and carry on with the cladding. Leave around 5 to 10 centimeters of clear space around your light fixtures when installing insulation.

## Dealing with the curve of the roof

Speaking of the roof, how does one go about making the join from the wall to the roof?

Well, and you're probably going to guess what I'm going to say here, but (all together now) there is no proper "one size fits all" answer with how to do it. When I was converting my camper, I tried lots of different methods of making a curved join from the wall up to the roof. The main option I went with was to add offcuts onto the ends of the beams that ran up the walls and along the roof to create thicker points for cladding to screw into as it curved away from the wall, naturally pushing the cladding outward but still giving it something to sit against.

This, however, is what my wise uncle would call "a bit of a chew on," which translated into proper English means "a pain to do." If making that perfect curve isn't something that is currently keeping you awake at night, then you can always just make a right-angled join that meets neatly by heading up one wall all the way to the roof and then marrying your first piece of roof cladding flush up to your new wooden wall.

As I've said before in this book, not all vans are the same shape and size, so it would be impossible for me to write down every method for cladding or boarding every different make and model. I converted a Vauxhall Movano maxi-roof with a fiberglass roof, and while the process will be similar for a Ford Transit, it won't be exactly the same.

My advice: Work with the contours of your van and do what feels most natural. Remember, this process isn't supposed to be stressful, so if you really can't get that curve to work, then go with a straight join and consider decorating the area with some artificial ivy, rope, or colorful bunting.

## Leaving room for a chimney

Not all of you may want to put a log burner into your camper vans, but I dedicate a section in Chapter 12 about how to install a log burner in your camper if you do want to complete those cozy log cabin vibes.

If you are thinking about installing a log burner or multi-fuel stove, then make sure you leave a cladding-free space for your chimney to exit your roof. I left a 16-inch (40-centimeter) square around the area I had set out for my chimney and drew a big cross on the underside of the roof where my exit hole would be.

WARNING

I've used the warning symbol here because this one's a biggie. Just remember that you want as little wood and insulation around your chimney as possible. It might seem overkill, but it pays to be vigilant when fire is concerned.

I get more into the topic of installing a log burner in Chapter 12, but just bear this in mind when you're cladding your roof.

# Installing Lights in the Roof

If you followed all the chapters from the beginning of the book to this point, then you should be at a stage where you have a full electrical system installed, including dangling spotlight lamp holders soldered into black and red wires on your roof. Now that you're getting onto cladding your roof and adding your insulation, it's time to shine some light on the situation once and for all.

Downlight housings come in different sizes, so it's worth picking a set that is as streamlined as possible. The space between your roof and your cladding will be limited, so the last thing you want is to have to modify your roof just to fit chunky housings. Measure the space between your roof and your cladding before purchasing downlights so you know you're getting the correct size. Let's take a look at how to get those downlights installed in your roof.

Things you'll need:

>> Downlight housing units (as many as you need for how many bulbs you are planning on installing)

» Downlight LED bulbs

» Drill

» Hole saw (this needs to smaller than the outside-facing of your downlight housing, but big enough for the bulk of the fixing component to fit through)

» Safety goggles

» Marker pen

**TIP**

Make sure the LED downlight bulbs you buy or have already bought fit into the lamp holders you have soldered into your wire run on your roof. It's going to be really annoying if you get to the final steps of installing your lighting and have to break off to go to the hardware store to swap them, so take a look now before you get stuck in.

**WARNING**

Double-check that your electrics are off before you do this, just to be on the safe side.

Once you've confirmed your LED bulbs will fit into your lamp holders, here's how to install your downlights:

**1. Locate the areas where you have soldered your lamp holders, and then hold up a piece of cladding underneath and make a small X using your marker pen to mark their locations.**

If there's one thing you're going to be amazed at by the end of this book, it's making crosses with Sharpie pens. This "X marks the spot" is going to give you a guide as to where you place the center of your hole saw when cutting the hole for your downlight housing to slot into.

**2. Put on your safety goggles, and using your hole saw inserted into your drill, cut a hole or holes in your piece of cladding for every X you have made.**

It doesn't matter whether you make this cut with the cladding installed on the roof or by taking the piece of cladding down and cutting it on a workbench outside.

**TIP**

If you do decide to cut your holes while your cladding is installed on your roof, then be careful not to cut into your lamp holder wires or the red and black wires on your ceiling. A hole saw will rip through thin wire in seconds, and this setback will only make things more fiddly as you replace sections of wire while cursing your rotten luck.

Obviously, it goes without saying that you need to make sure your electrics are turned off before you take a rotating metal saw blade anywhere near electrical wires. Turn your isolator key, remove it, and stick it in your trusty pocket for safe keeping.

Measure the diameter of your downlight housing unit or refer to the packaging before choosing your hole saw. If your hole is too big, then your housing will push up through your cladding.

You might look like a bit of a twerp wearing your safety goggles, but you'll look a lot sillier sitting in the emergency room with a swollen eye. A stray splinter could blind you, so get those goggles on and look after your eyesight!

3. **Once you've cut your hole, insert your downlight housing into your cladding.**

The lamp housings clip into place using two metal arms on springs that keep them locked into place. Bend each arm back, place them through the hole you've made in your cladding, then gently release them. They should now sit firmly against the back of your cladding.

4. **Repeat this process for every lamp holder that sits in line with the same piece of cladding.**

You should now have a piece of cladding with one or more downlight housing units installed.

5. **Grab an LED bulb and insert into the lamp holder.**

There's no right or wrong way to do this, so you don't need to worry about messing it up. Just insert the two little prongs on your bulb into the lamp holder and make sure they're in securely.

6. **Secure your bulb into place within your downlight housing using the thin circle of wire that comes with each unit.**

You see the circle of springy wire with what looks like two little ears on it? Once your bulb is pushed up into the housing, this piece of wire holds it in place, with the ears slotting into notches in the side of the housing. This will stop your bulbs from falling out and potentially smashing while you're driving around too!

7. **Repeat the previous steps for any other downlights you have throughout your van.**

Once you're done, make sure you have fuses installed in your fuse box, turn your electrics back on, and flip your light switches. If you want to make a momentous occasion out of it, you could say "let there be light" at the exact moment you flick your switch. Hopefully, if you've wired everything up right, you'll be bathed in warm light from your downlights. If not, you can always refer to Chapter 9.

# Using Cladding to Build a Cupboard Door

The last thing I want to touch on regarding adding cladding to your build is how to create the door for the cupboard you may have made space for in your false bulkhead wall back in Chapter 6. If you decided to make a false wall that is simply covered in smooth boards that you're going to paint over or otherwise decorate, then making your cupboard door is as simple as measuring the open space and cutting out a piece of board to those exact measurements.

If, however, you opted to clad your false wall just like the rest of your camper, then here's how to create a door for your cupboard with cladding:

1. **Count how many pieces of cladding meet the edge of your cupboard hole.**

   This will tell you how many pieces of cladding high your cupboard will be. If there are four full pieces of cladding next to your cupboard hole, then you'll need to use four pieces of cladding to make your cupboard door. Likewise, if there are only two and a half, then you'll need two and a half pieces.

2. **Measure the width of your cupboard hole and cut pieces accordingly.**

   Once you've measured the width of your cupboard, you should know how many lengths you can get out of one piece of cladding. Chances are good you'll be able to get at least two out of one piece.

REMEMBER

   If you are taking multiple lengths out of one piece of cladding, take the time to make sure the lines you cut are incredibly straight. Any wonky lines will stand out terribly when your cupboard door is closed, so cut slowly and carefully.

3. **Apply a thin layer of wood glue into the grooves of the pieces of cladding that the tongues of the pieces below will slot into.**

   If you have four pieces of cladding, working from the top, place glue in the grooves of the top three pieces, securing all four together.

4. **Allow the pieces to dry.**

TIP

   As your cupboard door will be opening and not locking into the row of cladding above it, you'll need to cut the tongue off your topmost piece of cladding.

5. **Clamp the piece of cladding to a workbench and, using your cladding jigsaw blade, carefully take the tongue off.**

   Alternatively, you can use a sharp chisel.

6. **Once removed, give it a quick sand down for a smooth finish.**

WARNING

   Chisels can also chop your fingers off if you're not careful, so go slowly and keep your hands away from the path of the blade.

**7.** **Use door hinges to attach your cupboard door to the part of your false wall above your cupboard hole.**

Using some small screws, affix the lower part of the hinge to your cupboard door and the top part to the piece of the cladding above.

TIP

If your screws are long and look as though they might poke out of the other side of your cladding, then double-up with a second piece of cladding so that your screw doesn't poke out and scratch you.

# Chapter **11**

# Creating Storage and Sleeping Quarters

Whether you're planning on living in your van full time, part time, or just on the odd weekend, you're going to need somewhere to sleep and somewhere to store all the essentials you'll be taking with you on your exciting adventures. For full-time vanlifers and outdoor enthusiasts especially, having ample storage space on board for everything from outdoor equipment to summer and winter clothes for rotation throughout the seasons is crucial.

In this chapter, you discover how to build the place where the magic happens — magical sleep, of course. You also discover how to effectively make the most of the available space under your bed as well as build cupboards to store your toilet, fridge, and other important belongings.

## Getting a Good Night's Sleep

I bet most of you are looking forward to getting in your van to seek out hot springs or find hidden glades in which to kick back and read a book. You probably aren't thinking about the benefits of sleep at this point, but statistically speaking, the one place you'll spend the most time in your van is in your bed.

We all love sleep. Scratch that; we all *need* sleep in order to function, especially if we're going to head out on the road and drive to new places, which is a key factor of traveling in a van, after all. You hear me say a lot throughout this book that there are times where you won't feel in top form and need to spend the day in bed or just have a long lie-in. You'll definitely have lazy evenings where you just want to curl up with your partner and watch a film or listen to an audiobook while watching the sunset.

To cut a long story with a hundred possible examples short, your bed is one of the most important elements in your build and shouldn't be overlooked. Because if you don't get a good night's sleep, you'll be grumpy and not end up enjoying your travels, and that won't do at all!

In the first part of this chapter, I give you an insight into the two main types of beds you can add to your build and then how I built the right one . . . er, I mean, how I built *my* bed (the right one).

# Deciding on a Static or Foldaway Bed

Toilets, showers, and beds usually divide the van life community. Everyone has their own opinion as to which one is best, though in truth and ignoring my little jab earlier, there is no real right or wrong answer. This is your build, and you should be able to design it however you want. That being said, in this chapter, I show you how to build a static bed, so deal with it, alright?

Okay, so you all knew that line was coming. I guess I haven't exactly hidden my feelings on the subject so far and probably won't as the book goes on. Still, in the interest of being impartial, let's compare static versus foldaway beds and look at the pros and cons of each type.

## Static bed

| Pros | Cons |
|------|------|
| Always ready to climb into | Takes up space that could be used for a seating area |
| Creates ample garage storage | Bedding can smell of cooking |
| Great place to relax | |

For me, there's nothing better than stretching out on a bed while writing. I also prefer having a sleeping area that's ready-made for me to jump into if I've been out all day. There's no setting up or messing around with bedding to be had with a static bed; just jump into bed and snore away. I suppose it helps that I had a high roof van — I was still able to sit up in my bed, even with it on a raised platform. If you have a smaller van like a VW Caddy or even a normal transit van, a static bed might feel like a waste of space.

One other great argument for building a static bed is the garage storage that comes with it. Having a bed in situ all the time means you have a place to store all your outdoor gear without needing to build extra cupboards in which to hide everything.

TIP

A big deciding factor on the static bed front is your height. The general consensus, and the method I use in the steps that follow, is that a static bed runs along the width of your van at the back of the main living area. This is for structural support from the metal beams running along your van wall, but also because you don't want a bed encroaching into the main living area. I took a double-sized memory-foam mattress and cut 4 inches (2.5 centimeters) off the length to fit it into my van. I'm 6 feet tall and managed to sleep comfortably at a diagonal, though most of the time I ended up curling up a little in the middle of the night anyway. If you want to go for a static bed, try testing one out first over a long weekend and see if you can sleep comfortably at a diagonal. Figure 11-1 shows what my static bed looked like in the back of my van.

**FIGURE 11-1:**
My raised sleeping platform was a cozy place to snooze with storage underneath.

## Foldaway bed

| Pros | Cons |
| --- | --- |
| More living space | Have to make your bed every evening before you get into it |
| Can build the bed coming out lengthways into the living space | Less storage space, including garage storage |
| Can be used as a sofa during the day | |

A pull-out or foldaway bed certainly gives you more space in your living room and is a better option if you think you might be entertaining others in your van. I didn't have people in my van that often for food and drinks, and if I did, we usually sat outside in warmer weather. The idea of having four or five people all chilling on my bed did feel a little weird to say the least.

Not having a static bed definitely does give you more options when it comes to sleeping positions. And, if you really can't sleep sideways, it's easy to implement a sliding bed that allows you to sleep in the main bulk of the living space at night and tuck everything neatly away during the day.

The main downside of a foldaway bed is the lack of storage space, and what storage space you might have implemented into your build by creating a sofa with a lift-up seat is usually used up by your bedding and pillows. A static bed enabled me to have a space to keep a winter duvet/comforter in a vacuum-packed bag, replacing it with the thinner summer option once the seasons changed.

**TIP**

If you're unsure what type of bed to go for, try spending a couple of nights in a few different campers and see how you get on with each style.

# Picking a Mattress

There's really only one perfect mattress for putting into a van, and that's a memory-foam mattress. They're easy to cut to size and usually come with an outer casing that can be sewn tighter to fit the new foam size or just tucked underneath the mattress itself.

Foam is simple to trim to size; I used a winning combo of a bread knife and a pair of scissors to cut my foam down to fit into the space. As I said in the last section, I bought a double-sized memory-foam mattress, retained the original width, and only removed 4 inches (2.5 centimeters) off the overall length. Don't just make a guess at how much you need to take off. Use a measuring tape to measure the width of your van (measured from your cladding and not the metal of the van wall) and then make a mark on your foam using a marker pen. Draw a line around the top, bottom, and edges of your mattress so you have a good idea of where you're cutting from all angles.

**WARNING**

You'll need a sharp knife to cut through the foam. Don't hack away at it; just take nice smooth strokes and take your time when cutting; otherwise you might end up taking off too much and have to glue bits back on again.

**TIP**

Condensation can build up under your bed, easily causing damp spots between your bed and the slats underneath. Condensation prevention matting placed underneath your mattress can help keep such dampness at bay. I bought some DRY-Mat Anti-Condensation Mattress Underlay online from a company called Ship Shape Bedding. It's essentially a semi-rigid sheet made up of micro springs that you can lay underneath your mattress that allows for air to constantly flow underneath it. You can wash it, cut it to size, and don't need to attach it to anything.

# Building a Bed in Your Camper

Okay, it is time to talk about putting your bed together. I should say at this point that I repurposed the flat-pack bed frame that I was sleeping on at the time into my van build. It was made of good wood and it made perfect sense not to waste it, so if you have a ready-to-assemble, flat-pack bed frame that you like, go ahead and repurpose it in your van!

I'm sure many of you have either put together a flat-pack bed frame or at least have seen one. These beds aren't expensive and come ready to assemble as a kit. Whether you're using your existing flat-pack bed or making pieces from scratch, you'll need the following supplies to make your bed supports and slats.

Things you'll need:

>> 3 wooden planks for the base beams (or the wood from your old bed)

>> 12 to 14 thin pine or spruce beams for the slats (or the bed slats from your old bed)

>> Square pine stripwood (2 lengths)

>> 3 1⅜ inch × 1⅜ inch (34 millimeter × 34 millimeter) wooden beams for support

>> Jigsaw

- » Drill and drill bits

- » Wood screws

- » Memory-foam mattress

- » Bolts and accompanying nuts

- » Tape measure

- » 3 angled L brackets

- » Pencil or marker pen

Now that you've collected all your materials and tools, follow these steps to build that bed:

1. **Measure the width of your mattress and place your three base beams (front, middle, and back) in place to gauge where they're going to go.**

2. **Draw lines on the metal ribbing of your van to create a template.**

   The beauty of this method is that you can make your bed as thin or as wide as you want. If you're traveling solo, then you can make your bed the size of a single or three-quarter mattress, or if you're planning on sharing with a partner, you can always decide on a custom-sized mattress and build your frame accordingly.

**REMEMBER**

   The wider your bed, the less space you'll have in the rest of your build. Also, if you're planning on storing bikes in your new garage area, measure your bikes and make sure your new bed is going to be wide enough to provide enough underbed storage for them that is accessible from the rear doors.

3. **Remove each base piece and drill a hole in either side.**

   Using a wood drill bit the same thickness as your chosen bolt, drill through each side of your three bed base pieces. Do this somewhere sturdy like on a workbench.

4. **Place the beams back in situ and mark the point where you made your holes on the metal ribbing of your van.**

5. **Remove the beams and drill holes through the ribs with a metal drill bit the same thickness as your chosen bolt.**

6. **Grab a marker and make a little dot through the holes you've created in each piece of wood, and then, with a metal drill bit the same size as your bolt, drill down through the metal ledge piece your base beams will sit on.**

**7.** Feed a bolt through your metal beam and the rib and secure with a nut, fixing your base beams in place.

This can be a little fiddly and you might drop your nut a couple of times. Tighten the nut with your fingers and then use a spanner or adjustable wrench to secure the beams in place.

**8.** Use existing slats from your bed or cut pieces of wood to size to make slats to fix into place on top of your bed beams.

**TIP**

If you don't already have slats that you can use from your bed (or want to keep your existing bed intact like a normal person), then the easiest method here is to get strips of pine or spruce and cut lengths that go across all three base beams.

**9.** Cut two pieces of wood approximately 2½ to 4 inches (6 to 10 centimeters) wide and use them as dividers to place between your slats. This will ensure your slats are spread out evenly.

**TIP**

Even if you are using anti-condensation webbing under your mattress, I suggest painting your slats with anti-mold paint, just to cover all bases.

**10.** Use wood screws to attach your slats to each of your three base beams.

**TIP**

Get your drill(s) and electric screwdriver back out again. Using the same method of drilling a hole, countersinking, and then using your electric screwdriver to insert your screws, add three screws into each slat and fix them into your front, middle, and back base pieces.

**11.** Glue a piece of square pine stripwood to your front and back base beams to stop your mattress from slipping off your bed frame.

Square pine stripwood is a small wooden baton that you can glue to your bed base at the front and back, keeping your mattress in place. This is especially useful when driving to keep your mattress in place on uneven roads or if you need to break quickly.

**12.** Measure the space between the underside of your bed base beams and the floor, and then take a piece of square 1⅜-inch × 1⅜-inch (34 millimeter × 34 millimeter) beam and cut to length.

**TIP**

Your base beams are secured into the metal ribbing on the side of your van, but it's still a good idea to support them in the center to prevent them from bending or drooping.

**13.** Screw the vertical support beam into place by drilling two pilot holes through each bed base piece into the support beam, and then fix into place using an angled L bracket.

If you just use one screw, there's a strong chance the support beam could pivot. Two will ensure that it stays exactly where it's supposed to.

Angled L brackets were my saviors during this build, especially for anything I wanted to screw into the floor. If you've never seen one before, then they are a piece of metal bent at a right angle with two screw holes on each part of the "L."

**14.** **With your support beam in place, attach an L bracket to the base of the beam and screw into the floor, securing it in place.**

**15.** **Repeat the support beam process on your other two base beam pieces.**

All that's left to do now is to grab your favorite comforter and some pillows, and bed down with the *Harry Potter* audiobooks playing softly in the background as you drift gently to sleep. I'll meet you in the next section once you've woken up!

# Creating Garage Storage

If you followed the previous steps to create a static bed, then you should now have ample garage storage space in the back of your van. Depending on the type of equipment you want to store, this space could be either be kept as open as possible for inflatable paddleboards and kayak, bicycles, kit bags, and more, or compart-mentalized into smaller sections by creating shelving or drawer units in the same fashion as the underbed storage you're about to get to grips with in the next section.

You can either make shelving between your bed support beams or make a storage unit from scratch. What I advise, however, is to avoid closing too many things off in the back of your van. Simple shelves composed of horizontal wooden beams with gaps in the middle will help air to flow around the back of your van, which will in turn reduce the amount of damp build-up.

No one ever wants to talk about dampness in a camper van. The truth of the matter is that it does build up in the back of your van on occasion, especially in the colder months. Keep some dehumidifying pods scattered around the back and try to air your garage area out on a regular basis. If you find that there's a real damp problem occurring on your back doors, then consider painting the lower half with anti-mold paint.

# Drawers, Cupboards, and Savvy Storage Solutions

No matter whether you're planning a year-long trip around Europe or just driving to Baja California for the weekend, storage is a key part of every camper conversion. My friends always remarked that my van felt a little like Doctor Who's Tardis: unsuspecting on the outside but great when it came to holding more items than should be humanly possible. Coincidentally, that's also how most of my girlfriends have described me over the years too.

**REMEMBER**

I want to reiterate at this point that I am not a carpenter; I'm a writer who has access to power tools and wood. If you are a carpenter, then you may well be able to take my ideas and make them better. But, if you're a novice to making cupboards and storage solutions like I was, then these ideas will serve you well for many years.

## Building drawers under your bed

Let's start with storage under the static bed. As I was living in a van full-time while traveling, clothes were something I wanted to make sure I was stocked up with. More T-shirts meant fewer trips to the launderette and more time on the road. If I'm being honest, I find launderettes quite peaceful, but they're not exactly a great place for making life-long memories.

I divided the space underneath my bed into three drawers:

>> One for underwear (and cables, passports, glasses cases, goggles)

>> One for T-shirts and sweatshirts

>> One for jeans, shorts, collared shirts, hoodies, onesies (yes, I had two)

Defining the sizes of each drawer was easy. I divided the overall space between the bottom of the bed base and the floor and subtracted the thickness of the softwood pine beams used to create the drawer frame to give me a general idea.

**TECHNICAL STUFF**

You can use drawer runners, but they have a habit of causing the drawers to roll open and bending or breaking when you're driving along after forgetting to lock them in place. And yes, this is yet another thing I experienced before rebuilding my underbed storage setup. I opted for creating a wooden frame using $1\frac{3}{8}$-inch × $1\frac{3}{8}$-inch (34-millimeter × 34-millimeter) pine beams and drawers made from plywood boards. It was a pretty easy process, mostly because I made most of it up as I went along.

Things you'll need:

» 1⅜-inch × 1⅜-inch (34-millimeter × 34-millimeter) wooden beams (cut to size)

» Drill and drill bits

» Screwdriver

» Wood screws

» Jigsaw

» Tape measure

» Plywood

» Wood filler

» Auto carpet

» Spray adhesive

To make drawers under your new static bed, follow these steps:

1. **Measure the available space under your bed.**

2. **Decide on your draw dimensions now to determine how high, wide, and deep you want each drawer.**

   You don't want your drawers to be as wide as the width of your van. You can see in Figure 11-2 that the frame for my drawers started at the edge of my toilet cupboard. I also left some room for a flip-up cupboard to the right of my drawers for storing items such as my removable table legs, yoga mat, and more.

REMEMBER

   Don't forget that you'll need to take the width of your beams between each drawer into account when you're deciding on your drawer height.

3. **Cut beams to make a complete box frame to fit underneath the space and screw them into place.**

TIP

   If there's one thing I've learned from converting vans and narrowboats, it's that nothing is ever truly straight. Make life easy for yourself and build this box in situ. Don't build a box and then slide it inside as it might not end up being the right shape.

4. **Taking your draw height measurements, place beams horizontally across the front of your frame to separate it into however many sections you want for your drawers.**

5. **Add more beams, this time running them vertically from the front to the back of your frame connected by your front and back horizontal beams for your drawer to run on, as shown in Figure 11-3.**

**FIGURE 11-2:**
This time, thinking inside the box is what the job calls for!

**FIGURE 11-3:**
Finished drawer compartments ready for drawers to slide into place.

Countersink all the holes that you make in the front of your frame before you screw these new beams into place. Once the screws are in, you can go over the heads with wood filler to hide them and make a smooth surface for painting.

6. **Apply wood filler, leave to dry, and then sand.**

7. **Treat your pinewood with teak oil and leave to dry.**

Now that you've built your frame, it's time to start making your drawers. I'm going to tell you how to make some simple drawers using plywood. They're light but sturdy and don't take Hulk-like strength to pull them out or push them back into place. Here's how to create them:

1. **Taking the height, width, and depth of each self-contained drawer segment, measure and cut out plywood pieces for your drawers, including a base piece.**

2. **Cut four batons from the 1⅜-inch × 1⅜-inch (34-millimeter × 34-millimeter) beam the same height as the drawer you are working on.**

   These batons will sit in each corner of your drawer and provide a means of screwing your different panels together.

**TIP**

   You can also use wood glue to hold the panels together, but I find using screws is much easier. We'll use both wood glue and screws for the base section, however.

3. **Screw each drawer panel into a corner baton, securing the front, sides, and back of your drawer.**

4. **Once complete, turn the drawer frame upside down and run a thin line of wood glue around the exposed edges.**

5. **Lower your base plate into place, drill, and then screw each corner into the corner batons underneath; leave to dry.**

6. **Cover over any countersunk screw heads in the front of your drawers with wood filler.**

7. **Once dry, sand to a smooth finish.**

8. **Vacuum out any dust from your drawers.**

   This isn't just good practice, but also it's going to provide a lean surface for the spray adhesive we add in the next step to stick to.

9. **Measure and cut your auto carpet, and using spray adhesive, glue it into place in the bottom and sides of the drawer for a nice soft finish.**

10. **Repeat these steps for your other drawers, working to the dimensions of each drawer compartment you have made underneath your bed frame.**

Let's "drawer" the line through this section now and move on, shall we?

# Building under-the-counter and overhead cupboards

Cupboards in vans usually go underneath worktop surfaces and/or at head height, attaching to the wooden ribcage beams you installed when creating the internal structure all the way back in Chapter 6. Remember screwing wooden beams into the horizontal metal ribs of your van? Well, those are going to come in handy now to provide support when screwing your cupboard sections to your wall.

I'm not going to go over the equipment you need for these next two sections, as you'll already have everything you need from building your underbed storage. Just glance back at the previous section if you're unsure as to what to use here.

## Under-the-counter cupboards

If you're looking to build under-the-counter cupboards from scratch, follow the steps outlined in the previous section, "Building drawers under your bed," to create a frame for your underbed storage. Measure the available space, use pinewood beams to make a box underneath the space, screw the beams into the floor and wall as you go, and then cut medium-density fiberboard (MDF) shelves to size for inside. Use pallet wood, painted MDF, or plyboard for your cupboard doors and attach using easy-mount cupboard door hinges on the outside. Voilà! You have an under-the-counter cupboard. See? All this messing about with wood has turned you into a craftsperson without you even realizing it!

## Overhead cupboards

Building overhead cupboards doesn't require many materials. Essentially, you're going to create a front frame that your door will attach to, add an MDF base to the bottom, screw the frame to the roof and the side of your false wall, and use some angled brackets to attach your MDF base plate to your back wall, before cutting a piece of wood to close off any exposed sides. Here's how to do it:

**1.** **Measure the area where you're going to install your cupboard.**

This will give you the dimensions for the front pinewood beam frame.

You can make your overhead cupboard as deep as you want, but when it comes to height, try to stick to the location of your wooden horizontal beam that you attached to your metal ribcage in your van back in Chapter 6 so that your angled brackets have something to screw into. Otherwise, your whole cupboard will be relying on your wall cladding for support. That might be enough if you're only storing spice jars in there, but it's not going to hold up if you're planning on storing heavier items inside.

2. **Using the same 1⅜-inch × 1⅜-inch (34-millimeter × 34-millimeter) beams you used to create the frame for your bed drawers, make a large rectangle the width of your desired cupboard.**

3. **Cut a piece of MDF the depth you want your cupboard to be and the same width as your rectangular frame.**

4. **Screw your MDF base plate into the wooden frame of your cupboard front.**

   Make sure the screws are long enough to pass through the MDF base and a good way into your rectangular frame.

5. **Screw some angled brackets to the back edge of your base plate.**

   These will be used to attach your base plate to your back wall.

6. **Screw the wooden frame of your cupboard front into your roof and your false wall.**

   The false bulkhead wall essentially acts as one side wall of your cupboard, saving you the job of having to make two side pieces. If, however, you opted for an open cab area without a false wall, then double-up on Step 8.

7. **Secure your MDF base plate to your wall using the angled brackets you attached to the edge that will sit against the wall.**

8. **Close any open edges with a piece of wood cut to size and screw or glue into place.**

**TIP**

If you're planning on building a toilet cupboard, then you don't even have to make a piece of wood to seal off this open edge. Measure the gap in-between your false bulkhead wall and your toilet cupboard and make the overhead cupboard fit in the gap. You can always put two (or more) cupboard doors on the front instead of one.

9. **Use cladding, MDF, or plywood to make a cupboard door(s).**

10. **Attach easy-to-mount hinges on both the outside front frame and the top of your cupboard door.**

11. **Use a bolt lock or a hook and carabiner system on the bottom to finish the cupboard off, keeping everything secure inside while you're driving.**

**TIP**

The underside of your cupboard's MDF base plate is a great place to glue jam jar lids for spices, pasta, and rice storage. By gluing the lids to the underside of your cupboard, you can simply unscrew the jars and grab the ingredients inside whenever you're cooking. Not only is this a savvy storage solution, but it also looks cool too!

REMEMBER

You don't have to build everything in your van; you can always use existing cupboards or dressers and integrate them into your build. My mum was getting rid of the old kitchen dresser that I had grown up with in my childhood home when I was building my van. Not only was this dresser a nostalgic part of my old life, but it was also a great bit of furniture boasting nine drawers, each with a finger hole cut out of the middle rather than handles to open them. By attaching bolt locks to the two bottom rows of three drawers on the inside, and carabiners and hooks on the top three drawers on the outside, I created a lockable drawer system that looked great and cost me very little money.

TIP

The moral of this convoluted story is that if you find an old piece of furniture that looks cool, perhaps an old art bench or a set of lockers from a science lab, make them a feature in your build and integrate them into your new tiny home. This is your van, after all, and you can make it however you want!

## CLEVER BIN STORAGE

Does the bin, or trashcan, need its own mention? Probably not, but I'm so proud of the bin that I built in my camper that I'm going to do it anyway.

After installing my mum's old dresser unit and building my under-the-counter storage cupboard, there was a small gap that I didn't really know what to do with. The answer? I screwed two drawer runners into the van floor and made a slide out bin with spare bits of plywood, cut to size to fit into the gap. The best part is that I built two compartments: a top compartment for refuse that lifted out, and a bottom compartment that sat on the runners to hold all my recycling.

To blend it into the build, I took some pieces of thick tongue-and-groove cladding I was given by a neighbor, stained them, cut them to size, and made a front facing out of them that, when the bin was pushed into the gap, sat flush with the front of the dresser unit.

This is one of the best bits about van life. You can get creative with what you have and come up with ideas on the fly. Remember, this is your conversion and not a professional build. Okay, it's going to look like the real deal while you're finished, but there's always something off-piste that you can do to fill a surprise gap. And if you have a gap that's not big enough for a bin, consider a slide-out plate rack or spice shelving unit. Bay leaves, anyone?

## Creating a spice rack

Like the bin I described in the sidebar, "Clever Bin Storage," the spice rack in my camper was another cool little feature that always caught people's eyes. Far from being complicated, this mobile spice emporium was made from spare bed slats — four to make the frame and two extra to make three shelved areas — and some broom handles to keep all the spices in place while driving.

TIP

To create one for yourself, use a jigsaw to cut the broom handles in half. Screw them down on the front of the spice rack at a height that still gives you enough space to slide a spice jar over it, and you've got some secure spice storage for any kind of off-road terrain.

## Utilizing bulkhead storage

If you've followed the steps in this book so far (which I hope you have; otherwise I would've just been talking to myself), then you should already have integrated a little bulkhead cupboard into your false wall in order to store items above your cab (the steps for which I outline in Chapter 6). I know people who have used this space for everything from keeping pots and pans secure to a place for their cats to hang out with a scratching post to keep them occupied. Feline fun aside, this is a great space to store objects like hammocks, cooking gear, sleeping bags, recipe books, a first-aid box, a pair of drumsticks, a sketchbook, some Harry Potter wands your friend Josh bought you, and a wallet full of DVDs (even though you don't own a DVD player).

And yes, if you thought that list was incredibly specific, I've just been sitting here stroking my chin trying to remember all the different objects in my bulkhead.

TIP

If you haven't gathered already, the bulkhead is a great place to stash miscellaneous items that don't really have a specific place. It's also a great area to put items that you use on a regular basis but that you don't want to keep out in your living area all the time, such as a smoothie maker, flashlight, or spare guitar strings. Okay, now that's definitely everything I had up there!

# Building a Toilet Cupboard

I know not everyone wants a toilet cupboard, but hear me out. Having a cupboard for your toilet isn't just a great way of keeping it hidden from view; it also provides a place for you to store other items such as your dirty laundry (literal, not metaphorical) and other useful equipment that might not come out on a daily basis.

A toilet cupboard is also a great privacy feature too. Even with the sliding door open or the curtains drawn back, I could back into the toilet cupboard and close the door with everyone outside being none the wiser.

Yes, I actually backed into this cupboard when I needed to use my cassette toilet. I know you didn't buy this book to think about me on the toilet, but sometimes life throws you these little surprises and you just have to roll with it. Think of it as a precursor to what's coming up in Chapter 15.

My toilet cupboard had two sealed compartments: a section that was the same height as me sitting down, and a compartment on top that was the same size as my 12-volt refrigerator. I saw a lot of builds on Instagram following a similar style after doing this, with people moving the fridge off the floor and up to head height for easy access. Moving my fridge to the top compartment also meant I could reach in and grab a drink from bed too, a handy feature for when I was feeling extra lazy!

You don't have to build a specific cupboard for your toilet. Many people use the same method I discussed earlier for building the underbed drawer frame to build bench seats that also house their toilets, but I wanted the extra storage space that came with the toilet cupboard.

It's time to grab your 1⅜-inch × 1⅜-inch (34-millimeter × 34-millimeter) softwood beams again, as you're going to use them to make the same kind of frame you made underneath your bed, though this time it'll be a lot higher.

For the purposes of this next section, I stick with my toilet cupboard design: a lower compartment for the toilet, and a smaller compartment at head height that housed my 12-volt refrigerator.

Twelve-volt refrigerators need air to flow around them. Double-check your manual to determine how much space you should have around your fridge once installed in a cupboard.

Here's how to build a toilet cupboard with a lower compartment for the toilet and a smaller compartment at head height:

1. **Place your toilet up against your van wall and sit on it (with the lid closed is fine).**

2. **Measure where your feet are and your sitting height and mark the area out using masking tape.**

   This might be easier to do with a friend who doesn't mind laughing at the thought of you sitting on a toilet.

The width of your toilet cupboard doesn't need to be much more than the cassette toilet itself. Just give yourself enough room to make pulling it out for emptying easy and stress-free.

3. **Measure the height of your fridge and add 1⅜ inches (34 millimeters) plus the width of your plywood combined twice to account for the shelf your fridge will sit on and the top of your fridge compartment.**

   This gives you the overall height of the beams you'll need to cut for your toilet cupboard.

4. **Cut four beams the overall height of your toilet and fridge compartments combined.**

   In most cases your van wall will be curved.

5. **Place one beam at the front of your proposed cupboard space against your static bed frame and one as far back as it will go before it meets your curved wall, again touching your static bed frame.**

6. **Screw them into your static bed frame so that they stand in place, also screwing the back beam into your wall for support.**

   Leave the other two lengths for now.

7. **Cut smaller beams the width of your cupboard space for the front and back of your cupboard.**

   I'll call these "width beams" from now on.

8. **Measure the overall width of your cupboard and subtract 1⅜ inches (34 millimeters) off each end to account for the vertical beams running up toward your roof.**

   This determines the size of the width beams you need to cut.

9. **Screw two width beams to the floor at the front and back of your cupboard.**

10. **Attach the two vertical beams you screwed to the side of your static bed into these new floor pieces using wood screws.**

11. **Cut two more width beams and screw these into the two vertical beams at the point where you have measured your maximum toilet sitting height (the place where your fridge shelf will be).**

    Don't just guess this measurement; grab your tape measure and check it three times to be on the safe side.

**12.** Screw the remaining two vertical beams into the width beams on the floor and at fridge-shelf height, making sure to screw the back beam into the wall for support.

**13.** Measure and cut four depth beams.

These should be the depth of your cupboard minus 1⅜ inches (34 millimeters) on either end.

**14.** Slot two beams into the two remaining gaps on the floor and screw them down.

**15.** Screw the beams into the corresponding vertical beams.

TIP

You'll need to use angled L brackets to affix these floor depth beams to the back vertical beams of your toilet cupboard. Again, I know I'm not a carpenter, but this worked fine for me.

**16.** Fix the other two depth beams into place in line with the width beams that will make the basis of the fridge shelf and screw into place.

**17.** Screw extra width beams into your depth beams to make a sturdy frame for your fridge shelf to sit on.

**18.** Once complete, cut a piece of plywood and sit on top and screw it into place.

Now you should have a sturdy shelf that your fridge can sit on. Don't go lightly on the beams when making your shelf here; the idea is to distribute the weight so your fridge doesn't fall down on your head while you're on the toilet!

**19.** Cut another two depth beams and two width beams and add to the very top of your toilet cupboard to complete your frame.

**20.** Add a second piece of plywood onto the very top of the frame to close it off, completing your fridge cupboard.

TIP

The roof of your toilet/fridge cupboard is a great place to store items such as a mixing bowl nest, salad mixing bowl, and a box full of chargers and other useful items that you don't know where else to put. Or at least it was for me, at any rate!

**21.** Clad or board the sides of your toilet cupboard.

Take care to follow the curve of your van when cutting pieces to close the sides of your toilet cupboard. Whether boarding or cladding, you can paint or stain the sides of your new storage space to match the rest of your build.

TIP

I fixed my spice rack to the side of the fridge compartment of the toilet cupboard so that it faced into my kitchen area (see Figure 11-4). On the other side in the bedroom area, I attached some pictures to make the bed feel cozier.

**FIGURE 11-4:**
Never leave home without plenty of spices, but don't try cooking with hand cream.

22. **Using medium-density fiberboard (MDF), measure and cut two doors for your fridge and toilet compartments.**

23. **Attach easy-mount hinges and secure in place.**

All that's left to do now is to add a couple of handles and you're done!

IN THIS CHAPTER

» **Choosing the right gas bottle**

» **Connecting your sink and water system**

» **Fitting an air-conditioning unit**

» **Deciding on which heating system is best for you**

» **Installing a wood-burning stove**

# Chapter **12**

# Useful Utilities: Gas, Water, and Heating

When you live in an off-grid tiny home, you don't have a gas or water supply that you can hook up to. Likewise, it's difficult to call out a heating engineer or plumber when your What3Words location is somewhere slap bang in the middle of the backcountry.

In this chapter, you discover the utilities you need for cooking, washing and drinking, keeping cool, and heating up your tiny home and how to hook them up. By the end of this chapter, you'll be one step closer to making, and more important — maintaining — a self-sufficient setup inside your camper.

## Connecting a Gas Bottle

Gas is most often used for cooking and keeping warm in a van, though some three-way fridges also run off your gas supply too. Knowing where to start and what type is best for your setup can all get a little confusing, especially if you've never done any kind of camping before. So before you start setting up your gas system, let's check out the different types of gas bottles on the market.

# Understanding gas bottle types

Most cooking burners are fueled by gas that you can store in a tank inside your van. The three main types of gas used for cooking include:

» **Butane:** Blue gas bottle

» **Propane:** Red gas bottle

» **LPG (liquefied petroleum gas):** Yellow refillable gas bottle

Butane and propane have been staples in the off-grid cooking and heating game for many years now. They're available to buy from most hardware stores, camping shops, and fuel/gas stations throughout the world. Butane is great for indoor use, whereas propane is perfect for outdoor cooking or storing outside. It has a lower boiling point and works better in colder temperatures.

REMEMBER

Standard butane and propane bottles aren't designed to be refilled. What's more, if you're traveling through Europe, the regulators and adapters for these bottles will change in the different countries you pass through. This means that if you run out mid-trip and need to change your bottle, you'll have to buy another regulator or adapter.

Many camper vans opt for a refillable LPG setup. These yellow tanks are designed to be refilled whenever you run out, meaning you don't need to find a safe space to recycle your old bottle or mess around with changing adapters. These bottles can be filled up with LPG gas from fuel/gas stations relatively cheaply. The bottles themselves cost more initially, though if you're planning on living in a van full time for long periods, then it's definitely worth the cost.

## A NOTE ON GAS BOTTLE REGULATORS

You don't hook up a burner directly to a gas bottle; you'll need a regulator in-between. The regulator attaches to the gas bottle and has a nozzle that you feed a gas pipe into. Regulator sizes and types vary from country to country, the type of gas you are using, and the size of bottle you have, so it's definitely not a one-size-fits-all type of deal. Speak to someone at your local camping store or check out camping forums or camping store websites in the countries you are planning on visiting to find out which regulators you'll need.

## Picking the best-sized gas bottle

The size of gas bottle you choose all depends on what size camper you decided to buy back in Chapter 3 and how much available room you have in your build. On a core level, a bigger gas bottle lasts much longer than a smaller one; therefore, I recommend going as big as possible every time.

In the U.S., vanlifers tend to use propane. These tanks come in three main van-suitable sizes: 11 lb., 20 lb., or 30 lb.

In Europe, there are three sizes of propane bottles — 3.9 kilogram, 6 kilogram, and 13 kilogram — and three sizes of butane bottles — 4.5 kilogram, 7 kilogram, and 15 kilogram.

LPG bottles come in smaller sizes still: 2.7 kilogram, 6 kilogram, and 11 kilogram.

While living static in my camper in York, U.K. for a year before traveling, I had a 15-kilogram butane bottle that I used purely for cooking, and it lasted me the entire year. I went through about one and a half bottles per year while traveling full time through Europe.

Yes, van life is much cheaper than living in a house!

## Securing your gas bottle

One of the best ways I found for securing my gas bottle while on the road was to use a ratchet strap attached to two brackets. This was simple to install and allowed me to securely tie down my gas bottle into the corner of the kitchen cupboard. It also sat behind my 25-liter freshwater canister, which was also strapped down in a similar fashion.

In other words, that gas bottle was going nowhere!

# Installing a Gas Drop-Out Vent

**WARNING**

Before you take another step, I need to talk about gas drop-out vents. If you're planning on putting a gas bottle in your van in either a cupboard or a lockable container, make sure you install a gas drop-out vent in the floor of your van next to your gas bottle. Make sure it's next to and not on top of your container and isn't covered by any other objects or materials.

Gas is heavier than air. As a result, if there is a leak from your gas canister, gas will fall and flow down your gas drop-out vent and away from your van. *I cannot stress enough how important a feature this is in your build.*

Gas drop-out vents cost around $10 (around £8) for two on eBay. That's $10 out of your entire budget for something that could potentially save your life if the worst happens, which is good value for the money if you ask me!

So as this is an incredibly important feature in your gas setup, I tell you how to install a gas drop-out vent in your camper before you make another cup of coffee or lose another drill bit.

Things you'll need:

» Drill

» Hole saw (this needs to be the same size as the tube of your drop-out vent, and depending on how much metal you need to cut through, you may need a couple of hole saws)

» Gas drop-out vent (make sure it's long enough to pass through the floor of your van)

» Cutting lubricant (such as WD-40)

» Goggles and mask

» Marker pen

To install a gas drop-out vent, follow these steps:

1. **Mark out where you want to install your drop-out vent.**

   This bit shouldn't cause you any trouble. Simply place the tube of your drop-out vent onto the floor of your van next to where your gas bottle is going to be situated and draw around it with a marker pen. This is the area you're going to be cutting with your hole saw.

2. **Put on your safety equipment.**

   I know that this should be a given, but I'm reminding you anyway because there's bound to be someone who gets too excited and wants to crack on with making sparks straightaway. Yes, I said *sparks,* so get those goggles on!

3. **Using your hole saw, cut a hole in the base of your van.**

   Sounds scary, doesn't it? Don't worry though; you've already made holes for your windows, and this hole is much smaller. This is where the cutting lubricant comes in handy. WD-40 comes as an easy-to-use spray, but any brand from your local hardware store will suffice.

TIP

The floor of your van is much thicker than its side wall. As such, your hole saw will have to work a lot harder. Cutting lubricant helps to cool down the area you are working with and keeps your hole saw nice and slick throughout the "hole" process. (See what I did there?)

WARNING

Don't forget that depending on where you're placing your gas drop-out vent, you may need to cut through a cupboard base, your wooden floor, insulation, and the metal base of your van. Take your time, go steady, and don't rush. While this might be a small hole, you don't want to be making a mess of the process and having to start again.

You might have to cut from both inside and underneath your van to make the hole for your drop-out vent. Make sure you're wearing goggles when cutting above your head as sparks or bits of metal may drop from the bottom of the van. Try not to cut with your face directly underneath the target area too.

**4.** **Once the hole is cut, place your gas drop-out vent through the gap and screw it into place.**

Some gas drop-out vent kits come with screws to attach them to the floor of your van, but by now you should have amassed screws of all shapes and sizes that will suffice. I used two cladding screws to secure my vent to the floor of my van and it has never moved an inch.

# Deciding on a Water Solution

Like gas, water is an essential item when living on the road. Not only do we need water to drink to stay hydrated in order to stay alive (quite a big point if I'm being honest), but we also use it for cooking, washing dishes, and washing ourselves. In this next section, I discuss all the different elements of your water system from storage to sinks, giving you everything you need to know to get a simple water setup in your tiny home.

REMEMBER

When I say simple, I really mean it. The water system tends to get overcomplicated in a van converter's quest to make vans as close to living in a house as possible. As such, you may find this setup to be a heck of a lot simpler than what is described in many other vans conversion books you might have read thus far, but sometimes going simple is the smarter choice for both you and your leisure batteries.

I'm primarily going to talk about the electric-free water setup that I implemented in my camper. I opted for as simple a setup as possible to make sure that — should there ever be a problem with my batteries or electrical setup — I could still get water. I've spoken to so many people over the years who have had problems with water pumps, be it leaks, motors burning out, or the pumps draining batteries. With this in mind, I plumped for using good-old-fashioned elbow grease, or in this case, as you discover in the coming sections, foot-pump power.

## Storing water

If there is one thing I've learned while traveling around the world in a camper, it's that you can never have enough water. It goes much quicker than you might anticipate, so it always pays to have more stored in the back of your van for an emergency.

Water can be stored both outside your van in underslung tanks that sit under the chassis, or inside in plastic jerrycans.

Once again, we come to another age-old debate in the van life world, and I'm guessing you already know which side of the fence I fall on with regard to which one you should use. To play devil's advocate and bump up my word count, let's discuss the merits and faults of each.

### Underslung tanks

Underslung tanks are perfect for storing large amounts of water. You can easily fit 70-liter or more tanks underneath your van, making them the perfect solution if you're opting to put a shower in your van. One thing to remember is that whatever size freshwater tank you opt for, you also have to install a greywater (wastewater) tank that is the same size.

**WARNING**

I discuss this point in Chapter 15, but as an early warning, remember that you can't — and shouldn't — empty your underslung water tanks whenever and wherever you feel like it. There are designated camper van disposal points for both wastewater and toilet waste, but you'll discover all about those in due course.

My main bugbear with underslung tanks is that, apart from having to drill more holes in the bottom of your van for pipes and the extra hassle that comes with hooking up water pumps to your 12-volt electrical system, they lower the clearance of your van significantly. That means that if you're planning on doing a lot of driving on rough terrain, you'll need to raise your suspension in order to keep your tank away from any pesky rocks or logs that could damage it. And I'm not talking about off-roading in the outback here, but stranger things have happened, especially when going over uneven ground.

## Plastic jerrycans

As you might have guessed, I opted for the no-nonsense plastic jerrycan option inside my camper, a no-nonsense, easy-to-fill-and-clean solution that sat inside the cupboard directly underneath my sink. With one 25-liter jerrycan for freshwater connected to my tap and another for wastewater connected to the sink, I could fill up at any tap and carefully pour my wastewater down any drain I came across by hand, which was much more convenient than waiting to find a disposal point!

Over the course of the next few sections, I let you know how I connected it all together using some food-grade waste piping, pipe clips, and a sink waste disposal kit.

TIP

You don't have to store your freshwater jerrycan under your sink. In fact, you can keep it in your garage space at the back of the van and opt for a much bigger tank. This might mean a bit more pumping on your part if you opt for the foot pump I describe, but it's an option if you're planning on spending a lot of time in the middle of nowhere and won't know when you will come across the next water point or stream to fill up again.

**WARNING**

If filling water storage up from a natural water source, always use a filter like the LifeSaver Jerrycan to filter out any viruses or bacteria.

# Choosing a faucet

Before you can hook everything up, you first need to pick a faucet (or tap, depending on which region of the world you're currently reading this book in).

**REMEMBER**

As I said earlier, I describe the water system I installed in my van, and I opted out of including a water heater and pump in my build. From having spent time living on a narrowboat, I know that water pumps are loud and aren't especially suited to stealth camping. Though to be fair, neither is a narrowboat.

What's more, a water heater just felt like something else that would take power from my batteries when my sink was sitting right beside my burner and kettle. I could fill the sink with cold water while my kettle was boiling and create a nice temperature for washing up without having a noisy pump disturbing the peace of the countryside.

Because of my choice to only have a cold-water feed coming into my sink, choosing a faucet was incredibly easy. I only needed a faucet with one feed and one lever, essentially on and off. Though, as my chosen pump method was a foot pump, water only ever flowed when I was at the pump. Not only that, but it gave my calves a nice little workout too.

# Picking your pump

I know I've said it a lot in this chapter already, but water really is one of the most important things you need for living off-grid. How many of you leave a tap running needlessly when you're in your house, probably when you're cleaning your teeth or waiting for it to warm up before washing up? In a van, that's literally precious water flowing down the drain, and with a 12-volt pump, it's all too easy to let it run willy-nilly. Old habits die hard, which is why you need to put your foot down and make a change.

If you haven't guessed already, that was a nice little segue into talking about the Whale Babyfoot manual foot pump.

I installed the Whale Babyfoot pump in my camper at the very beginning of my van life journey and it stood the test of time and heck of a lot of pumping. It might have "baby" in the name, but this little piece of kit is super strong and incredibly durable. This pump can produce 8 liters (2.11 gallons) per minute through human-pump power. To explain that in everyday terms, you can get half a mug of water from a single pump. One pump is also enough to rinse the suds off your dishes when washing up, something I seem to be forever doing! Figure 12-1 shows the water setup I had in my camper van.

**FIGURE 12-1:** My wastewater jerrycan is on the left, my freshwater jerrycan is on the right, and my foot pump in the middle.

# Installing a sink

Sinks come in all different shapes, styles, and sizes. Whether opting for a standard chrome camper sink or the quintessential baby Belfast sink (also known as a "farmhouse" or a "butler" sink), the general process of cutting a section out of your worktop and making space for pipes underneath is essentially the same.

I've always wanted a Belfast sink in my house, so much so that this was the very first thing I bought from eBay for the van build . . . even before the van itself. At $15 \times 15 \times 15$ inches, it was perfect for the space and a great deal. I would have been stupid to miss out on it, so it sat under my desk at work and then in my dining room for about three months until I was ready to install it.

Things you'll need:

>> Sink

>> Cardboard (for making a template)

>> Marker pen

>> Measuring tape

>> Jigsaw and jigsaw blade

>> 4 angled brackets

>> 1 piece of wood the approximate width and length of your sink for your sink shelf

>> Quick-drying silicone sealant

Here's how to install a sink in your camper (for the purposes of this section, I refer back to how I installed the baby Belfast in my own camper):

1. **Measure the size of your sink.**

   This might seem like a pointless step if it says the dimensions on the box, but just like the Matrix, sometimes things can be different to what they seem. Measure everything just to be on the safe side. It'll also give you an idea of where any curves or wider points are situated.

2. **Mark out the dimensions on your worktop.**

   Make a cardboard template first and then draw around this. It will give you a chance to hone the corner shaping down so that you don't make any mistakes when it comes to cutting out your sink space.

3. **Cut the area out for your sink to sit in.**

   Take your time with this and go slowly. There's nothing worse than cutting too much off and being left with a massive gap you need to fill up with sealant.

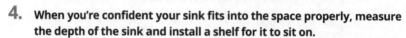

   For a Belfast sink, make sure you cut three sides to create a U shape to slot your sink into. This will leave the front face of the sink on show.

   Even after cutting out space for your sink with your jigsaw, the gap might still be a little snug when you try to dry fit your sink. Use sandpaper to sand the space down by hand until your sink fits.

   You might have seen Belfast and butler sinks in tiny homes and shepherd's huts that have the worktop coming over the top of them. While there's nothing wrong with this, I'm not a massive fan of that look and prefer having the edge of the sink flush with the surface of the worktop. It looks much less cluttered to me, and while the overlapping method means you don't have to be as precise with your measurements, I still think taking the time to get it right looks much more impressive.

4. **When you're confident your sink fits into the space properly, measure the depth of the sink and install a shelf for it to sit on.**

   Take care when picking the height of your sink and don't forget to take the width of your countertop into account too. Check out Figure 12-2 to see how I tackled it.

**FIGURE 12-2:**
Prepping the area for my baby Belfast sink.

5. **Cut a hole in the shelf for the waste connection point to sit in.**

   If your cupboard is already in place, then use your L-shaped angled brackets to fix your sink shelf into your cupboard. If you can remove your cupboard, drill from the outside into the sides of your shelf to hold it in place. Don't overthink this step too much, but if you're cutting a piece of wood especially for this purpose, make sure you make a neat cut. One edge will be on show underneath your sink, so take the time to get it right.

6. **Seal around the gap between the sink the worktop with quick-drying silicone sealant.**

   It's a good idea to fill the sink half-full of water before doing this; otherwise the silicone could crack due to the added weight of the water when you're doing your washing up.

   Don't get trigger-happy with the sealant. Dampen your finger and run along the top to remove any excess.

TIP

## Installing the water system components

Now that you've installed your sink and got your jerrycans in place, the next step is to hook everything up.

Things you'll need:

>> ½-inch (13-millimeter) food-grade non-toxic hose piping

>> Hose clips

>> Baby Belfast sink waste kit

>> Waste piping

>> Drill

>> Hole saw

WARNING

Don't throw the screw caps from your jerrycans away; you're going to create a hole for your pipes to fit down through them.

## Installing your faucet and foot pump

Follow these steps to install your faucet and foot pump:

1. **Using a hole saw that is the same size as the bottom of your faucet screw, make a hole in your worktop for your faucet to sit in.**

2. **Dry fit your faucet, but don't screw it into place just yet.**

3. **Position your foot pump in your desired location.**

4. **Measure a length of blue hose from the right nozzle on your pump to your freshwater jerrycan and another length from your left nozzle up to where your faucet will be sitting.**

5. **Run pipe clips down over the pieces of hose and secure them into place over each nozzle on your foot pump.**

6. **Using a drill, make a small hole in the cap of your freshwater jerrycan screw cap and feed your blue hose from the right nozzle on your foot pump down through it.**

   This hole only needs to be big enough for your hose to fit through; otherwise the water in your canister won't be sealed properly. If you find that your hole is a little too big, then seal around the gap with some food-grade silicone.

7. **Connect the other length of blue hose from the left nozzle to your faucet and screw in place in your worktop.**

   Now, with your faucet in the open position and your foot on the pump, you should have water flowing.

Make sure to have a cup underneath your tap if you try it out at this point; otherwise water will go everywhere until you hook your waste up in the next section.

## Connecting your sink to your wastewater jerrycan

You're on the home stretch. Let's get that waste pipe set up, and then you're good to go! Follow these steps to connect your sink to your wastewater jerrycan:

1. **Fit the drain/plug hole to the sink, screw in place, and tighten.**

   The drain will have a large screw that connects to the waste pipe on the other side. Your waste pipe will join up to the part of your sink that sits through the shelf you made to support it in your cupboard.

2. **Attach a piece of waste pipe to the underside of your sink waste and feed it down through the cap of your wastewater jerrycan.**

   Again, this hole needs to be just big enough for your pipe to fit through. Any more, and you might have odors seeping out into your van. Use some sealant to close off the gap if it ends up being too big.

   Now you have a fully working sink system, all without 12-volt electrics!

**WARNING**

The following sections cover utilities that aren't crucial to your van build and are therefore classed as "optional extras." If you do decide to add air-conditioning, a diesel heater, or a log burner into the mix, then complete these steps before you clad, add insulation, or install wires, as you will be cutting holes in your roof. Alternatively, plan accordingly and leave these spaces clear until you have finished installing your chosen devices.

# Crank Up the A/C!

When things start to heat up, you need to be able to cool down your space in a jiffy. For some, opening windows and creating a through draft is enough to cool down your internal space with ease, especially when you're parked by the ocean and taking advantage of that fresh sea breeze.

But what happens when you're parked in the city on a still day and your van is hotter than the Gobi Desert? No number of pocket fans will help you in that situation, and if you want to avoid a one-way trip to Melt Town, you need to crank up that air-conditioning unit and get your chill on.

In other words, it's time to discover how to install an air-conditioning unit inside your van. (I really should have just said that in the first place.)

## Picking the right air-conditioning unit

Air-conditioning units come with different BTU ratings. (BTU stands for *British Thermal Unit.* The meaning of that abbreviation is irrelevant right now, but it might help you out on the next pub quiz or if you're trying to impress someone at a dinner party.) According to some research I did for this chapter with my good friend Google, 12,000 BTU is the equivalent of 1 ton of cooling. An average guide to go by when cooling an average-sized house is that you'll need around 36,000 BTU, or 3 ton of cooling.

But we're not cooling a whole house, we're cooling a van!

To calculate the BTU rating you'll need for any space, take the length and the width of that space and multiply those numbers together to get the square foot measurement. Then, multiple that number by 25. For example, if your space is 12 feet by 6 feet, giving you a total of 72 square feet, then 72 square feet × 25 BTU gives you a total of 1,800 BTU. That means a 5,000 BTU air-conditioner will more than suffice for your space.

If you were converting a bigger vehicle like a bus that was 24 feet × 10 feet, giving you a total of 240 square feet, then 240 square feet × 25 BTU gives you a total of 6,000 BTU. That means a 6,000 BTU air-conditioning unit would be perfect for the space.

TIP Pick an air-conditioning unit that runs quietly for stealth camping and try to find as lightweight a unit as possible. And of course, it's important to pick a system that is kind to your leisure batteries too.

## Powering an air-conditioning unit

Remember when I said that I bought a household fridge and tried to run it off my inverter, but it kept draining my batteries? Can you also remember how the 12-volt alternatives were much better when it came to drawing power but way more expensive?

Well, the same goes for air-conditioning units. You can buy units that hook up to your inverter or plug into your sockets that you've connected to it, and while they are less expensive than the 12-volt alternatives, you certainly can't run them as long.

The price difference is dramatic, however, with the 12-volt alternatives costing four or five times more than the household electric voltage rated models (120V/240V). Still, to give your batteries a break and to get the most out of the energy you've stored from the sun, it's worth spending the extra cash and getting a 12-volt model that you can integrate into your existing 12-volt system, especially if you're planning on keeping your camper around for a good long while.

Dometic offers a great 12-volt air-conditioning unit called the RTX 2000 that only draws around 19 amps in Eco mode. There's also the Mabru 12V rooftop air-conditioning unit that pumps out 12,000 BTU and uses 22 amps on its lowest setting. This one is easy on the ears too, with a noise rating of 33 decibels compared to the RTX 2000's 70 decibels.

## Installing air-conditioning in your camper

Enough chit-chat and number crunching; let's look at how to install an air-conditioning unit in your van. For the purposes of this section, I talk about installing the Dometic RTX 2000 12-volt air-conditioning unit.

Things you'll need:

>> Dometic RTX 2000 (this comes with all bolts, accessories, and templates, as well as a wires)

>> Custom-made RTX 2000 adapter (see Step 2)

>> Sharpie

>> Jigsaw

>> Metal file

>> Isopropanol

>> Rustproof paint (Hammerite or Rust-Oleum)

>> Sikaflex sealant (you might need a couple of tubes of this)

>> Sealant gun

>> Masking tape

>> Torque wrench

>> Hand saw/multi-tool

**WARNING**

You need to get a friend to help you with this one. Don't try to tackle it on your own; it'll only end in tears. Even the lightweight air-conditioning units aren't exactly "light," so take your time lifting them and call in some muscle power from a friend to help. Also, you're going to lift something heavy while climbing up ladders, so *please* be careful. I would advise having some extra people to hold both your ladder and your friend's ladder as you lift. Maybe get the whole family round to help with this one.

**TIP**

If you don't feel comfortable lifting your air-conditioning unit up ladders, then consider hiring a winch to get your unit safely onto the top of your van.

To install an air-conditioning unit in your camper, follow these steps:

1. **Pick an area on your van roof where you want to install your air-conditioning unit.**

   Typically, the air-conditioning unit goes either in the middle or the back of the van depending on where you've put your solar panels. Decide now and make sure you're happy with your decision; once that hole is cut, there's no going back!

2. **Place your pre-made adapter into position.**

The Dometic RTX 2000 comes with a rubber gasket that you can use to create a seal around your air-conditioning unit once it is sat in the hole you've cut, and while it does the job, it's a little fiddly. I spent a lot of time researching air-conditioning installation methods and came across a company called DIYvan via a YouTube video posted by van converters, Our Thriving Life.

DIYvan sells template adapters specifically for the RTX 2000 air-conditioning unit. Essentially, you glue this adapter to your van roof, and then the RTX 2000 sits neatly inside it. It also adds extra structural integrity to your van roof and helps take the weight of the air-conditioner.

The adapter costs around $200 (about £167), but it's well worth it to take the stress out of sealing off such an important piece of equipment and weather-proofing your van. DIYvan makes them for all different types of van brands and roofs and they ship internationally.

So for the remainder of this section, that's the method we'll follow.

3. **With your pre-made adapter in place, draw around the inside of it with a sharpie.**

   You've done so much sharpie drawing throughout your build so far that I'm not going to insult you by telling you how to draw a line.

   Okay, maybe I am. Use a thin sharpie so you don't end up following the inner edge of a thicker line and cutting your hole too small.

   Don't forget to draw around the cable entry hole in the adapter too.

4. **Using a jigsaw, carefully follow your sharpie line to cut a hole in your van roof.**

   Take your time with this; you can't add metal back on once it's been cut off.

5. **Cut across the corners diagonally and go back once the main bulk of the hole is out to get a proper round finish on them.**

   Go carefully around the cable entry hole that you're making too.

6. **Once you're done, file down the edges to make them smooth before dusting off any metal shards.**

7. **Clean the area with isopropanol, then once dry, apply some metal paint such as Hammerite or Rust-Oleum to rustproof the area.**

   Isopropanol is strong stuff, so wear a mask and gloves when using it.

8. **With your adapter back in place, place masking tape on the roof of your van around the edges.**

9. **Remove the adapter and run a good amount of Sikaflex sealant around the area between the inner edge of your tape and the edge of the hole that you cut for your air-conditioning unit to sit in.**

My friend Andy always uses the phrase "gob it on." This basically means "the more the merrier" when it comes to using adhesive sealants. Apply liberally and wipe off any excess that squeezes out when you position your adapter back in place.

10. **Weatherproof your adapter by adding a layer of Sikaflex around the edge that meets the van and run your finger over it to smooth.**

11. **Once done, tape a plastic bag over the hole into your van and weigh the adapter down with something heavy like a couple of logs or weights.**

Leave it to dry for 24 hours.

12. **Grab your Sikaflex and run a line around the top of your adapter and then lower your air-conditioning unit into place.**

13. **Press down and remove any excess sealant that spills out.**

Again, leave this to dry and form a tight seal.

14. **Install the bars that come with the RTX 2000 on the underside of your van roof.**

These bars essentially bolt to the ribs on the roof of your van and help to secure the air-conditioning unit in place. Use the template that comes with the unit when drilling holes for attaching the bars in place.

**TIP**

If you already added pine beams to the metal ribs on your roof, then cut slots for your metal bars using a hand saw or multi-tool. Hold the bar up to the desired point, draw around the area that needs to be removed, and make a slot in the wood so that the bars sit flush with the metal ribs on the roof.

15. **Place and tighten the bolts using a torque wrench.**

Follow the specified tightening torque and refer to your instruction manual to determine the correct bolt length measurements.

16. **Feed your wires down to your battery bank terminal and follow the steps used in Chapter 9 to both connect the positive feed up to your isolator switch and earth to the side of the van.**

The RTX 2000 comes with an 80-amp fuse and holder along with the positive and negative feed that you can run down to your isolator switch (positive) and wheel arch (negative).

17. **Hook everything up, and bask in the glory of your "cool" achievement.**

# Getting a Handle on Heating

No matter how well you insulate your van, you're still going to need a heat source from time to time when the temperature drops. Maybe you're planning on doing what I did and living in a van full time in your city through a cold winter, or perhaps you're planning a trip to the outer reaches of Alaska or even the Outer Hebrides. Either way, having some form of heating in your van is important for creating a comfortable living space no matter the weather.

I've previously spoken with people who have woken up with frozen hot water bottles in their beds and ice on the inside of their windows during the winter months. You wouldn't stand for that kind of goings-on in a house, not nowadays at any rate, and you don't have to put up with it in a van either.

In the sections that follow I talk about two of the heating formats I've used in a van throughout my van life adventures: a diesel heater and a wood-burning stove.

Some of you may be wondering, "Why isn't he mentioning a gas-powered heater?" The answer is simple. These heaters blow through your gas bottle much quicker than if you were just using it for cooking. I like to keep all my elements for one specific thing, two if you count diesel for the heater and the engine. And considering that the diesel heater I chose only pulls 0.1 liter of diesel an hour on the lowest setting and still keeps the space warm overnight, it's a much more cost-effective and easier solution than continually swapping gas bottles.

So let' have a little look at a couple of pros and cons when it comes to diesel heaters versus fires, alongside a rundown of each.

## Heating with a diesel heater

| Pros | Cons |
| --- | --- |
| Heats your space without using much diesel or electric | Costly to fit and not something I would recommend fitting yourself |
| Fast heating source at the push of a button; also comes with a cold air mode | |
| No lighting kindling with cold fingers | |
| Timer function to come on at a certain time before you wake up just like the central heating in a house | |
| Can be installed into your main diesel tank or a separate tank | |

Don't get me wrong: I love having a log burner in any tiny home. Still, when your thermostat is showing −10 inside your van because it's covered in snow and your hands are cold from messing around building a snowman with your mates after a long shift at work (yes, this is another story from *Captain Sebastian Hindsight*), the last thing you want to be doing is messing around lighting a fire and throwing kindling around while shouting "why me?" (I did that bit too.)

As I've mentioned already, I removed the log burner in the van to meet the requirements for full-time European travel before the U.K. left the E.U. The replacement: an Autoterm 2KW diesel heater fitted with an exhaust muffler to help when stealth camping in cities.

Yes, a black box inside the shoe cupboard didn't have the same cozy feel as crackling logs and an orange glow, but there's something about having instant heat and a timer setting for when you wake up for work in December that never, ever gets old.

The Autoterm 2KW is a relatively cheap heater, but it does the job perfectly. In all the time I've used that heater, I've hardly ever had it above 4 on the power rating scale for long periods of time. I bought mine from a company called Mellor Online back in 2018 after having a lengthy discussion with a sales assistant about which would be best for my build and the ins and outs of all the different models. They ship worldwide too, so get in contact to chat about the best model for your conversion.

The main downside to a diesel heater is that, depending on where you are based, they can be quite expensive to fit. Back when I lived in York, U.K. (take a minute to give it a Google; it's very nice), I was quoted £1,000 (around $1,200) by a mechanic to fit it (not so nice). In my mum's village at the local coal yard and car garage, however, a mechanic quoted me £200 (about $240). So if you have a relative in a sleepy little place that doesn't even have a Post Office, then go get your diesel heater fitted there.

# Connecting a diesel heater to your electrical system

While the process of drilling into your vehicle's diesel tank, positioning your 12-volt electric pump, and fitting your exhaust is something that I would advise you getting a mechanic or auto-electrician to complete, hooking the diesel heater itself up to your batteries is no harder than anything that you've done back in Chapter 9 when you put your electrical system together. In fact, it's exactly the same process.

Just like you did with your solar and plug wire, use conduit to protect the positive and negative feeds from your heater as you run them to your main isolator switch. Hook the positive end to the right terminal on your isolator switch (looking from the back — the one that the batteries aren't connected to) and earth the negative wire to your wheel arch.

**WARNING**

The Autoterm heater had a "plug and play" connection system, with the control display unit and 12-volt pump plugging into adapters that popped out of the main heater unit itself. Refer to your instruction manual for assistance when it comes to plugging in components.

## Warming up your space with a wood-burning or multi-fuel stove

| Pros | Cons |
| --- | --- |
| Makes any camper feel like a log cabin | You'll need to find somewhere to store your logs |
| No need to rely on electricity or diesel; keep warm at any time | Some companies refuse to insure campers with wood burners |
| Great as an extra cooking space and for cooking jacket potatoes | You'll need a place to empty out ash from the ash pan |
| Keep in all night and get going again the next day | The initial smoke produced when lighting a fire isn't great for stealth camping |

In the beginning, camper van conversions are like blank canvasses, and you're a nomadic Bob Ross. You can put anything you like into your little world, a cupboard here, a crocheted throw there, but the important thing is that you fill it with things that make you happy.

For me, having a wood-burning stove made me think back to my childhood, sitting next to a roaring fire while playing video games with my parents. And, from speaking to lots of other camper owners and enthusiasts, I know a lot of other people have had the thought about putting a stove in their rolling homes too.

There is no feeling like having a log burner or multi-fuel stove in your van. It seems so weird yet so right at the same time — a quirky feature that immediately turns a metal box on wheels into a homey space. Sometimes I would just sit with a cup of tea by the open fire door while listening to an audiobook or warming my toes while writing an article. And, as I mention in the pros list earlier, it's also another hot surface that you can use for boiling a kettle or cooking sauces!

Smokeless fuel isn't expensive when bought through a coal merchant, and if you hone your fire skills, it's easy to keep a fire burning all night long and get it going again in the morning. You can also burn dead wood that you find in a park-up spot too; just don't pull greenwood from living trees.

WARNING

Of course, you shouldn't drive with a fire lit in the back of your van, so always make sure it's fully out before you move on to your next destination.

TIP

It might seem odd, but trust me when I say that people simply don't care if you have smoke coming from the chimney in your van. I remember lighting mine one day and looking out the window while a woman walked past reading a book and listening to music through headphones, and she didn't even bat an eyelid. I know not everyone who walks past your van will be feeding their senses so frantically, but the truth is that most people are too wrapped up in their own worlds or rushing to get somewhere to see or even care that you're lighting a fire in your van. Hopefully, this will give you a little bit more confidence when it comes to staying warm during cold days. Get those flames roaring!

# Adding a Wood-Burning Stove

Just like the baby Belfast sink, I knew I wanted to have a log burner in my van from the very beginning. I might have removed it because of insurance purposes while traveling around Europe, but it proved invaluable while living in the U.K. through a really cold winter. And plus, it was a cool talking point when people were around for a nosey around the conversion.

There's something great about sitting in bed reading a book and listening to logs crackling and seeing the glow from smokeless coal. I bought a stove from eBay for £86 (about $103) and fitted it myself, along with all the necessary safety features, fixtures, and fittings.

REMEMBER

As long as your stove/wood burner meets the safety regulations in your country, then it's perfectly fine to install inside your van.

TIP

I got all the elements I talk about in the sections that follow from a website called Glowing Embers here in the U.K. Not only do they have every product you could ever possibly need for a stove installation, but the customer service was impeccable when I needed help with specific parts and installation tips. Glowing Embers ships throughout the U.K. and worldwide, so get in touch to chat about your specific stove needs.

# Important parts of your stove setup

Here's everything you need for a stove installation along with a little bit of information as to what each bit does and why it's integral to the build.

Before I go any further, I want to talk about airflow. Fires draw in air in order to keep burning. If you run out of oxygen in a small space, then carbon monoxide builds up, and that's something you *do not* want to happen. The effects can be fatal, but there are numerous ways to prevent this situation from ever happening.

For starters, install a gas drop-out vent underneath your fire. Air will be drawn from outside of your van, thus preventing a carbon monoxide build-up. Likewise, it's also a good idea to keep a window open a crack to keep air flowing into your living space. This could be in the cab or by using one of the windows in your living space.

Keep that air flowing; that's the most important thing you need to remember.

## Stove

Obviously, this bit goes without saying. It would be pointless installing everything else without the main attraction, after all. Look for a unit that comes with fire-bricks pre-fitted and one that has all the necessary safety ratings for your country and/or state.

## Twin insulated flue

It won't surprise any of you to know that I was extra safety conscious with the flue in the van. Then again, when you're dealing with a box full of flames and a metal tube passing close to wooden surfaces, I guess it pays to be a little more like me.

So why did I opt for a twin insulated flue? Well, it's a heck of a lot safer than using exhaust piping or a standard flue as it has a thick glass mineral wool lining that insulates the pipe and prevents heat from transferring to other surfaces. The wooden wall behind my flue never got hot, making it money well spent in my book!

The thickness of the flue you purchase ultimately depends on the diameter of the hole at the top or back of your fire. I bought a flue with a 5-inch internal diameter, and because it was twin insulated, that meant that with 2 inches of glass mineral wool, the overall diameter was 7 inches. Okay, so it looked substantial when installed, but it certainly turned a few heads and gave me peace of mind when I went to sleep at night.

The type of stove you get will determine which flue connector pieces you need when connecting your flue up to your stove. A potbelly stove, for instance, won't need any elbow joins, whereas a stove like the one I bought with a flue connection point at the back needs a 90-degree elbow piece to connect it up to the main length of flue passing through your roof.

It took two pieces of flue, one that was $1 \times 1$ meter and one that was $1 \times 30$ centimeter long to make it through the roof, as well as a 90-degree elbow bend to fix it to the back of the stove, all made by Shield Master and bought through Glowing Embers. Shield Master products are self-locking and clasp together with push locks, so there's no need to cement around them and ruin the look of your new flue.

Make sure to place your flue at least 8 centimeters away from the nearest surface and secure it in place using a flue bracket. While you won't need to use fire cement around the joins in your flue, you may need to use some inside your stove at the flue connection point. Check all seams and joins carefully when you first light your fire and use fire cement to close off any gaps.

Always keep at least one carbon monoxide monitor near your wood burner. I had one on the wall behind the stove and one in the bedroom area just to be on the safe side.

## Flashing

Flashing isn't that thing that you see people doing when they streak across a football pitch . . . not in this sense, at any rate. Flashing looks a little like a rubber traffic cone crossed with Gandalf's hat, and it goes over your flue at the point that it exits your van roof.

You're going to need a high-temperature flashing kit that can cope with the temperatures your fire will be outputting. Just like flues, these come in different sizes but can be cut to size too. Glowing Embers also provides a fixing kit with screws, screw caps, and fireproof sealant.

## Fire rope, sealant, and cement

I've already touched on a few of these elements, so I figured it was time to give them their own section. Fire rope, sealant, and fire cement are used to block off areas that smoke might emit from and also to protect other surfaces from coming into contact with heat. You'll need lots of all three when installing your flue and flashing, especially fire sealant.

Envirograf fire sealant is heat resistant up to 1200 degrees, so grab some of this to use around the exit point where your flue passes through your van roof and for your flashing.

## Rain cap

Every chimney needs a top hat, right? The rain cap stops water from flowing down into your chimney, but you can also get stormproof caps if you live in an area where the weather is more violent than two gators playing Street Fighter. Mine looked more like the hat worn by the cat in Dr Seuss' *The Cat in the Hat* after a couple of months of driving under low-hanging branches in the Yorkshire Dales, but it still did the job.

## Aluminum sheet

For an extra bit of protection (and because it looks cool), take a ⅛-inch (3-millimeter) piece of aluminum and used it as a finishing sheet to finish off the exit hole where your chimney leaves the van roof. Not only will it help with heat transference, but it's also helping to support the chimney and adds extra stability to that section of roof.

## Stand and stone

Heading back down into the van, a fire stand and stone for it to sit on are important parts of your stove setup and the parts you need to think about first. Having a solid base for your fire is key and can be done pretty easily with some clever use of pallets.

I used a wooden pallet for a stand with a block of Rivenstone on top to create a fireproof surface that wouldn't transfer heat. It doesn't need to be any more than 2-inches (50-millimeters) thick, just something that will do the job of a hearth should coal or embers fly out.

When using stone, make sure to finish it with some stone sealant. This will protect it from stains and make it much easier to clean if you spill anything. You can pick stone sealant up online or from your local hardware store.

The holes in the pallet allow for air to flow up through the gas drop-out vent, thus making your fire draw easier and keeping you carbon monoxide–free.

# Installing your wood-burning stove

Now you've got all the components; let's get to work installing your stove!

1. **Bolt your stove to your stone, then screw your stone to your pallet base.**

   Some stoves come with a bolt hole for you to secure them down to a surface. Others may have a foot with a plate that you can drill through in order to bolt them to your stone. If you don't have either, then speak to a metal worker to ask if they can weld a bracket to one or two of your legs. That's the stove's legs, not your own.

**TIP**

   You'll need to use a hammer drill when drilling down through your stone. Get a friend to keep the area around where you are drilling lubricated with a hose, and place something underneath around the spot to support the stone as you drill down. This will minimize the risk of snapping your stone in half as you add pressure.

**REMEMBER**

   When drilling a hole through your stone, you'll need to use a masonry bit the same size as the bolt that you are using to secure your stove down. I recommend using no bigger than a 6-millimeter masonry bit here.

   The same goes for drilling holes to screw your stone to your pallet. Use screws that correspond to your chosen drill bit. I recommend a 4- millimeter bit for making screw holes.

2. **Mark the area you're going to place your palette/stone stand.**

3. **Using a hole saw, add a gas drop-out vent into your floor.**

4. **Secure your pallet to the floor of your van.**

5. **Follow the same steps for adding a gas drop-out vent at the beginning of this chapter.**

6. **Screw your pallet down in at least four places to make sure it's fully secured to your van's subfloor.**

7. **Attach your 90-degree elbow join to the back of your stove (optional).**

   This is an optional step as your stove might connect to your chimney from the top rather than the back. If it connects from the back and you need to use an elbow piece like I did, then use a couple of easydrive screws to secure the elbow piece to the lip of the flue connection point on the back of your fire and seal over with fire cement. Check out Figure 12-3 to double-check what this elbow join looks like attached to a stove.

**FIGURE 12-3:**
My twin-insulated flue and elbow piece attached to the back of the stove.

8. **Attach a fixing bracket to your wall to help secure your chimney.**

   It's recommended that you use a fixing bracket to support your chimney every meter. It's unlikely you'll have more than one meter of flue inside your van, so one fixing bracket should be enough.

9. **Fix one piece of flue to the top of your stove and your 90-degree elbow join and lock in place.**

   As I mention earlier, Shield Master products lock into place without any need for fire cement. Simply slide one onto the other and clip into place to lock.

   Now comes the part you've all been waiting for or perhaps dreading: cutting another hole in your roof. Don't panic, though; I talk you through the entire process and show you that there's nothing to worry about.

**WARNING**

That being said, please be careful when using power tools on the roof of your van. Place your ladders on a level surface and have someone hold them just to be on the safe side.

**TIP**

Before you start cutting a hole in your roof, put a plastic bag over the end of the length of chimney sticking up from your fire so debris doesn't get stuck inside.

**10.** **Using your smaller piece of flue, draw around the bottom of it with a sharpie to make a template on your roof.**

This is the simplest way of getting the circumference of your chimney correct the first time without messing around with measuring tapes or a compass.

**11.** **Using your drill, make a hole inside your circle big enough for your jigsaw blade to fit in.**

Make sure your hole is big enough for you to fit the blade in comfortably and that it doesn't overlap your chimney circumference line.

**12.** **Carefully follow the line with your jigsaw to cut out the circle.**

It's a good idea to use a blade with thin teeth such as your aluminum cutting blade, especially if you have a fiberglass roof that could crack easily.

**13.** **Dry fit your smaller flue piece through your hole.**

This is just to see if your hole is big enough. You're not fixing anything together just yet, but if it fits, then take a break and have a biscuit to celebrate.

**14.** **Taking your smaller flue piece and sheet of aluminum, draw around the flue to create a circle the same diameter.**

**15.** **Cut out the circle using your jigsaw.**

This finishing plate will go up flush against your roof, or as flush as possible depending on the curvature of your roof.

**TIP** Use a thin-toothed aluminum blade when cutting through your aluminum sheet for a clean finish.

**16.** **Place your smaller piece of flue through the hole in the roof and your aluminum sheet.**

**17.** **Attach the smaller section to the bigger piece already locked to your stove and attach your finishing plate to the underside of your roof.**

Lock the pieces of flue together using the same method.

**18.** **Attach your finishing plate to the roof by bolting it through the roof of your van as you did with your solar panel fixing kit or by using heat resistant glue.**

**19.** **Feed fire rope and fire sealant into the gap between your chimney and the edge of the hole you fed it through.**

If you can, packing a little rope and sealant in here will help to further reduce any heat transference into your roof. Now, you should have your stove in place on its stand with a chimney sticking out of your roof. All that's left to do is to attach the flashing and pop your rain cap in place.

As I mention earlier, the flashing kit from Glowing Embers comes with some easydrive screws, making attaching your flashing to your roof an absolute breeze. Flashing kits have an aluminum strip around the edge, making it easy for you to push it down to mold around the contours of your van.

TIP

When placing your flashing over your chimney, use a little washing up liquid as a lubricant so you don't tear it.

20. **Using adhesive sealant such as Sikaflex, apply a layer to the underside of your flashing and press into place on your roof.**

The more the merrier here; you can always clean up the excess that squeezes out with a wet cloth as you are screwing your flashing down in the next step.

21. **Using the easydrive screws from your flashing kit, screw down through the aluminum strip into the roof of your van.**

As you drill down, the screw will lock itself into place and fill the hole you've created with some of the sealant underneath the flashing, further weather-proofing your new fixture.

22. **Place the caps for each screw included in your flashing kit onto each easydrive screw.**

This is to stop the screws from rusting and for preventing any pesky leaks from dripping down into your van.

TIP

If you're not too concerned about how the roof of your van looks, pop a bit more sealant over the top of each cap to fully cover them.

23. **Place the rain cap onto the top of your chimney and lock in place using the same method as your other flue pieces.**

The finishing touch!

Now all that's left is to step back and marvel at your handiwork.

# 3

# Living Your Best Van Life

# Chapter **13**

# Changing Your V5 Form and Insurance

For all the U.K. readers currently making their way through this book, you've come to a very crucial part of the conversion process that, while a little boring compared to building beds and cupboards or heading out to your first beach park-up, is still a necessary element to consider in your van build. Changing your van's classification with the Driver and Vehicle Licensing Agency (DVLA) is something that provides multiple benefits for you as a driver, and while it's not actually a legal requirement, registering it with the DVLA has multiple benefits for you and other drivers out on the road.

In this chapter, I explain all about the U.K. V5 form, registering your van as a camper with the DVLA, and also the benefits that you can take advantage of, many of which will be kind to your pocket. There's a sidebar with information on registering a van in the U.S. too, and if you live outside of the U.K., you can always stick around to learn something new about how things work on our little isle!

## REGISTERING A VAN IN THE U.S.

In the U.K., vans are registered as "motor caravans," and in the U.S., they're registered as RVs. (For anyone not up on their acronyms, that's *recreational vehicle*.) As the U.S. is so vast, the registration requirements vary so much from state to state. Each state's Department of Motor Vehicles (DMV) office is where you will find the registration requirements for the state in which you want to register your van. Do a Google search for "[state] DMV" to find a link to that state's DMV website.

Just like registering your van as an RV, insuring your van is a process that changes between states too. And, as I mostly talk about DIY conversions in this book, be aware that insurance companies have different requirements to be able to properly insure your camper once complete. A good tip is to keep all your receipts for the equipment you've bought for the van, including the van itself, to prove how much the van is worth. Always shop around with different insurance companies to get the best deal and make sure that all your needs are met before signing.

# What's a V5 Form?

Let's get the boring bit out of the way first, shall we?

The V5 form is basically the blueprint for your vehicle's history. It's proper title is the V5C form, but you'll often hear it referred to as the vehicle's *logbook*. This document legally registers your vehicle with the DVLA. That's the Driver and Vehicle Licensing Agency for anyone not living in the British Isles.

The V5 form has all the information about your van's life since it rolled off the production line. It shows everything from the date it was made to the original color of the vehicle and engine size. You'll see the original manufacturer on there too as well as who currently owns the vehicle.

If you've ever bought a secondhand vehicle in the U.K., you will have filled in a segment of a V5 form to send off to the DVLA to change ownership of said vehicle. What you might not have seen is the section to change the vehicle classification; it's not something that comes up that often, after all.

# Why It's Important to Change a Vehicle's Classification

I get onto the nitty-gritty parts of how to change your van's designation to a camper in a minute. But first, I want to explain why it's so important to make sure your vehicle classification is correct when you're driving on the roads.

The DVLA keeps track of all vehicles on the roads. That includes your granny's Fiat Punto, your uncle Derek's tractor, and the panel van you're currently converting. They log down the body type of each vehicle and therefore what that vehicle looks like, including key features that separate it from other vehicles. Imagine the dog car from the movie *Dumb and Dumber*. That V5 form would state that it was "covered in hair with big dog ears" under the distinguishing features section.

REMEMBER

Registering your panel van as a camper van keeps all your records up to date with the relevant authorities so that your vehicle can be correctly identified if it goes missing or is involved in an accident. Now, I know that those are two things that you probably don't want to be thinking about at this stage, but sadly they happen all too often, so it's better to be safe than sorry.

# Is It a Legal Requirement to Change My Panel Van to a Camper?

It isn't a legal requirement to change the designation of your van to a camper, but the benefits that I'm about to talk about are worth it if you're planning on spending a lot of time traveling around in your vehicle. You *can* still use your converted vehicle as a camper van, but you won't be able to insure it as such unless the right criteria are met.

The rules have changed since I converted my first van. Back in 2017, the criteria were there to basically make sure people weren't sticking a blow-up bed in the back of a van and getting cheaper insurance for their "camper." Now that van life has become such a big movement, however, the rules and regulations as to what constitutes a converted camper van have changed, and you'll have to meet the conversion criteria I outline later in this chapter if you want to become a bona fide camper owner.

WARNING

It's up to you to make sure the changes you make to the vehicle are safe. Adding a diesel heater tank or installing a roof vent aren't things that come up on your MOT (Ministry of Transport test), so it's down to you as the owner to make sure those things are properly installed and safe to use.

# The Benefits of Declaring Your Van as a Camper

There are multiple reasons why you should consider changing your panel van to a camper van, all of which help to make your life easier while out on the road.

# Cheaper insurance

Yes, I thought I would start with the biggest plus point first. Car and van insurance isn't cheap by any stretch of the imagination. If you're buying your first van and haven't had a car before, which was the situation I found myself in, then the price of insuring it will make you feel a little sick in the stomach.

As an insured panel van, I was paying around £900 ($1,075) a year for my vehicle to be legally insured while out on the road. Once I reclassified the van as a camper and sought out specialized camper van insurance, however, that bill dropped to £220 ($263) a year. That's a dramatic saving and one that makes a big difference if you're planning on doing some long stints of living or traveling in your van.

**REMEMBER**

If you're planning on spending a lot of time traveling outside of the U.K. in your camper, then double-check how long you will be insured in certain countries before you set off. Different insurance policies dictate how long you can spend outside the U.K., and now that the U.K. has left the European Union, you'll also need to have a Green Card for Schengen Zone areas. I touch more on this as you move on through the book, but keep it in mind while approaching insurance companies.

# Increased speed limit

Did you know that a large panel van like a Mercedes-Benz Sprinter or a Vauxhall Movano legally must drive 10 miles per hour (mph) slower than the legal speed limit on most roads?

That surprised you, didn't it?

More specifically, anyone with a Category B driving license that allows them to drive vans up to 3.5 tons must adhere to different speed restrictions when out on the road.

Here's a breakdown:

>> If you're traveling in a 20, 30, or 40 mph zone in a van, then you can drive at the same speed as a car.

>> If you're on a single carriageway displaying the national speed limit of 60 mph, then you must not exceed 50 mph.

>> If you're on a dual carriageway displaying the national speed limit of 70 mph, then you must not exceed 60 mph.

>> Vans can still travel 70 mph on a motorway.

You can be fined and get points on your license if you don't adhere to these rules.

**TIP**

This fact is something that surprisingly few drivers know, which is why you'll often get people honking when you're driving a van at 50 mph in a 60 mph zone. While you're still converting your vehicle, there's no reason why you can't get a "my vehicle is limited to" sticker to alert people while on the road.

When you register your panel van conversion as a camper van, however, the speed limits revert back to that of a car. That's:

» 60 mph on single carriageways

» 70 mph on dual carriageways

## Cheaper contents insurance

Depending on how long you're planning on spending in your van or how much you're thinking about taking with you, you might want to investigate contents insurance.

Some people already have existing insurance for their mobile phones and laptops, but camper van contents insurance covers all types of possessions and costs a lot less than contents insurance for a panel van. Just like all insurance companies, it pays to shop around to find the best deal for you and the items you want to cover.

## Cheaper ferry tickets

The last benefit I want to touch on is something that many of you will be doing in your camper vans at some point in your lives, and that's catching a ferry. Ferry tickets for camper vans are usually cheaper than commercial vehicles that might be carrying goods, so reclassifying from a panel van to a camper can save you some precious pennies if you're planning on doing a lot of travel overseas.

# How to Legally Change the Vehicle Type from Van to Camper Van

Many folks online have said that it's difficult to get their van reclassified as a camper van. In my personal experience, I had no trouble whatsoever and found the process to be very straightforward. My vehicle was reclassified on the first try; you can't get any simpler than that!

TIP

I give you all the details you need in this section, but for additional help with your application process, go to www.gov.uk/government/publications/converting-a-vehicle-into-a-motor-caravan/converting-a-vehicle-into-a-motor-caravan and keep the page open for reference while you're reading.

First, to reclassify a vehicle as a camper van, it has to be one of the following vehicle types to begin with:

>> Ambulance

>> Box van

>> Insulated van

>> Light goods/light van

>> Livestock carrier

>> Luton van

>> Minibus

>> MPV (multi-purpose vehicle)

>> Panel van

>> Special mobile unit

>> Specially fitted van

>> Van with side windows

For the purposes of this chapter, I'm going to carry on referencing a panel van, as that's the main vehicle we've been focusing on so far in this book, but at least you now know where you stand if you own one of the vehicles listed here or are planning another conversion.

Second, when you send off your classification change request, you need to submit a completed checklist that notes which of the external and internal conversion criteria you have met.

REMEMBER

Take pictures of all the modifications both inside and outside your camper. Number them on the back and write as much information as you can give as to what the picture is showing. For example:

> *1. Flip-up table that locks into place via two bolt locks set into the wall. When not in use, the table is secured into position via a bolt lock and a magnetic strip.*

It's little extra steps like this that show you're serious about your conversion and have put in the extra effort to create a proper "motor caravan" that abides by the rules.

# External conversion criteria

Certain characteristics are common to camper van conversions that set them apart from other vehicles. It's not rocket science; even if you've never owned a camper before, you can probably tell that they have windows, doors, and most commonly a type of decorative decal that features a nature scene or some flowing logo printed on the side.

The DVLA wants to see some, but not all, of the following integrated as part of your camper conversion. The first three items noted here are the easiest to implement into any van build, but let's take a look at the whole list.

>> **Windows:** For your van to be considered a motor caravan, it needs to have at least two windows in one side of the main body of the conversion. They don't both have to be large windows; one can even be a privacy window. As long as they let daylight in, then you're good to go.

>> **Entry into the living quarters:** If your van has a sliding door that leads into your living area, then you've already got this one covered. Plus, if you have a window in the sliding door, it counts toward your overall window count for that side.

>> **Camper van-style decals:** Strangely, this is one of the cheapest external modifications that you can make, though it's also something people choose to use least. Putting decals on a van makes it look more like a camper (which is the whole point of this section), but many people who like to boondock or stealth camp think that it gives the game away. If you go down the decal route, chose something simple and easy to install.

>> **An awning:** Retractable awnings are some of the most widely used products in the camper van world. They're simple to use, adjustable for keeping off rain and creating shade, and pack away with the turn of a handle. Fiamma is one company that sells great awnings that are affordable and easy to install.

>> **High-top roof:** A high-top roof isn't something that you can add onto your build, but if you've already opted for a vehicle like a Vauxhall Movano Maxi Roof, then this is one checkbox you can tick immediately.

Pop-top roofs don't count as high-top campers. For a camper to be a high-top, it must have a permanently fixed roof.

**WARNING**

**REMEMBER**

Once again, you don't need all of these to change your van's classification. Just tick off the ones you have on your checklist. I recommend having two or three of these on your camper, with windows being the most recognizable camper feature and luckily one that is covered earlier in this chapter.

# Internal conversion criteria

While you don't need all the external modifications to turn your panel van into a camper, you *do* need to make sure you've ticked off all the following internal conversion criteria in order to get that sweet V5 form classification change. Luckily, these four requirements are what anyone looking into full-time van life needs to live a comfortable life anyway, so if you've followed the steps in the previous chapters, then you won't have any extra work to do.

Internal conversion requirements include:

>> **Seating and a table:** If you've got a flip-up cupboard that turns into a table or a swing table attached to a wall, then you already have this section covered. As long as the mounting feature is permanently attached to your bedframe, wall, or the floor of the van and is near a permanent seating arrangement, you'll have no problems.

>> **Somewhere to sleep:** You won't get away with just having a sleeping bag or a hammock in the back of your van. The bed in your camper needs to be an integral part of your living space and can either be a static bed or a sofa that converts into a bed. Either way, it needs to be permanently attached to the van wall and/or floor, so don't forget to take pictures of where it's attached when sending off your conversion checklist. (If you're converting a Luton van with a space above the driver's cab for a bed, then this section doesn't apply.)

>> **Cooking facilities:** Cooking on the go doesn't have to be hard (that's something I go over in Chapter 15), and provided you have at least a single-ring burner or a microwave, then you can get your van converted into a camper.

REMEMBER

If you're using a gas canister, then this needs to be secured in its own cupboard and have a gas drop-out vent installed for safety. If you get your gas from a remote supply, then the supply hose needs to be fixed to the vehicle structure securely.

>> **Storage:** You'll need cupboards or lockers to store food and clothes. As long as they're secured down to the walls and floor of the van and you can take pictures of them for the checklist, then you've got another criterion covered.

# Chapter **14**

# Bringing Along the Comforts of Home

L iving in a van doesn't mean you suddenly have to live a technologically deprived life. Nor does it mean you have to give up your favorite hobbies or live an uncomfortable life sitting on a plastic chair with a frown on your face. Van life is an extension of your life; it enables you to do all the things you enjoy doing and more, whether that's kicking back with a video game or working up a sweat to your favorite exercise channel.

In this chapter, I tell you how to connect to the Internet in your van and what items you may want to consider incorporating into your tiny home setup. You'll also find some good tips on creating personal space and setting boundaries for a healthy friendship or relationship too.

# Internet, TV, and the Digital Nomad Lifestyle

In today's world of remote working, binge-watching, and social media surfing, it's no surprise a lot of people ask me about how to incorporate what has become an essential everyday element — the Internet — into their van builds. The concept of the *digital nomad* refers to a person who lives a nomadic lifestyle while still working — perhaps logging into the office network remotely from the beach in Baja or taking orders for handmade goods from the depths of an orange grove in the Spanish countryside. Over the course of this section, I tell you all about how to access the Internet in your van so that you can keep connected to the world while you're traveling across it.

I know that the whole idea of van life is to get out there and see the world, and I have every faith that you will do a lot of exploring and embark on many adventures while out on the road. Having said that — and this is something you've probably heard me say often in this book — there will be times when after a long hike, all you want to do is lay in bed with a cup of hot chocolate and just give your brain up to the latest episode of *Rick and Morty* or that bizarre game show where contestants have to guess whether something is a real object or cake.

You will get ill at some stage too, so prepare yourself mentally for this. Van life isn't a cure-all for ailments, and just like living in a house, you might catch a cold or have a dodgy stomach every now and again, so it's important to have those home comforts to keep you occupied while you are recuperating.

**TIP**

If you haven't thought of it yet, get a little box to use as a medicine cabinet. Pack some ibuprofen, paracetamol (acetaminophen), cold and flu medicine, throat lozenges — anything you can think of that might help with ailments while off-grid. And check out Chapter 16 for tips on what to include in a first-aid kit.

## Connecting to the Internet

The main question many of you have probably been asking yourself is, "Can I live without Wi-Fi?" My friends still can't believe that I lived without conventional Wi-Fi for almost five years, but I honestly didn't miss it at all.

Okay, so I wasn't trying to get online to play gaming tournaments on the PlayStation 5, but I still managed to upload articles, YouTube videos, FaceTime friends and family, and play the mobile version of Ticket to Ride on the iPad with my mum while on the other side of the world.

In the following sections I outline the main methods of getting onto the Internet while traveling in a van.

## Hotspotting

By far the most popular and easily available method of getting onto the Internet while traveling is by hotspotting off of your mobile phone's internet connection. All smartphones have a mobile hotspot function that essentially turns your mobile into a Wi-Fi emitter, allowing you to hook external devices capable of accessing the Internet, such as laptops and tablets, up to your existing 3G, 4G, or 5G mobile connection.

I took a prepaid sim card with unlimited social media allowance and 45GB of data per month on the road with me and never ran out. This was my main source of internet connectivity when I was living in a van while static in the U.K. too, and I used it for everything from watching Netflix on the iPad to uploading pictures for articles.

TIP

Before you start hotspotting off your mobile, make sure your data plan has a tethering allowance before you rely on it as your main internet source. Also, find out if your plan has any tethering restrictions, and if so, what they are. My mobile plan gave me free streaming through hotspotting via tablets but not laptops, so look out for any clauses that could potentially catch you out.

WARNING

Whether using your mobile phone's internet hotspot connection or hooking up to the mobile Wi-Fi router I discuss next, it's important to ensure that your chosen plan allows for data roaming, especially if you live in the U.K. now that the country has left the E.U. No matter what country you live in, double-check how much of the data you have will work outside of the country in which you set up the plan, as sometimes the amount can decrease by up to half.

## Mobile Wi-Fi routers and motorhome Wi-Fi

Mobile telecommunication companies such as T-Mobile and Vodafone offer mobile Wi-Fi router packages that basically do the same job as your mobile hotspot but don't drain the battery of your phone. You can charge these up via a portable power pack or the USB charging port you hooked up to your fuse box all the way back in Chapter 9.

Motorhome Wi-Fi is essentially a fancier version of the mobile Wi-Fi router. These devices often come with screens to show you parameters such as data used and data remaining, as well as an option to check messages and configure settings straight from the unit itself.

### Public Wi-Fi

Many restaurants and fast-food outlets have free Wi-Fi. The same goes with public Wi-Fi hotspots in town centers, museums, and other public buildings. A Wi-Fi extender amplifies these Wi-Fi signals and enables you to use them from the comfort of your van so long as you are not parked too far away.

Likely the most used facilities by vanlifers on the road are public libraries and hotel foyers. The public library could be one of the most tranquil institutions left in the world, and who could resist the comfortable seating and air-conditioning in a hotel foyer?

## Can I still watch TV on the go?

Absolutely. In fact, I binge-watched many TV series while traveling around the world. I even hooked my Nintendo Switch up to the monitor I brought with me a couple of times on rainy days when I decided to spend the day in bed. It's a tough job, but someone's got to do it!

Let's talk about the actual practice of watching TV first. As long as you have an internet connection, you can log into all the regular streaming services such as Netflix, Disney+, Prime Video, and more. I even had the streaming television service Sky Go on my laptop to watch my favorite movies and Italian football matches from time to time.

**TIP**

In some countries, certain content isn't available at all. I tried logging into one of my streaming services to watch some shows in California that I had been previously watching in Milan and they wouldn't play, so consider downloading all your shows to play them offline before you travel. Also, downloading shows uses less data than streaming them. Okay, so you'll need to put a little forethought into what you'll want to watch, but you'll thank me at the end of the month when you still have plenty of internet data left.

When it comes to TVs, you have three choices available:

>> You can purchase a 12-volt TV and wire it up to your fuse box.

>> You can purchase a standard, slimline monitor and plug it into your wall sockets powered via your inverter, removing it from sight and placing it in a cupboard when not in use.

>> You can purchase a mini projector and screen to hook up to your phone, computer, or tablet.

**TIP**

If you really don't want to watch content on a laptop, I recommend opting for a mini projector and screen combo. As long as it has an HDMI port, you can still hook up a Nintendo Switch for some Mario Kart multiplayer gaming or a Blu-ray player to watch *The Lord of the Rings* extended editions once the sun goes down.

Can you tell I did a lot of this on my travels?

If you want to watch TV in a more conventional sense (not via an internet streaming service), you'll need to purchase a TV antenna to tune in to the TV channels in your local area. However, if I'm being perfectly honest, this is a pointless exercise nowadays, especially when all the shows you could ever need are on demand. It also saves having an antenna sticking off your roof like some sort of budget spacecraft, another thing that might get snagged in tree branches while you're parking in forests.

# Other Things You Can Do in a Van That You Can Do in a House

I'd bet good money that a lot of you skipped straight to this section to figure out how many things from your pre-van life would stay the same once you move into your van. And to be honest, I don't blame you. Change of this magnitude can be daunting for the best of us, but don't worry. There are still so many things that you did in your previous life that don't have to change once you downsize.

Here are a few of the biggies that I get asked about on a regular basis.

## Yoga

As long as you have a yoga mat, you can do your routine inside or outside your van on a comfortable surface no matter the terrain. I had a standard-sized yoga mat that fit in my main living space diagonally. Come rain or shine, you can still stay supple and Zen wherever you are. Plus, if you have a high-roof van, you can even do headstands and the warrior pose with ease.

## Listening to music

As long as you have a portable Bluetooth speaker or a nice set of headphones, then listening to your favorite tunes doesn't have to stop. Neither does listening to the radio, thanks to Digital Audio Broadcasting (DAB) digital radios and mobile apps dedicated to your favorite stations. Okay, so you might not be able to listen to your town's local station on the other side of the world, but you won't have any trouble tuning into BBC1 from Cambodia or Planet Rock from New Zealand.

## Wood carving

The best bit about wood carving on the go is that you can pick up wood that you find along the way to play around with. Who knows? This could be the start of a new career!

TIP

Be sure to either sit on the edge of your van and cut outside, or carve over a blanket inside that you can shake off outside once you have finished; wood shavings have a habit of getting everywhere.

## Art

Whether drawing on an iPad or painting on an easel, your passion for art doesn't have to stop while living in a van. Paint with the door open to re-create the stunning vista you are parked in front of or draw a scene from a parallel universe on Procreate. The possibilities are endless!

## Gaming

The Nintendo Switch is the perfect gaming companion for off-grid adventures due to its hybrid nature. I often tackled a few shrines on The Legend of Zelda: Breath of the Wild or had a race on Mario Kart while playing in handheld mode. Hooking the dock up to my monitor meant that I could play a bit of Super Mario Odyssey when the rain was lashing down against the van roof and see the action on a bigger screen.

## Working out

Whether doing weighted squats on the yoga mat or triceps dips off the edge of your step, there's no reason why you can't keep your exercise routine going once you hit the road. Store your weights in the back of your van and pump iron in the best-looking outdoor gyms around.

## Playing an instrument

I took an acoustic guitar on the road with me (see Figure 14-1), and although I managed to avoid any "kumbaya" moments around the campfire, I did enjoy playing guitar to sheep and horses while camping in the wild. Acoustic instruments such as violins and guitars along with woodwind instruments are the best bets for packing into a tiny home. Still, if you have the space, there's nothing to stop you from bringing a portable practice amp along for the ride and hooking up a keyboard or a bass guitar.

**FIGURE 14-1:** I like to think that Kermit the Frog was playing his banjo alongside me just out of shot.

**TIP**

If you're stealth camping, just put on some headphones. You can still enjoy the sounds of your funky music while still staying off the radar of the people around you.

## Cooking oven-based goods

The Omnia Oven is one of the most used van life cooking utensils, but before I got my hands on one, I used my RidgeMonkey for all my oven-based goods. This deep-fill sandwich toaster was made for fisherman to cook up their catch at the side of the river. When closed, it keeps the steam in and is perfect for making everything from paninis to pizzas and Yorkshire puddings.

Yes, it was nice to whip up cinnamon buns and make olive bread in the Omnia Oven, but it was equally as amazing to stick fish fingers and chips or a bag of chicken nuggets (basically what my mum calls "beige food") in the RidgeMonkey from time to time. No matter how much you may enjoy cooking, there may be times when you want to eat quick-and-easy comfort food, and these two genius bits of culinary equipment provide the solution every time.

# Thinking of Your Van as a Tiny Home

You've completed your van conversion, and now it's time to add some home comforts to make it truly feel like home. But what should make the cut and what comes under the category of "going overboard" with the décor?

## What to bring into a small space

You've likely heard of folks who like to pack "everything but the kitchen sink" when they travel, and I'll be the first to agree that it's important to pack enough belongings and items for a long trip away. It's also important to remember that a tiny space can become cluttered very quickly, so bringing the essentials on board and leaving unnecessary items behind or giving them away in order to avoid temptation is key.

### Less is more

Of course, what you bring into your van all depends on the size of your vehicle. There's no point in considering whether you can fit a surfboard inside your VW Caddy camper, for example. But regardless of size, I always go for the "less is more" school of thinking in a tiny home, making sure there is a place for everything, and that everything goes back into its place when not being used.

I didn't bring that many appliances or utensils from my house into the van with me. The blender and mixing bowls took up residence on top of the fridge, the pans sat in a hammock under the sink, and household tools made their home under the bed in the back of the van.

Ah, the back of the van — that magical Tardis filled with opportunity and equipment for all your recreational activities. While my living area was kept largely clutter-free bar a fruit hammock that mostly held bags of crisps, the garage area played host to skateboards, a body board, an inflatable paddleboard, a football, a skipping rope for workouts, and a hammock for pulling out and attaching to a tree. Check it out in Figure 14-2.

**FIGURE 14-2:**
A place for everything, and everything in its place.

The main point to take away here is to split your belongings into three sections:

» Things you can't live without

» Things you'd like to use in your free time

» Things you'll never use that need to go to a charity shop immediately

While it's pointless to hold onto that desk lamp Auntie Irene bought you four Christmases ago, packing your rollerblades and running shoes with the prospect of some exercise is a great idea. Likewise, large ornaments like an oversized wine bottle replica of the FIFA World Cup will quickly become a nuisance in a tiny space, but useful items like a pair of ladders slotted down the length of your van in the storage area for cleaning solar panels definitely have a place in your new lifestyle.

## Clothes and shoes

Shoe lovers should look away now, because what I'm about to tell you may prove to be very distressing.

I only took three pairs of shoes into the van with me: walking boots, Vans Hi-Tops, and running shoes. That's it. If you're in the habit of going out to fancy restaurants, then you might want to take a dressy pair of shoes with you, but the reality is that whoever you are, you don't need any more than three or four pairs. They'll only get in the way and take up valuable storage space.

Clothes, however, are a bit of a different story. More clothes mean fewer trips to the laundromat, which means more time in nature and away from cities where you can roam freely. Bikepackers might take two pairs of underwear and two T-shirts on a trip, but I had boxer shorts, socks, and a T-shirt for every day of the month. Yes, my clothes drawer was pretty big, but it was definitely worth it knowing that I could go a full month without having to do any washing.

TIP

Laundromats are easy to find, thanks to apps like Park4Night. You can see their location, plot the coordinates, and plan a trip on the way to your next destination. I visited a launderette around once a month to wash bedding (I took two sets with me and rotated through the month), jeans, and any muddy items, leaving the rest to the Scrubba wash bag and some warm water when parked at a water filling station.

TIP

If you're planning to be on the road through multiple seasons and have plenty of storage space in the back of your van, then it's a great idea to have plastic boxes for a winter and summer clothes rotation. I kept sweaters, jeans, and fleeces in the back in favor of vests and tees in the summer and rotated when the weather got colder. The same goes for coats too; you might not need that sheepskin-lined Levi's denim jacket in the middle of summer, but you'll certainly be glad to have it when the temperature drops.

## Making your van feel like home

We've all seen van conversions on Instagram that have piqued our interest, saved pictures to Pinterest of builds that have inspired us to head out on our own adventures, and scoured Google for the best-looking tiny homes. But what is it that truly makes a van feel like home? Is it the choice of cladding or the cupboard placement, or is it the soft furnishings and quirky ornaments, the tiles behind the fire, and the little figurine of Chewbacca holding an ice-cream cone stuck to the fridge that we remember the most?

I think you know the answer to this one.

Here are some of the things that I included in my build to make it feel less like a wood-cladded box and more like a cozy, country house on wheels.

## Blankets, cushions, and a good duvet

My mum could have made a fortune from all the requests I received on my Instagram page about the crocheted blankets on my bed. She went through a stage of crocheting heavy woolen blankets in different colors just for fun, so much so that I ended up taking four of them on the road with me and rotated them, keeping spares in the bulkhead. Not only did they provide that homey touch, but they were incredibly warm too, the perfect addition to a night around the campfire with newfound friends to ward off the evening chill. There were also nights in the mountains while stealth camping when I used all four on top of my duvet to create a cozy cocoon I didn't want to leave.

Speaking of a duvet, having a quality duvet with quirky bedding makes any van instantly feel homey. It makes your bed feel more like a permanent fixture than just having a sleeping bag thrown on top of a mattress. Add a few printed cushions into the mix (don't go mad with the scattering; this is a tiny space after all), and you've got yourself a great place to kick back and relax with your favorite Netflix show.

## Pictures and signs

I'm not suggesting you hang a replica of the *Mona Lisa* in your camper, but those walls you've just put up are perfect for small prints. If you have enough space, you can even put a canvas up in there.

One of the reasons I called my van "Vincent" was that I had a canvas of Vincent van Gogh's *Starry Starry Night* acting as a cover for the window hatch I put into the front wall of the main living space. I filled the back of the canvas with rockwool and held it in place with auto carpet. I then added some hinges to one edge and a clasp to the other, and fixed it in place. Not only did this keep the inside private for stealth camping, but also it added a touch of color and a focal point inside the living space.

The same goes for signs. Instead of creating a backsplash behind the sink with colored tiles, I opted for using small metal signs my mum had hanging in her kitchen, each bearing old advertising slogans for Marmite, Danish Bacon, Bisto, and other quintessentially British items. Above the sliding door I put a wooden "Diagon Alley" sign that I bought from Glastonbury Festival and that used to hang above the door in my old house. I figured the views I was about to see were going to be pretty magical, so why not give them the wizarding touch?

These signs were imbued with so much nostalgia that they instantly brought happy memories to mind every time I saw them. It didn't matter whether I was in a forest in Slovenia or broken down in Italy; they made me smile and think of friends and family. Check out Figure 14-3 for a peek at how I decorated Vincent with various signs and paintings.

**FIGURE 14-3:**
There's no place
like home!

## Ornaments, memorabilia, and important trinkets

I'm not one for clutter, but I've certainly picked up my fair share of little figurines and small ornaments over the years. As I like to cook, I placed some of the best ones on top of the spice rack so that I would catch a glimpse of them whenever I reached for the oregano or the cumin. The same goes for the tickets to *Harry Potter and the Cursed Child* that I stuck up in the toilet cupboard or the Harry Potter wand my mate Josh bought me that I placed under the Diagon Alley sign. (I dare you to spot the Harry Potter nerd.)

**REMEMBER**

If you haven't guessed already, making a van feel homey isn't about adding the best Instagram-able features; it's about filling it with things that make you, you. Pick things that make you happy, things that represent your character, and things that remind you of all the awesome stuff you have done in your life so far (see Figure 14-4).

## Handmade blackout curtains

If you have the ability and patience to wield a sewing machine or know someone who can, then I definitely recommend ditching the motorhome blinds and making your own blackout curtains. Pick some cool fabric, line it with blackout material, and make curtains with a loop that can slide along a curtain rod made from a broom handle. It couldn't be simpler, and nothing says getting cozy for the night like drawing the curtains the good old-fashioned way.

**FIGURE 14-4:**
Check out how crowded the top of that spice rack is. Eric the egg timer barely had any room to move!

## Musical instrument

I've played guitar since I was 10 years old, so having a guitar in the build was a must for me. Again, this is another element of my personality that I added into my rolling house; it's not just there for show. If you play the banjo or violin, for example, having your instrument out and ready to play at a moment's notice when the feeling strikes is another means of making your van feel like a little slice of home.

## Plants

Plants make any space feel more relaxing, though they have a tendency to fall over when you're driving around. Consider making a shelf that you can affix plant pots down with Velcro or attach some hanging plant pots that you can remove and place in the cab with you while driving.

# Creating personal space when traveling with a partner or friend

Traveling with a partner or a friend can be an enjoyable way of seeing the world. But while seeing new places and sharing sights with another person is an incredible way of making memories, it also means you're sharing a tiny space with another human.

I've both lived solo in my tiny home and shared a space with others throughout my van life adventures, and the one thing that I feel is really important to consider when sharing your space is to develop a method of having alone time. Even if you're traveling with your best friend or long-term partner and with all the good will in the world on your side, sooner or later, after spending so much time with that person in one tiny room, you're bound to do something that will annoy them.

Now, if you're reading this section with a partner and you have just eyed each other warily wondering which one of you will end the relationship while driving through the middle of a forest in Nicaragua, then please don't worry. I'm writing this now to avoid that scenario from ever happening. Living in a small space can be tough and will test any kind of relationship, so it's important to put the steps in place to make sure you have enough "me time" to recharge and switch off, just like you would in a conventional house setting. Not only is having regular alone time a healthy practice for your own mental well-being, but it's healthy for your friendship or relationship too.

I think one of the best pieces of advice I give friends or couples traveling together on the road or living in a tiny space is to be open, honest, and transparent with each other at all times. There is no "cooling off while you're at work" or packing your bags and going to your parents' house for the weekend; problems have to be dealt with straightaway to avoid anything escalating. If something is irritating you or you have a problem, talk it out in a calm fashion. It's all about give and take, so keep in mind the other person's thoughts and feelings as they will yours, working together as a strong unit to reach a compromise everyone is happy with.

**TIP**

One of the easiest ways to create space while living in a tiny home is for you and your partner or friend to head off and do different things, perhaps a walk to the beach with your favorite book, a run along a mountain path, or a peruse around the local town. You'll find that when you return, you'll both have exciting things to talk about and can spend time describing everything you saw to each other over dinner.

Inside the van is a little trickier; it's all about creating specific zones for you and your partner to relax down in. One of you might sit drawing at one end of the van while the other plays a game on the bed at the other, each immersed in something that brings each of you joy without the other person being involved. Again, it's not being antisocial; it's an important part of winding down and recharging. Put those boundaries in place and set time aside if not every day, then at least every two to three days.

**TIP**

A good pair of overhead noise-canceling earphones help when living with another person in a small space. Perhaps you're on the bed listening to your favorite podcast while your friend or partner is chatting to their family on a video call. Remember, it's all about compromise, working together, and sharing the room . . . literally.

Don't be afraid to broach the subject about spending time away from your friend or partner with them. If you're worried about their reaction, then just explain to them calmly why you want to put these measures in place and that it isn't because you don't enjoy spending time with them. Talk about the benefits of down time and why it is important for the both of you to focus on things that you enjoy separately in order to be a stronger unit together.

## USING THE TOILET WITH ANOTHER PERSON ONBOARD

How close are you to your friend or partner? Close enough to listen to them wee while you're in the van with them? How about close enough to be in the same room when they go for a Number 2? There are certain instances for which the "hear no evil, speak no evil, see no evil" monkeys come into play, and this is one of them. Smell no evil could be another in this instance, as nothing escapes the senses in a tiny space.

Some of you won't be bothered by this at all. Heck, if you've changed nappies, then the smell of poop isn't going to bother you one bit. Others might be worried about this factor alone the most, however, especially if you're in a new relationship and still getting to know one another.

My advice: Time it so that one of you goes for a walk while the other person is doing their business. If the weather is rubbish or it's dark outside, then sit in the cab and give the other person some privacy. And if all else fails, lay on the bed with your head out of the window. If you can't see or hear it, then it's not happening, right?

# Chapter **15**

# Managing Life's Essentials: Cooking, Showering, and Going to the Bathroom

By embracing van life, you open yourself to the possibility of a complete change of lifestyle. But some aspects of your life are going to stay exactly the same no matter whether you're boondocking in the Canadian Rockies or wild camping in the South of France. I am, of course, talking about eating, keeping clean, and going to the toilet — essentially, the basic things you need to do to look after yourself on a daily basis. But don't worry; you can do them all very easily while living in a van.

In this chapter, I give you inside information into what it's like to cook, wash, and go to the bathroom inside your van, as well as some tips on dealing with some unsavory van life problems.

Don't be squeamish; we're all friends here.

# Cooking in a Van

If you're culinary minded or consider yourself a foodie, you've definitely come to the right part of the book. Here I give you lots of tips on how to whip up tasty treats in a van, including information about some utensils that I can't live without on the road.

## Choosing the right stovetop

Picking a stovetop (or burner) is a crucial part of your kitchen setup. Stovetops come in many different styles, types, and shapes. In the following sections, I tell you about three of them that I have used over my van life journey.

### Single-burner portable stove with gas cartridge

For many people who just take their campers out on weekends or on short trips, a one-hob burner for warming up soup or packet meals might well be enough. I've always carried one of these around with me just in case my main gas bottle runs out, and it's helped out when I've boiled up pasta a few times.

Little single-burner (one-hob) stoves usually use a butane cartridge slotted into a compartment. They aren't the most cost-effective solution for full-time van life, but if you have a VW Caddy conversion that you only use once in a blue moon, then this could be a great solution.

My main gripe with the single burner is that if you want to cook a meal with multiple parts, everything ends up taking a lot longer, as each component will need a separate turn on the burner. Pasta, for instance, or a pork stir fry with meat, vegetables, and noodles, ends up taking forever, which is not good when you're hungry after a long drive.

### Two-burner gas stovetop with grill

The two-burner gas stovetop with grill system is a great all-around option. This was the first type of burner I had in my van, and it allowed me the freedom to whip up Bolognese on one hob and pasta on the other. (I do eat more types of food than pasta, I promise.)

The grills on these burners can sometimes be a little hit and miss, so it pays to buy a reputable model from a company like Vango. I loved cooking sausages on my grill for breakfast on wintry Saturday mornings.

### Three-burner stovetops

As you might have guessed by now, my personal preference is the three-burner stovetop. I need all the pan space I can get when I'm making meals, especially when the Omnia Oven is taking up the middle hob. (Don't worry, you hear all about the Omnia Oven shortly.)

If you like to cook or are planning on cooking for multiple people you might come across on your travels, then the three-burner propane stovetop is definitely the option I recommend. My Vango three-hob burner has never let me down once and gives me ample space for using woks, griddle pans, and more.

## Hooking up your burner

Remember back in Chapter 12 when I first mentioned gas regulators? Regulators are little devices that go straight onto your gas bottle that then hook up to the gas hose leading to your burner. Regulator sizes and types change depending on where you are in the world, what size of gas bottle you've bought, and what type of gas you're using. Check out `www.flogas.co.uk/gas-bottles/regulator-selector`, a handy website I show people when getting in-depth with regulator types and for keeping sharp on regulator safety.

There isn't much to hooking up your burner to your gas regulator. All you need to do is purchase a gas hose kit from a hardware store or by visiting Amazon or eBay and then follow these steps to hook it up:

1. **Slip two tightening gas hose clips over your hose and let them lie loose.**

   It's best to do this now; otherwise, you'll have to remove your hose and put them on again.

### GAS DROP-OUT VENTS

I speak about the importance of gas drop-out vents in Chapter 12, but it's such an important section that I wouldn't be able to sleep soundly at night unless I added an extra sidebar in here for good measure.

If you've got any type of gas bottle in your van — propane, butane, or LPG — then you need a gas drop-out vent as an extra and crucial safety measure. Because gas is heavier than air, if there is a leak, the gas will flow out through your gas drop-out vent and away from your van. I know it might seem like a little thing to overlook, but it's so important if anything goes wrong with your gas setup. So head back to Chapter 12 to get the information on how to install your drop-out vent if you haven't already!

2. **Attach one end of your hose to your gas regulator and one to your burner.**

TIP

The nozzles on both your regulator and your gas burner might look a little like a miniature loud hailer or megaphone. All you need to do is push your hose over these nozzles as far as they will go. You might need to twist your hose round a little as you push; just make sure it's as tight as it can be.

3. **Using a screwdriver, tighten the gas hose clips as tight as possible to ensure a secure connection to both your regulator and your burner.**

You'll feel when the clip is as tight as it will go. Be careful not to piece your hose with your screwdriver. The walls of the hose are pretty thick so you should be fine, but just pay attention at all times to be on the safe side.

WARNING

If you smell gas at any point, shut off your regulator and reassess your setup. Always perform any gas bottle changes or burner changes with a window or door open so that you have plenty of fresh air in your living space.

# Cooking like a pro on the road

Good workers never blame their tools, which is why I'm about to reveal some of the best gear for cooking on the go. The only thing you need to be blaming from now on is how tight your pants are after all the good food you're going to be making and eating!

## XL RidgeMonkey

The XL RidgeMonkey compact sandwich toaster is possibly the most versatile piece of cooking equipment I've ever used on my van life adventures. This little piece of genius was originally designed for fishermen to cook up their catch on a jet burner at the side of the river. The camper van community quickly claimed it for themselves, however, realizing that this little portable oven could take the place of a standard oven and much more.

I've made calzones, chicken Kievs, enchiladas, veggie burgers, lasagnas, Yorkshire puddings, and many more oven-based dishes in this thing over the years, and it's never let me down! I also use mine for frying the perfect egg, haloumi, and tofu too.

## Omnia Oven

If you want to go one step further and bake bread and cakes, cook chicken thighs, or make incredible stews or roast potatoes, then you need an Omnia Oven. This doughnut-shaped stovetop oven changed everything for me, especially while living in a camper van during the COVID-19 pandemic lockdowns. Cooking cake and bread in this oven was so simple, as was making meals like shepherd's pie, pasta bakes, and more.

The Omnia Oven works through convection. Heat is drawn up from the hob through the middle of the oven and passes up and over the food inside, providing heat all the way around the oven and creating an even bake.

**TIP**

With both the RidgeMonkey and the Omnia Oven on board, you won't be short of tasty treats to eat and intriguing recipes to try out.

## Nesting bowls

Mixing cakes and kneading bread can get a little messy when you're trying to use pans and mugs. That's why nesting bowls are such a great idea.

Nesting bowls, as you might have gathered from the name, nest inside one another. Joseph Joseph makes a great set that includes a large mixing bowl, colander, sieve, smaller pouring bowl, and a set of cup measures all inside the largest bowl. The measuring cups are perfect for measuring (go figure) out baking ingredients, sushi rice, sauces, and much more.

## Bialetti moka pot

I think I've dropped the Italian card a lot throughout this book so far, so it won't be a surprise that I traveled everywhere with a Bialetti moka pot on board. And yes, it was red, white, and green . . . when in Rome.

This stovetop espresso maker is the perfect companion at breakfast time or before a long drive. It doesn't take up a lot of space and stows away in a cupboard or drawer easily, providing budding adventurers with an energy boost boasting sumptuous flavors at the drop of a hat.

## Handleless pans

You'll have a hard time cooking without any pans, making them a bit of an essential item when it comes to stocking up your kitchen. The only problem is that they can be quite bulky, so grabbing a set of handleless pans that pack away neatly can really make cooking in a van a lot easier.

**TIP**

I stored all my pans in a pan hammock underneath my sink. It was a good way to use space that would have otherwise been wasted and freed up a drawer for more dry ingredients.

## BioLite kettle set

I'm pretty sure the late great Muhammed Ali was said to "pour like a kettle, cook like a pot." Maybe that was the BioLite KettlePot . . . who knows?

This little piece of equipment can be used for both brewing up tea or cooking soups and stews, and is another genius space-saving utensil for tiny-home lovers. It also has an insulted handle to keep your hands scorch-free.

## Knife set

No matter your dietary preferences, it pays to have a trusty knife set on board for preparing food. As you know, I'm all about making life easy for myself, so having a good bread knife as well as a sharp blade for slicing everything from tomatoes and tofu to chicken and chorizo is essential, especially when you love food as much as I do.

## Handheld food processor

I know that I've spent a lot of time talking about electrical food processors, but I couldn't complete this discussion without throwing a metaphorical spanner in the works.

Zyliss makes a neat little manual food processor that is great for chopping up onions or making dips in your camper. It makes mincemeat (literally) of food prep and works your arm out at the same time. Just pull the hook and back like a miniature rowing machine, and you're good to go!

# Figuring Out Bathroom Activities

Okay, it's time to address the elephant in the room: looking after our hygiene and going to the toilet. They're both important things that we do every day, and you still have to do them when traveling around the world in a camper van.

I've traveled through the U.K., mainland Europe, and the U.S. in a camper van, washing everywhere from hot springs to public showers, and even using a plastic box filled with water from the kettle. (That plastic box shower wasn't amazing, but I did cover the floor in enough drips to warrant me giving it a quick clean at the same time. Every cloud . . . .)

During my work as a travel writer and automotive journalist, I reviewed more camping toilets than you have probably had hot dinners. Yes, I mean that; I didn't even know there were so many portable toilets out there in the world before I started writing about and living the van life.

The point I'm trying to make here is simple — there are so many shower and toileting solutions out there that combat all the "problems" you might be thinking about when heading out on an off-grid adventure that there really is nothing to worry about . . .

. . . unless a bear spies on you while you're taking a shower, that is, but I guess you can't prepare for every eventuality.

## The age-old shower debate

Like the static bed versus rock 'n' roll bed debate, the argument of whether to have a shower inside your van or not is a topic that divides vanlifers all over the globe. Showering, like going to the toilet, is something we usually do on a daily basis. It's ingrained into our daily routine just like eating and sleeping, so I can understand why needing a shower might be a big deal for some people. However, in my experience — and from speaking to many other vanlifers on my world travels — you will not use that shower you're thinking of installing.

For starters, let's talk about water storage.

If you're planning on carrying enough water for a shower, then you'll need an underslung tank below your van, making it much harder to go off-grid on uneven ground. If you do make it off-grid, then you won't be able to stay there long as showers use up water incredibly fast.

Second, showers take up a lot of space in a camper van build. I know it might make your sprinter van feel more like home, but it's also going to dramatically reduce the amount of space in your living area. While there are retractable options that include shower curtains that can be removed when not in use, there's always the worry of getting the inside of your van wet.

So on that front, in the following sections I outline some more van-friendly shower options to consider implementing into your van life setup in order to stop people from pinching their noses when you do your weekly grocery shop. These solutions can be filled on an ad-hoc basis from faucets or filled with hot spring water; the choice is up to you!

### RinseKit

The RinseKit portable shower has been keeping nomads clean for years now. This little portable tank comes in varying sizes, the largest holding up to 4.5 gallons (17 liters) of water and weighing about 60 lbs. (27 kilograms) when full, making it the perfect solution to store in the back of your camper. The RinseKit auto-pressurizes to 50 PSI in just 20 seconds, giving you six minutes of shower time. Add in a hot-water adapter for all the comforts of home.

### Solar shower bag

What could be better than having a scenic shower? Solar shower bags are essentially water bags that heat up from the sun's rays. Alternatively, you can fill them with a mixture of cold water and hot water from the kettle to get the same outcome. Hang them from a tree or tie one to a broom handle wedged into an opening in your van.

### RoadShower

Remember I said that there were plenty of products out there catering to the needs of vanlifers? The RoadShower is a great example. It is a portable shower designed to attach to a van roof rack that heats up via the sun's rays. Choose from 4-, 7-, or 10-gallon options depending on how big your van is. Attach a hose and shower whenever, wherever, filling up at water outlets that you pass on your travels.

### Hozelock PortaShower

Yes, you read that right. The same people who make the sprayers you might use in your garden to get rid of weeds also make a portable shower perfect for van life. Create pressure by pumping up the canister, and voilà! Enjoy a three-minute shower anytime. Just fill it up with two parts hot water and one part cold water, then prepare for a good rinse down!

**TIP**

If you want to maintain some sense of modesty around other vanlifers at campsites, then consider getting a little pop-up pod to stand in while using your chosen shower.

# Going to the toilet in a van

Would you believe me if I told you that the question I was asked most often by people from all over the globe when traveling in a van was "How do you go to the toilet in that thing?" Not "How many countries have you traveled to?" Or "What is it like seeing the world from your front door?" No, always straight to the toilet.

It's not hard to understand why, really. It's something we all have to do on a daily basis. I've probably written part of this book while on the toilet, and you might be reading this chapter on the toilet right now.

Good, now that we've cleared that up and no longer have any secrets between us, let's crack on.

Going to the toilet in a van is a little different from going to the toilet in a house, I admit. Still, it's not a scary process and the outcome is exactly the same. Plus, it saves you from heading out into the forest in the dead of night when you need to do your business, squatting next to a sleeping bear or on a mound of fire ants.

**WARNING**

Listen, this next section is going to feature a lot of toilet humor . . . literally. Going to the loo isn't something everyone likes talking about, but I'm going to make it as approachable and light-hearted as possible, so please don't poo-poo my jokes, okay?

## Picking the right porta-potty

It might surprise you to know that just like van life, porta-potties aren't a "one-size-fits-all" situation. Well, they don't actually fluctuate in size that much in all honesty, but there are certainly different styles and types to consider when planning your build.

### COMPOSTING TOILET

For the eco-conscious camper, the composting toilet is a great addition to your setup and one that doesn't need much maintenance while using. Essentially, these toilets separate your liquid and solid waste into two separate compartments ready for disposal.

You might not know that solid waste, also known as poop, has to remain dry for it to break down into compost. If it's mixed with urine, it won't break down and will remain whole. Please don't ask me how I know this; I don't want to relive that experience ever again, so just take my word for it.

Because liquid waste takes up much more volume inside your toilet, it's possible to go much longer without emptying the solid container. Some leading composting toilets used in campers and boats such as Nature's Head composting toilet have a urine container that needs emptying every three to four days and a solid waste container that can hold a month's worth of poop. That makes composting toilets a great option for anyone looking to go off-grid for long periods of time.

**TIP**

Here's another useful fact: Urine can be safely deposited onto flowerbeds. Our bodies might not need it, but urine contains potassium, phosphorus, and nitrogen, which just so happens to be the nutrients plants need to thrive. Just make sure to do this on flowerbeds away from water sources, and ask any garden owners before you go pouring your pee onto their property.

Solid waste can be emptied into a compost heap and left to break down over time. The main problem is finding a compost heap while traveling on the road. They're not impossible to find, but it might take some prior planning when deciding on your route. The alternative option is burying your waste just as you might while camping or throwing it away in a plastic bag, which does kind of defeat the point of this entire exercise.

Hold up though; I know what you're thinking. Isn't all that poop going to start stinking up your van?

Well, in a word, no. There are lots of tips and tricks such as using sawdust, coconut core, or chestnut shavings to keep those smells at bay, all while kickstarting the composting process. Composting toilet setups usually include a fan that sits in the side of your vehicle to help filter out smells and aid the composting process.

Yes, I have written a lot of articles about toilets in the past. Some even say that I'm a leading figure on the subject, though I really don't want that spreading around.

### CHEMICAL TOILET

Chemical toilets are much more common in most camper van builds. You might know them as cassette toilets, and they usually comprise of an upper and lower compartment.

The upper compartment is the bit with the seat. It's also the bit where any liquid that you choose for flushing your waste into the bottom chamber sits. Some toilets have a push-button flush, while others have a pump-action flush. They both do the same thing, but the pump-action flush toilets are usually cheaper.

The bottom container is a sealed chamber where your waste is held. It's sealed to stop smells from emitting into your van and keep everything inside where it belongs. When it comes to emptying, it includes a spout with a screw top for pouring your waste into the relevant receptacle.

## Combatting odors

The most common way of combatting odors in toilets is by using chemicals. Notice I said *most common* and not the thing I would do. Don't worry, I get to that in a second.

You've probably seen these chemicals in camping stores: little grey bottles with pink and blue labels on them for the corresponding parts of your toilet. The general rule of thumb is that the pink liquid goes into the flushing compartment at the top, and the blue liquid goes into the tank at the bottom. Now, lots of people will tell you that chemicals are the only option for keeping chemical toilets smelling nice. I guess it's in the name, so it's an easy assumption to make.

Toilet chemicals aren't cheap, however, especially if you get the eco-friendly ones that are nicer to the environment, which should be a given in this day and age. That's why I skip chemicals all together and use something much cheaper — less than 70 cents a box, in fact.

My solution? Ordinary washing powder, the kind you use to wash your clothes in either a Scrubba wash bag or at a launderette.

The enzymes in washing powder break down your waste and stop it from smelling, keeping your toilet fresh and eradicating the need for harmful chemicals. With some spray for the top half and washing powder in the bottom, you can keep a clean loo for a fraction of the price and not have to worry about stocking up on toilet liquid or staining everything in sight when a bottle inevitably spills (which it will; it always does).

## Figuring out where to put your porta-potty

This answer might seem like a bit of a cop-out, but there really isn't a right or wrong place to put your porta-potty in your camper van build. The great thing about them is that they are pretty easy to slot in anywhere and can be integrated into a number of features to hide them from view.

One of the simplest solutions is to put your toilet underneath a bench seat. It can either be accessed by taking the top of the seat off or kept in place by a small door with a bolt latch, allowing you to pull the toilet out into the middle of the room. This option, of course, is better if you're traveling on your own and don't have to worry about a friend or partner witnessing (and hearing) you doing your ablutions. You've really got to be close with your friends or partner to have them sit in on that spectacle, which means they're probably going to have to sit in the front of the cab or take a walk outside while you are, as my mother puts it, "writing out your will."

Another option is putting the toilet inside a cupboard. That's the option I went for in my build, building a cupboard that was just high enough to sit up in if I backed into it. When not in use, the cupboard housed dirty laundry bags and other bits that could be stored away for transit. This allowed for some privacy when people were walking past the windows and I had forgotten to close the curtains, and I preferred the idea of not having to slide the toilet out of a chair or messing around with anything when I needed to go.

Once again, I'm all about ease when it comes to life's necessities. Make things simple for yourself, and van life will be so much easier.

## Disposing of toilet paper

Toilet paper takes up a lot of space inside your cassette, and when spending a lot of time off-grid, you need all the toilet space you can get. I know that there is special paper that dissolves in the liquid that we should all be using, but chances are you're going to skip the expensive stuff and buy four rolls from the local supermarket every time you do a food shop, and that stuff doesn't break down as much.

While traveling around Sardinia, I managed to go ten days without emptying my toilet by doing my Number 1s outside and Number 2s in the van, depositing toilet paper in a separate bin next to the toilet.

The thing is, there are far more places to bury toilet paper or bins to dispose of it in around the world than there are camper van waste disposal points. This keeps your toilet space free for the business that matters, keeping you away from towns and cities for longer.

## Emptying grey and black waste

At some point on your journey, and more regularly than you might realize, you'll have to empty your grey and black waste. To clarify:

> » *Grey waste* is the wastewater from your sink.

> » *Black waste* is the contents of your cassette toilet.

Emptying these two tanks might not be the most exciting job in the world and may well feel a little odd at first, but after a while, both of these jobs will become second nature.

How to empty grey waste:

**1.** **Locate your wastewater emptying receptacle.**

Mobile apps such as Park4Night or iOverlander list designated wastewater disposal points in your area. These can be everywhere from car parks to specifically designed camper van waste disposal areas.

**2.** **Carefully empty your wastewater down the drain.**

Wastewater disposal points are usually drain channels in the ground that run into a main drain. If you have an underslung water tank, then simply drive over this drain and open your tank.

If, like me, you opted for a jerrycan system for both fresh and wastewater, then simply lift your cannister to the drain and pour it down manually.

**3.** **Use freshwater to flush out your tank or canister.**

It won't hurt to use some cleaning products here too to keep everything smelling nice and fresh.

**WARNING**

This next bit isn't a section you're going to want to read while having your dinner. Also, you might want to wear some gloves. And don't wear your favorite jeans or white trainers. Trust me; you'll thank me one day.

How to empty black waste:

1. **Locate your toilet emptying receptacle.**

   Once again, apps such as Park4Night or iOverlander list cassette toilet emptying spots in your vicinity. These could be located in supermarket car parks, gas stations, or designated camper van waste disposal areas.

2. **Remove the bottom cassette from your toilet.**

   The cassette part of your toilet usually releases by pushing a button or pulling a latch. If you haven't traveled in a camper or used a cassette toilet before, then be warned: This bottom chamber can get very heavy when full, especially if you're using it for liquid waste too.

TIP

   Check your toilet on a regular basis to make sure it isn't going to overflow. Some of the more expensive models come with a level meter to monitor how full they are, but it's just as easy to open the lower chamber up with the flush handle and have a look with a flashlight. A toilet overflowing is one of the worst things that can happen in your tiny space, as is finding out that you have a full toilet in the middle of the night when you really need to go.

   And before you speculate, yes, I am giving you the gift of hindsight here. And yes, both of these situations were as bad as they sound.

3. **Carefully pour your waste down the drain or chute from the spout on the cassette.**

WARNING

   Be sure to pour carefully; pour too fast and you'll end up having to take a cloth to your boots.

4. **Swill the cassette with water a couple of times to fully empty out all the waste.**

   Most cassette toilet emptying receptacles have a tap specifically for flushing the cassette with water.

TIP

   It's always a good idea to carry a length of hose with you to make the filling process easier.

5. **Use some eco-friendly cleaning products to clean the cassette.**

6. **Using a small cup, pour some washing powder into the cassette and mix with some water to dissolve it in.**

   I used an old espresso cup for this (surprise, surprise). Pour a couple of cups of powder into the cassette before adding a touch of water.

7. **Make sure the space is left clean and tidy for other users.**

This is a common courtesy that all vanlifers should adhere to. I have spent too many hours of my life unblocking receptacles or cleaning up a space before it's even fit for me to use, and contrary to popular belief, I've got better things to be spending my time on.

**REMEMBER**

Leave a toilet cleaning drain or receptacle as you would expect to find it, and if you're unsure how that should be, the answer is as clean as a whistle.

# Coping with Common Van Life Problems

Have you ever come across a problem in your house that has made you tear your hair out? Perhaps you found a rotten beam in the loft or damp behind the freezer in the kitchen. Sometimes annoying things like this just can't be avoided, and they happen just as easily in a terraced house in Basildon as they do in a million-dollar condo in Miami.

Van life is an incredible way to live and acts as a medium for you to get out and see the world, but it isn't a magical way of life with zero stresses or worries . . . no matter what Instagram might make you believe.

**REMEMBER**

Stuff will go wrong while you're on the road. However, when things go wrong, that doesn't mean you have failed. People don't talk about the bad stuff on social media, so I'm going to talk about it with you right here, right now.

I've had ants in my garage area, mice in the bulkhead, damp on the back doors, and a leak coming down through my sliding door. But then again, my dad has had all these things happen in his house, so when you put it into perspective, it's not really that big of a deal. In this next section, I cover a few of the most common problems that crop up while living in a van and how you can both deal with them and prevent them from happening again in the future.

## Dealing with damp

Living, breathing, and cooking inside a tiny space means you're going to build up a lot of moisture inside your camper van. For those of you who aren't aware of what I'm talking about, I'm referring to the black spots of mold you might see on certain objects from time to time.

**TIP**

Keeping air flowing through your camper by opening windows is incredibly important, as is allowing that air to flow around your living space.

But you've spent all that time insulating your van to make it warm, so why is this still happening?

Well, condensation is one of the biggest culprits when it comes to damp. If you're in a cold climate and the front of your van is toasty but no heat is getting into the back behind your drawers or sofa, then you're bound to create some condensation, which will slowly lead to damp. If it's not dealt with, damp can create a musty smell that isn't pleasant. What's more, mold spores can affect a person's breathing too, so it's good practice to keep on top of damp before it has a chance to build up.

As I said earlier, this will have happened to all the vanlifers you see on social media at some point, even though a lot of them won't admit it. Black mold can usually be cleaned off very easily with some mold killer spray and a cloth. Still, here are some other neat tricks I've picked up from living the van life full time that you should implement into your build to help prevent damp from becoming a problem.

## Condensation prevention matting

Condensation prevention matting is a semi-rigid structure usually used on boat beds that sits between the mattress and the bed base to allow air to flow between them. As I first mention back in Chapter 11, DRY-Mat Anti-Condensation Mattress Underlay from Ship Shape Bedding is one such example of matting you can use under your van's mattress. By slotting some of this underneath your mattress and your bed base or slats, you can help prevent black mold from building up under your mattress.

## Dehumidifier pods

Portable dehumidifier pods are used to draw moisture from the air and are small enough to stick into pretty much every nook and cranny inside your van. I've used these for years, mainly during the winter in places in my van that are prone to damp (for example, in the garage area and the bulkhead).

**TIP**

Use a little bit of Velcro to keep them from tipping over and replace as necessary.

## Damp-proof paint

In the end, I repainted the lower half of my van doors with damp-proof paint. Essentially, damp-proof paint contains a water-reactive agent within the paint itself. It's not foolproof, but it does stop damp from building up as quickly.

# Combatting pesky leaks

For those of you who haven't been to the United Kingdom, rain is usually the main weather forecast all year round. It's raining as I write this section now, in fact. And I don't just mean drizzle; I'm talking torrential, sideways, soak-you-to-the-bone kind of weather, which means that the U.K. is a perfect place to discover spots where a van might leak.

One of the biggest culprits for leaking is the sliding door. This is such a common problem that Fiamma created a mini gutter called Drip Stop. This little lifesaver is basically a stick-on gutter, similar to what you have around the edges of your house to help rain drain off your roof. It comes with adhesive strips and sticks directly onto your van, channeling water away from your sliding door, windows, and any other problem areas. I've used this on both campers and narrowboats, and it works great every time.

# Getting rid of pests

There is a chance that you're going to have unwanted guests living in your van at some stage, especially if you're parked up in one spot for a long period of time or like keeping your doors open in the summer.

## Ants

Ants have a habit of arriving uninvited, but with a van conversion that looks as good as the one that you have built, can you really blame them?

Use coffee grinds, paprika, or lemon peel along with juice of the lemon to repel ants humanely. You can also use chili pepper too. If the problem has escalated to the point of no return, however, plenty of ant repellents are available from hardware stores around the world that can be used as a last resort.

## Mice

Like ants, mice are also in the habit of showing up unannounced, especially in the winter months. I had a couple trying to make a nest in my crisp stash; they obviously didn't know not to get between a man and his stock of salt and vinegar snacks!

Take a scroll through eBay or Amazon, and you'll find many options for catching mice humanely. Place them in and around the affected areas and check back regularly. Be sure to let the mice out away from your van, too, so they don't sneak back in, and keep the cheese out of reach of little paws.

# Chapter 16

# Enjoying the Great Outdoors

Traveling through the great outdoors; that's one of the main draws to this lifestyle and could well be the reason you bought this book in the first place. Building your camper is only part of the journey; the real fun comes when you get to test it out in nature and live the life you've been dreaming of since I started waffling on in Chapter 1.

There are so many things to consider when heading out on the road in a new country or into unknown territory. How do you keep your belongings safe? Where can you park, and will the police move you on? What's the deal with boondocking? In this chapter, you find answers to all these questions, as well as key information on living and maintaining a self-sufficient lifestyle on the road and how to complement your van life adventures with exciting activities.

# Complementing an Ad-van-turous Lifestyle

When describing van life to people, one of the things I say the most is that "the whole world is your front garden." I know, it's a little cliché, but it's also incredibly true. Opening your sliding door onto rolling fields or a winding river doesn't just fill your life with lovely views and opportunities for taking lots of photos for your walls. Having beautiful locations right on your van doorstep provides immediate access to adventure, whether that's hiking, paddleboarding, climbing, swimming, or any other hobby that gets you out of bed and into the fresh air. In this first section, you discover how living in a van complements a healthy, outdoor lifestyle and the benefits that can have on your mental health.

## How van life promotes an outdoor lifestyle

While I consider a camper van to be "home" while out on the road, for me, my van is also a conduit between myself and nature. Bringing the outside into my living space is one of the things I love the most about van life. Having the sounds of the ocean or the tweeting of birds accompanying normal tasks like cooking or working instantly fills me with a sense of calm that I just can't get anywhere else.

Before I go any further, let's take a minute to be completely honest with one another here: Vans are small spaces. We all know that; it's what you signed up for when you bought this book, so this shouldn't be a shock all these chapters in. The truth is, no matter how cozy and homey you make your new house feel, you're not going to want to stay in it all the time, and that's completely natural for any home situation.

I'm speaking from experience here when I say that you *will* begin to yearn to get outside more and more while living in a van, often just returning to your trundling home for meals and to sleep. You'll find yourself sitting out in the open more even when it's colder, itching to get out for walks and spending your time scrolling through Atlas Obscura to find new and exciting places to visit in your area.

**REMEMBER**

There is absolutely nothing wrong with feeling like this. Don't think that you're going against van life if you find yourself wanting to be out of your van in the open more and more and spend less and less time inside your van reading or playing on the Game Boy; that's the whole point of this lifestyle!

### Looking after your well-being

I want to take a moment to talk about something that's incredibly important to me: mental health. There were times while living in a van when I felt anxious, and days when I was very aware that I was living in a small metal box on wheels.

Anxiety can strike like this in a house, in a caravan, or in a tent just as easily as it can in a van; it's an unavoidable part of life. And although all the people you see on Instagram might be smiling and happy while holding coconuts sporting little umbrellas, I want you to know that van life isn't a cure-all for mental health problems.

However, being in nature *can be,* and it's a heck of a lot cheaper than therapy. When you live in a house, it's too easy to say, "The woods are a drive away," or "I've got too much work to do; I can't afford any time to get outside." When you live in a van and the forest path is literally a step away, there are zero barriers and zero excuses not to look after yourself.

**TIP**

The best advice I can give you if you're feeling a little low or feeling that you don't have enough space — which as I've said, *will* happen from time to time — is to just get out and walk. Stick to a path and let your feet do the decision-making, or maybe pull out your paddleboard and take a couple of laps around a lake before meditating on the shore. Van life is all about making "you time" and enjoying life, so make sure to put some time aside to look after yourself along the way.

## Utilizing your spare time

What's that strange feeling you're experiencing? Could it be that new yogurt you bought from the supermarket? Or maybe you finally had a good night's sleep? While it could easily be both, I'm talking about the feeling you might get when for the first time in a long time, your time is completely your own. Somebody should put that line on a T-shirt and give me 10 percent of the profits.

Cleaning one room in your van is much easier than looking after a whole house, and even if you are still working, you don't have to worry about your morning commute to the office anymore. Your days will feel longer, your schedule hopefully much less pressured, which means that before long, you're going to look for extra things to do.

What a position to be in, and as I've said throughout this book and in countless articles beforehand, it was this spare time that helped me to turn my passion for writing into a full-time career. But alongside that, it also allowed me time to go out for a run or to take my paddleboard to the ocean. Instead of doing yoga stretches inside, I did them on clifftops before sipping a coffee on the beach, feeling the sand between my toes.

You won't believe how productive you can be when you take a ten-minute break to go paddleboarding while writing an article, either (see Figure 16-1)!

## Outdoor activities suitable for van life

So what are some of the activities and hobbies that you can take on the road with you? Let's start with a simple one: running. You might want the Lycra leggings and earbuds to complete the look, but all you really need to get out on a good run is a pair of running shoes. Stick on some shorts, plan your route, and head out on a tour of the local area. Going for a walk is even easier; just don a pair of trainers or hiking boots if you're heading into rough terrain and start exploring.

Skateboarding and roller blading are other outdoor activities whose equipment you can store away pretty easily. Bring along a fold-up scooter, or even a pair of ice skates if you're heading to colder climates too.

Most of these activities can be done both in the city or the country. Still, the beauty of having a house on wheels is that you can drive to locations specifically suited to certain hobbies and interests. You can park as close to a mountain or cliff face as humanly possible, removing the need to drag all your gear with you on public transport. The same goes with water sports such as surfing and paddleboarding (see Figure 16-2). I've even seen people kitesurfing and setting up paragliders that were stored in little trailers pulled behind their vans.

In essence, there isn't really anything you can't do while living in a van. From climbing to canoeing and drone flying to donkey trekking, the world is your oyster.

I wouldn't advise traveling with a donkey though . . . just think of the additional food bills!

FIGURE 16-2:
Boondocking with friends at the edge of Lake Como, Italy.

## Taking outdoor gear on the road

I know you're probably thinking, "You just spent all that time talking about how vans are tiny spaces and now you're going to tell us to fill them with even more stuff?" Well, in essence, yes, but stick with me.

How many of you have played Tetris before? Slotting those blocks into place and making them fit together neatly is pretty satisfying, right? Well, when it comes to taking outdoor gear on the road, you'll need to harness your inner block-dropping nerd and make the most of your garage space.

In the back of my van, I held two skateboards, a football, a body board, and a 12-foot inflatable SUP (stand-up paddleboard) that, when packed up, slotted down the side of my ladders. For a time, I had a fold-up bike in there too!

While I'm on the subject of the garage space, let's talk about storing equipment in there. I've looked at lots of conversions over the years that utilize bike holders bolted to the floor of the van under the bed area. By removing the wheels and locking the frame into place, you can easily fit two bikes under your bed and out of sight of thieves. The same goes for any other outdoor equipment that packs down such as inflatable SUPs or kayaks, items that would otherwise take up the entirety of your living space.

The garage storage space is also the perfect place for climbing equipment: ropes, portaledges, bouldering mats, chalk bags, and more. If you don't have a garage space, then smaller items like ropes that can be wound up tightly can be placed neatly inside bench seats in the main living space alongside running gear, tennis rackets, and more.

Bike carriers are incredibly common in the van life world, with models either attaching to the towbar or a ladder on the back doors. I did a lot of walking when I was traveling through Europe, but having a bike on hand meant that trips to the local shop were much quicker and way easier for carting back lots of fresh goods for my evening meal.

Surfboards, however, tend to be the exception to the rule. I've seen boards of different sizes inside living spaces, on the top of vans, and hanging from racks on the side. They're possibly the coolest outdoor sports accessory that you can take with you while living the van life, an opinion that probably stems from the fact that I'm envious of anyone who can surf even the tiniest bit.

**TIP**

If you fancy taking up paddleboarding or surfing, then it's much cheaper to take a SUP or a surfboard with you than renting equipment along the road. It might seem like a big expense initially, but having the ability to just park and get out on the water at a moment's notice for free when the feeling strikes is incredibly exhilarating and a novelty that won't wear off.

# Boondocking and Wild Camping

Is van life really as simple as just rocking up to any old place and living your life? Are there rules? And how do you find places to park?

If I had a pound, euro, or dollar for everyone who has asked me those questions over the years, I'd be set for life when it came to paying tolls on my travels. It's completely understandable; the concept of just living anywhere is, to most of us, incredibly alien. We save to pay rent or buy a house that provides stability for us, and is surrounded by familiar comforts, noisy neighbors, and that meowing cat that never shuts up. So the idea of being in deadly silence in the middle of a forest for the first time with no meowing cat might be an incredibly daunting and bizarre notion, one that you have no idea how to actually begin to understand.

Don't worry; over the course of this next section, you find out about the art of boondocking or wild camping. By the end, you'll probably be able to have your own show about boondocking on TV with Bear Grylls.

# What is boondocking and wild camping?

*Boondocking* refers to taking your camper and parking it on land that isn't part of a campsite, essentially driving to a spot in nature and setting up your own camp spot for the night. In the U.S. this practice is called boondocking, but in Europe and the U.K. it's more widely referred to as *wild camping*.

Before I go any further, I want to share my thoughts on campsites. I'm not saying that there's anything wrong with staying at a campsite as opposed to boondocking; they certainly have their place and provide safety and stability, especially when traveling with children. That being said, for me, van life is more about getting out and exploring the world, parking up in remote areas away from a guy who is trying to impress his new girlfriend by playing an Oasis song badly on the guitar and making up all the words.

Once again, if you think that's a niche reference, it's because it's true and happened the only time I stayed in a campsite on the outskirts of Venice.

TIP

Usually campsites are a safe bet, however, in places near major cities, and especially when the camping resources talk about the potential for break-ins in an area (like they did while I was trying to find a place to park near Venice). Don't rely on them all the time when traveling, though, as you won't experience everything the world around you has to offer, especially as there are so many free areas to stay in so easily.

# Rules and regulations

Specific rules and regulations on boondocking vary from country to country. Still, there are some common themes that run throughout the practice of boondocking that you should bear in mind before heading out on your wild camping adventures.

## Leave no trace

This one isn't a hard rule to grasp, but you'll be surprised how many people don't follow it. I'm willing to bet good money that you have been taught to clean up after yourself throughout your life thus far. It's a constant that is prevalent in all our lives — washing the dishes, putting things away, taking out the trash, and so on.

Sadly, you'll find some people just don't care about keeping nature clean for others, and I've done everything from litter picking on the side of a mountain to cleaning out a stone trough underneath a tap that someone had decided to empty their black water tank into in the hope the contents would pass down a minuscule pipe into a drain.

And yes, black water is the waste that comes from your porta-potty, just so we're all on the same page here.

TIP

Leave no trace doesn't mean "don't have fun"; it just means leaving a camping area in a state that you would like to find it in. If you're making a fire pit on the beach or in a forest, use stones to make a circle that will control the flames and cover over it with earth or sand once you have finished. If you make any rubbish, take it with you and deposit it in the nearest bin, and if "nature calls," do your ablutions away from the parking area and bury it, making sure to throw out or burn any toilet paper you use the next chance you get.

## Be mindful of others

One of the great things about parking up in the middle of nowhere is that you can be as loud as you want. If you're having a laugh with a friend with some beers and there aren't any houses nearby, then feel free to get out your portable speaker or play some guitar.

If there are houses nearby, however, then use your common sense and judge each park-up spot as you find it. This is especially true if you're stealth camping. I remember parking up outside a science laboratory once and was laughing away while watching something on my laptop when a security guard knocked on the door and pointed to a sign that said "we can see and hear you." The whole thing felt a little like a scene from a horror movie, so I drove off quickly and didn't go back.

REMEMBER

Boondocking and wild camping are generally tolerated by most residents in the places you visit. If you're from out of town and just park on the side of the road for a night or two, it's no different than just parking your car outside of a friend's house. Problems arise when you cause a disturbance or give local councils a reason to ban campers and motorhomes from the area. Use your head, be respectful, and keep a low profile around built up or inhabited areas.

WARNING

In some countries, you might be be fined for actually "making a camp." Parking up is fine, but erecting awnings and putting out plastic furniture is a big no-go. If in doubt, just sit on the edge of your van and don't attract too much attention.

## CAMPING LAWS IN YOUR AREA

The main snag you might come across when looking for a spot to boondock or wild camp are the camping laws in the area in which you are visiting. "No motorhome parking" signs have started cropping up in more and more places, especially since the COVID-19 pandemic, but don't let this bother you. (I discuss the various apps you can use to plan ahead when finding places to park in a little later in this chapter.)

Wild camping is a bit of a grey area in the U.K. in the sense that it's not technically allowed. Still, I lived in a van in Yorkshire for just over a year with no problems whatsoever and know many people who still do. One of my favorite park-up spots was right next to a police station and I was never told to move along. If you're heading into Europe, boondocking is also illegal in Slovenia and Greece, but I and countless others have wild camped there without any problems.

Most places with camping laws have them to keep areas of natural beauty clean and tidy, just like I mentioned at the beginning of this section. If you keep yourself to yourself and look after the area, then you won't have any problems. I was only ever moved on by the police a couple of times while traveling around Europe, and one of those was for my own safety. Sometimes authorities might want to see your travel papers or do a random search of your van, but that depends on what areas you are traveling through or into. Just be polite, upfront, and friendly, and you shouldn't have any problems.

# Picking the Perfect Park-Up Spot

Like most things in life, there isn't an exact science to picking the best park-up spot. You need to consider many different factors, from the availability of sunshine for your solar panels to the view out of your back door while you're eating your evening meal. Over the years, I've parked everywhere from the cusp of lakes and rivers to natural hot springs built into baths by the Romans. I've parked in sand dunes in Sardinia and along the California coast, basking in beautiful views while drinking an espresso and watching the world go by.

Equally, I've spent many nights in car parks with a concrete patch as a front garden outside my sliding door or tucked up between delivery vans outside of warehouses. The perfect park-up spot isn't always picturesque; it can simply be useful, in a good location, or just surrounded by other people in a place that makes you feel safe. Or (slightly) more important than all of those, free.

The fact remains that one of the main reasons we vanlifers boondock is to see the world from our sliding doors or look at the stars from our beds. The other is having direct access to places where we can get out and explore, areas near nice walks, or places to swim.

Location is key and plays a big part in my adventures. Because van life is synonymous with an outdoor lifestyle (as you discovered earlier in this chapter), I tend to opt for places on the coast near the ocean or mountainous areas, places where no matter where I am in my van, I have a beautiful view to look out on. In the following sections I offer some tips on how to find those perfect parking spots in a variety of different scenarios.

## Useful resources and apps

There are so many resources out there to help you find a good parking spot. Take the pressure out of planning your route and picking a place to park; van life is supposed to reduce stress and not increase it, after all.

### Park4Night

If there's one app that I have used more than any other on my travels, it's Park4Night. Searching for new and exciting locations to call home for a day (or in the case of Sardinia, ten days!) both in my current area and on my proposed journey became a regular part of my routine.

Park4Night has a handy quick search function that gives users the chance to pick specific facilities or areas rather than searching through an entire map. Pick nature spots with a minimum rating of four stars or search for the nearest laundromat without being distracted by other symbols.

**TIP**

I often discard any place rated three stars or fewer. That might seem a little snobbish, but after the story you're about to read in "Going with your gut" a little later on, you'll see why.

### iOverlander

iOverlander works in a very similar fashion to Park4night but is designed more for travel through the U.S. and Canada. With over 30,000 camping spots registered throughout the U.S. and over 11,000 in Canada at the time of this writing, it's a one-stop-shop for vanlifers looking for a place to spend the night in these areas.

Whereas Park4Night has more European appeal, iOverlander covers every continent and spans locations from Belize to Qatar to Fiji and beyond. Find waste disposal spots, free camping locations, laundromats, campsites, and more via the helpful icons that pop up whenever you zoom into your chosen or current location.

## Wikicamps

Wikicamps is primarily used in Australia and New Zealand but has since become available in the U.S., Canada, and the U.K.

Set the easy-to-use search filter to find the type of campsite or park-up spot you're looking for and discover everything there is to know about that location right from your smartphone screen. Wikicamps also comes with some cool extras like a compass and a handy trip planner that you can use to make custom maps.

## Google Maps and Apple Maps

Google Maps and Apple Maps don't need any introduction in this day and age. I'm sure most of you have used one of these apps when planning a trip along the freeway or heading down country roads to your friend's new house in a sleepy little village somewhere. Some travel apps like Park4Night allow you to link straight up with Google Maps and Apple Maps and open up your proposed route straightaway. Others require you to input coordinates in order to direct you to the specific location pin shown.

More than just directing you to specific locations, however, Google Maps and Apple Maps allow you to search the area around you using satellite view to find bodies of water, forest glades, and other places you can reach via camper.

If you come to your chosen boondocking area and it's full, then using satellite view to find areas in the immediate vicinity is a great way to still enjoy the spot you've been looking forward to visiting without having to come back another day. There are usually other areas nearby that you can stealth camp in very easily, so do a little research before you drive off in despair.

## TomTom Go Camper

I don't know what I would have done without the TomTom Go Camper navigation app while traveling. Google Maps and Apple Maps are great, but they don't always take you down "van friendly" routes.

The TomTom Go Camper app allowed me to put in my vehicle's dimensions including the van's height in order to eliminate routes that I wouldn't be able to drive down or through. It's simple to follow, uses bold colors, and has downloadable maps for every continent. I used it in both Europe and the U.S. and it never let me down once!

# Finding a place to stay for the night

So now you know how to search for exciting places, but picking one is a different ball game entirely. How do you decide which forest park-up is the best, which one will give you the most comfortable night's sleep, and which one you'll feel safest in? Is it possible to know all these things just from looking at a picture on an app, or do you need to go there to experience them firsthand to find out?

I don't know why I'm asking you; you're supposed to be coming to me for the answers!

**WARNING**

Before I go any further, I want to talk about how important it is to find a parking spot before nightfall. Always try to park before it gets dark so that you can get a proper lay of the land and find out what kind of area you are parking in. The last thing you want is to be woken up at dawn by a police officer telling you you're boondocking in the middle of a marketplace and in the way of someone's stall. This one didn't happen to me, but I know a couple of people who have found themselves in this situation.

**TIP**

I know it's not always possible and sometimes unavoidable if you've had a long trip, but finding a parking spot during daylight hours is always preferable, especially when it comes to determining whether the spot is safe or not. And, it pays to use the resources and apps I mention earlier to find out some information about a place before you arrive too, as daylight doesn't always provide all the answers.

I'll never forget the time I parked in a quiet spot by a stately home (the kind of place you might see on *Downton Abbey* or *The Crown*) while exploring Europe. It was only about 6 p.m. when I went to sleep, and it was still light outside, but I was feeling ill and needed the rest. Five hours later, I was woken by the police telling me that I had to move for my own safety because I was parking in a dangerous sex-trafficking zone! It's the one and only time it ever happened, and I hotfooted it back to a safe place I had stayed in the night before. The moral of this story? Always check and take heed of the comments and reviews left by users on Google Maps and apps like Park4Night to your advantage if you're from out of town.

**REMEMBER**

You'll hear me say this a lot throughout this chapter, but always go with your gut when making decisions when it comes to park-ups. No matter how rationally you think about that descent or that precarious-looking path, if your instincts are saying leave it alone, then leave it well alone. It doesn't matter whether you saw someone on Instagram who had reached the end destination you're heading for; if you don't feel comfortable, then pick another spot further along and don't risk it.

## In the heart of nature

The first time you arrive in a forest park-up spot in the middle of nowhere might feel a little daunting. We've all seen horror movies set in the deep dark woods, but the reality is that most of the time you're either sharing these spaces with other vanlifers looking for a little peace and quiet, or the local wildlife who are quite good at keeping to themselves.

When you arrive at a camping spot in nature, the first thing you should consider are your solar panels. If you're thinking about staying in one place for a few days, then will you have enough power in your leisure batteries if you park under a forest canopy without any sun hitting your panels? If not, then finding a space on the outskirts of the forest or a gap in the trees might be the best bet to keep your batteries topped up on the go.

The next thing you might want to look for is an even place to park. Full disclosure here: This never bothered me too much as I've slept on hills and slants throughout my entire van life, and there's always tire levelers that you can use to create a more level surface for sleeping on.

**TIP**

Don't take on the challenge of reaching a forest park-up that you don't think your vehicle is capable of. I've come across so many steep inclines or gravelly descents while driving a long-wheelbase panel van that I've almost tackled but thought better of at the last minute. The same goes for sandy tracks that look as though you might slip or slide around on them or roads that are flooded or riddled with pot holes.

Unless you're driving a 4x4 with all-terrain tires that can easily cope with everything Mother Nature throws at you, then it's really not worth the risk of getting stuck in a place where you might not come across someone who can help for hours.

Your approach to nature park-ups will strongly depend on where you are in the world. If you're traveling around Northern Italy, for example, then it's highly unlikely that a bear is going to stumble upon your campsite and try to break in to steal the Ben & Jerry's from your fridge-freezer. If you're boondocking around Lake Tahoe or in the middle of a national forest in Montana, however, then this is a much bigger possibility.

**REMEMBER**

It's not a bear's fault if it breaks into your camper because you left some toothpaste out on the front seat. Bears don't know that toothpaste isn't edible; all they know is that it smells nice and want to investigate further. Keep them and yourselves safe by keeping all food and scented items out of sight in cupboards in your van.

Some campsites have bear lockers to keep food locked up in. These aren't there for fun or to make for a cool photo; they're there because bears also frequent those areas, and they aren't looking for a cozy place to pitch a tent. Follow the rules for the safety of the bears, yourself, and other campers.

**TIP**

You can also hang food in a bag out of reach in a tree or use a bear-safe lockable coolers when out in nature.

## By the beach

I think one of the main reasons many folks want to get into van life is to see sandy beaches and park by the ocean. I'm sick of the number of times I've written "I parked by the waves" in this book already, so you're probably starting to feel the same way. All I can do is apologize and admit that it's probably going to happen many more times yet.

The truth is that, as humans, we're drawn to water. It usually calms us, cools us, makes us feel at peace. It probably has something to do with the fact that we're about 60 percent water ourselves, so it's only natural that we want to get in it, listen to it, and look at it while drinking it.

Sand, however, is your camper van's arch nemesis. While it's good to roll around in and make castles with, it's tough to drive on and may often result in you getting stuck and needing to be pulled out by something much bigger.

**TIP**

A lot of beaches have parking lots that are possible to stay in overnight. Alternatively, park near the beach and walk around on foot until you find out where the hard ground suitable for parking on is. If you're currently stuck in sand and have turned to this book for guidance on how to escape, then skip ahead to the safety equipment section that follows. Alternatively, use this book as a spade and buy another copy when you get back home.

## City park-ups

Many cities have designated spaces for campers to park in, especially in Europe. The bays will usually be bigger, and some might even come with power outlets and water supplies.

If you have a smaller camper like a medium-wheelbase Ford Transit or a VW Caddy, then you have much more choice when parking as your vehicle should easily fit into a regular spot. Plus, you're going to blend in much easier than a Toyota Tacoma with a Four Wheel Camper on the back of it.

Stealth camping in a city is much easier if you're simply "parking" and not spreading your stall out with barbecues, camping chairs, and fold-out tables. Blend into your surroundings and do everything possible not to stick out like a sore thumb!

Many supermarkets offer 24- to 48-hour stays for camper vans with the hope that you will do your shopping there. Some even have water and disposal facilities too.

Parking in the city in the U.S. isn't tricky; you will find so much space down residential areas and in car parks that you shouldn't have a problem finding a place to pull up for the night. And if all else fails, there's usually a comfortable parking bay at the local WalMart.

## Stealth camping in a city full time

Of course, not everyone wants to travel in a van. For some, van life provides a legitimate place to live full time. Perhaps you're saving for a house or just can't afford conventional accommodations right now, or maybe you're sick of handing all your hard-earned cash over to bills and rent at the end of the month. Tiny homes are still homes, and van life provides a place to call your own for very little money.

I tell everyone I speak to about van life to live in their van in their home city before they head out on the road. It means that they still have all their friends and family around them as a safety net should anything go wrong or they discover any teething problems with their vehicle.

I know I've mentioned this before, but working full time while living in a van really helped me to save up an emergency fund for any emergencies while traveling. Luckily, I didn't have to dip into this too much apart from a problem with my diesel pump in Italy, living off my freelance work as I traveled. Still, knowing that I had money for any "worst-case scenarios" really helped me to sleep soundly at night while on the other side of the world.

## FINDING A FILL-UP SPOT

Using the apps I mention earlier in this chapter, it's easy to find what I've referred to throughout this book as "camper fill-up spots" dotted throughout the state or country you are traveling through. These spots are places where you can park for a designated amount of time while filling up water, emptying your waste tanks, and doing your recycling at the same time. Check signage to find out how long you can stay in each place; I've seen signs that have stated 23-hour stays only and some that have allowed for anything between two weeks to a month.

Okay, that's enough of the tips. How *do* you go about stealth camping in a city full time?

Well, my advice is to pick a few different spots and to circulate between them. When I lived in my van in York, I moved between three different locations. I'm not going to share them for obvious reasons, but one of them *was* near the scary science lab I mentioned earlier in this chapter.

Industrial estates are quite a common place for vans to park from time to time. People in the nearby housing estates park their cars there overnight, and you don't tend to get people walking through that often. I would sometimes hear people say, "I see this van everywhere; I wonder who owns it?" while I was brushing my teeth or reading, but they never commented about the smoke coming out of the chimney.

REMEMBER

As I've said before, people are quite often wrapped up in their own worlds to notice what you're doing. As long as you don't write "someone lives in here" on the side in bright neon lettering, you shouldn't have any problems.

TIP

Like boondocking in inhabited areas situated beside natural beauty hotspots, just be mindful of your noise when parking in an industrial estate or near houses. Don't worry about getting in and out of your van; people open and close car doors all the time. Just don't do anything that might attract unwanted attention like playing music incredibly loudly or listening to a funny program near a scary science lab.

I wonder if they can still hear me now?

# Free camping in the U.S.A.

Not to be confused with Bruce Springsteen's classic hit.

If you're lucky enough to live in the U.S., then you have lots of areas where you can camp for free with very few restrictions. Let's take a look at the three main types of places.

## Bureau of Land Management (BLM) land

BLM land accounts for a whopping 245 million surface acres of land in the U.S., and it's all free to camp on. If you like getting away from civilization and into the heart of the wild with no one around for miles, then BLM land is definitely the place to do it. The main rule of leave no trace applies as always, as does a time frame of not staying longer than 14 days in one place.

If you're heading out into BLM areas, remember to take lots of supplies with you. There's no guarantee that there will be any amenities, so packing a water filter for drinking water is a must. Some areas might be better suited to an off-road 4x4 setup, so do your research before heading out to see if your vehicle can cope with the terrain.

## National forests

National forests work very similarly to BLM land in the sense that they're free to camp in and you don't need to book a slot. Some areas do require a camping permit just to help regulate the number of people using the space.

As always, make sure that you do your "business" away from water sources that other boondockers or animals might use. Be vigilant for bigger animals and always let someone know your proposed location before heading off-grid. Don't forget to follow the advice I mention earlier when it comes to protecting your food from bears too.

## State and national forests

State forests and national forests are very different entities, so make sure to do some research on your destination before setting off. State forests tend to have a lot more regulations that need to be adhered to and many require permits before you camp. If in doubt, speak to a ranger or email a park office to find out the necessary information for your stay.

# Free camping in Europe

Europe is a bit of a mixed bag when it comes to camping. I've traveled all over mainland Europe, and the rules on boondocking vary from country to country. In some places, it can be a bit for a free for all, while other places like the U.K. have a pretty firm stance on where you can and can't camp.

Here are some of the places to look out for while traveling around Europe.

## Aires

The one constant that I've come across during my travels through Europe is the fact that most countries have designated camper van parking areas or fill-up spots, called *aires*, that have drinking water, waste disposal, and sometimes electrical hookup facilities for a cost. Sometimes, aires can be in the middle of cities, and sometimes you'll find them next to lakes or in the middle of fields. There are lots of guides online as to where you can find aires, as well as via the apps mentioned earlier in this chapter.

Oh, and if you happened to be staying at the same aire as me in Spain where I found the free-to-use showers and used up all the hot water, I'm still not sorry. That was probably one of the top five greatest showers of my entire life!

## Supermarkets

Some supermarkets will allow camper vans to park for up to 48 hours, which can be good if you just need to settle down and do some work or have a long sleep after partying with friends. A lot of the Intermarchè supermarkets I stopped at in Portugal had toilet emptying and water fill-up facilities, and as a result, I ended up doing a big weekly shop in the store at the same time.

**TIP**

Some supermarkets require you to pay for a token or "jeton" before you can use the camper facilities. You might have to ask inside the store, so use a translation app if you're not comfortable with the local language.

## Brit Stops

The clue is in the title here. Brit Stops operates in the U.K., specifically in Britain, and aims to give people traveling in campers a safe and secure place to spend the night. The organization has partnered with over 1,100 hosts across the U.K., including pubs, antiques centers, farm shops, and so on, and each location is listed in both a printed guide and an app.

While it's free of charge to stay at these places, the general idea is that people staying at Brit Stops will end up going to the host's establishment for a meal or drink, or perhaps buy some fresh local produce, thus helping business owners and giving something back to the local community too. It isn't a requirement, but it's nice to give something back.

In many ways, it's the same as supermarkets offering camper van parking and emptying facilities mentioned earlier, though Brit Stops are usually in nicer locations than city car parks.

## National parks

Laws for staying in national parks vary from place to place too. The Lake District in England, for example, has rangers who will tell people to move if they park in certain areas. The Yorkshire Dales National Park, however, has lots of spaces for campers to sleep for the night.

Likewise, the Schwarzwald or Black Forest technically has a strong no camping stance, but I and countless others have successfully stayed the night there without being moved on. The same goes for Portugal; the Guarda Nacional Republicana (or GNR) often patrol forests to make sure that you aren't damaging the wildlife or setting out "camp." If you are simply parked, then they will often leave you be and allow you to stay for 24 hours.

In summary, overnight camping in most national parks in mainland Europe is tolerated. It's tougher in the U.K., but not impossible. Do some research and look to parking apps for more advice.

### Allemansrätten: The right to roam

Some of the more relaxed areas of Europe like Scandinavia (Norway, Denmark, and Sweden) follow the idea of *allemansrätten*. What this essentially means is that every person, be they a native citizen or a visitor to the country, has a right to use the space around them. That includes the air, land, and water. So even if a space is privately owned, it can still be used for camping or recreational activities.

Scotland also has a right to roam policy that allows for wild camping in areas of natural beauty, which is why it is so popular with travelers from across the globe.

Just because you have the right to be in a place doesn't mean that you can take advantage of it. Remember the leave no trace rule and be respectful to both the land and others around you.

# Tips for blending in

It might be tempting to paint your van bright pink with polka dots or to create a mural of your favorite Marvel characters on the walls, but that'll certainly draw attention to your rig.

My advice is to keep your van as boring and as bland as possible on the outside. It doesn't even matter if it looks a little old and dirty; how often are you going to look at the outside of it anyway? A van that looks uninspiring on the outside is sure to have nothing interesting on the inside, right? Even if it has camper van windows installed, you'll blend in a lot better.

If you have the money, however, I recommend spraying it a dark blue-green color, almost verging on black. White vans tend to stick out like a sore thumb in forests, especially if people are using flashlights at night. So if you're planning on stealth camping, then a paint job might be worth the money.

As I've also mentioned in previous sections, not putting out camping equipment and keeping everything self-contained inside your van is a great way to blend in. If you want to open your sliding door, park in a manner so that it doesn't open out onto a road or a place where pedestrians might see into your van.

TIP

You might have designs of creating a big Instagram following while traveling in your van. You might even want to put a logo on the side to make it look cool. I always advise against branding your vehicle, and I would certainly advise against putting your Instagram handle on the side of your van too. All it takes is anyone with a smartphone to type in your handle and see everything you've got inside your rolling home, from laptops and drones to that nice watch you got from your last Instagram campaign. Travel smart and safe; don't advertise what's going on inside your van to everyone who passes.

One of the best ways to blend in is to just be confident and to not make a big fuss out of anything. It also helps if you don't fall out of your van while burning your hands on your log burner as you try to empty your ash into a bucket, either. Yes, it hurt a lot.

## Park-up etiquette

When you park at an aire or in a forest, don't park too close to the person next to you. If you hit it off and become firm friends, then there's no reason why you can't move a little closer. Still, some people have come away for some peace and quiet and to not speak to other campers, so it's important to respect their privacy until you are told otherwise.

If someone leaves a parking spot and takes everything with them, then that space is fair game and up for grabs. If, however, they leave some chairs or other equipment behind, then it means that they're coming back and will be returning to said space.

It's fine to put up hammocks, do a bit of spoon carving, and chat with friends outside, but just like when parking next to other houses on streets or by natural areas, bear in mind that not everyone wants to hear your music on the speaker or your rendition of "Stairway to Heaven" on the guitar.

Don't leave rubbish, but do assist others if you see them cleaning up an area. It's a great way to meet people and make friends too.

Don't empty your water right under your camper, and don't put your black waste in that trough I cleaned up in Sardinia, because it took me ages and I still have nightmares about it!

# Staying Safe While Off-Grid

One of the biggest things you need to consider when parking in new places is safety. And that's not always just from external sources. Sure, you might quite rightly feel threatened by a group of people holding baseball bats while screaming bloodcurdling cries, or if you see a camper van with a smashed window in the parking bay two spots down from you. But sometimes, you might just get a feeling that something isn't quite right, even if you can't see anything untoward.

And, if there's one thing I've learned from living in a van over the years, it's that you should never ignore such feelings. If you don't feel safe, then you won't enjoy your time at the park-up. You won't sleep, and you'll be tired the next day, thus potentially putting yourself and others in danger while out on the road.

Take a look at the pearls of wisdom I've included in this next section and discover some tips and tricks about staying safe and looking after your well-being on the road.

## Going with your gut

It's time for another travel story, so grab a cup of coffee and try not to fall asleep. . . .

While traveling around Spain, I wanted to visit a place called Finisterre, a place the Romans thought was the very end of the known world. With its iconic lighthouse and rock finger stretching out into the sea, it's a stunning sight to behold and well worth a visit. On my way, I decided to park at a location by a lake for the night. It was in the middle of nowhere, miles from the nearest café, shop, or house, which wouldn't normally put me off in the slightest. Still, something about this place just felt off. There were car parts strewn on the ground and a weird locked shed that I didn't like the look of, as well as hills that were quiet . . . *too quiet.*

To be honest, there was probably nothing wrong with that spot. The car parts might have been from an enthusiast who used the space for renovations, and the shed could well have held equipment for a local boating club. Still, I had a bad feeling about it from the very beginning, and after eating a sandwich, I turned around and drove back in the direction from which I came.

This only happened a couple of times throughout the entirety of my time spent traveling in a van (the other was in an area where I thought people were shooting guns, but it turned out to be a fireworks festival), but I'm still glad I went with my gut and listened to the little alarm bell inside my head.

There is absolutely no shame whatsoever in leaving a place because you don't like the feel of it. You're not "chickening out" and you're certainly not failing at van life. It's nice to get out of your comfort zone, but it's also fine to have limits and stick with what makes you feel safe.

## Warning signs to look out for

When it comes to physical signs to look out for, it's not too difficult to spot red flags that shouldn't be ignored.

If you see lots of broken glass in a car park, it's a sure sign that thieves have been operating in the area. Similarly, I've seen listings on park-up apps that have advised against entering car parks due to nails and glass being scattered on paths and roads to stop campers in their tracks, thus making them easier targets when it comes to breaking in.

If you see clear plastic packets on the ground around where you're parked, that could be a sign that people have been taking drugs in the area too. Likewise, as I mention earlier, some areas are used for sex trafficking both during the day and night, so if you see people sitting on plastic chairs by the roadside, I wouldn't advise parking nearby.

Some of you might have found the previous paragraphs a little hard to read, and I'm sorry if you did. The truth is that as much as we wish they didn't, these things do go on in the world. All I can do is give you an idea of what to look out for so that you can stay out of danger while on the road.

Sometimes cars will pull up close to you while you're parked out in the wild or in a car park. This happened to me quite a lot while I was boondocking, and nine times out of ten the cars belonged to teens who had come to a secluded spot to spend some time with their friends. I imagine they were also a bit weirded out by a camper van with English plates hanging out in their usual haunt, but I never got out to ask them.

On occasion, people would pull up next to me and play music till 3 a.m. Well, the joke was on them, because I used the time to catch up on article writing or playing a bit of Mario Kart, knowing that I had the luxury of sleeping in the next morning. That's also how I developed an insatiable love of Portuguese techno music, but that's a story for another book.

# Five extra security features to add to your camper

The truth of the matter is that if someone is determined to break into your van, then they'll try their very best to have a good go at it. While you can't account for every eventuality, you can make your van look less appealing to burglars by adding extra security features to the outside.

TIP

When you're thinking about upping your van's security features, you should think about both stopping people from entering your vehicle *and* from driving away with your tiny home. It's bad enough losing your belongings, but when you live in a vehicle and your vehicle is gone, you suddenly lose your entire world.

REMEMBER

A lot of thieves are chancers looking to see what they can find on a whim. They undoubtedly know that they won't have a lot of time to search through your van, and the likelihood is that they will pick vans that look easy to break into. With this in mind, the following safety features have a dual effect as both visual and physical deterrents.

My thought process has always been that if a van looks like it will be a hassle to break into, then people will leave it alone. So far, I've never had any problems with break-ins, so my overcautiousness seems to have paid off!

## Thule sliding bolt lock

The Thule sliding bolt lock attaches to the outside of your van on either the sliding or rear doors. Attaching to either side of a door join, the bolt prevents the door or doors from being opened when clicked and locked into place. It's easy to install in any position and height too.

TIP

Take your time with the template. You're going to be drilling holes into your van door to install the bolt lock, so try to get the installation right the first time; otherwise your door might end up looking like a slice of gouda.

## Master Lock van padlock and hasp

I used a Master Lock padlock and hasp on the rear doors of my camper as an extra security measure for protecting the outdoor equipment in my garage space. Not only that, but having another lock on the back doors, which happened to be right next to where I slept, made me feel more secure once inside the camper for the night.

TIP

If you can, park so that your back doors are against a wall or bush whenever you leave your van for the day. That way, with the extra security provided by your Master Lock, you can enjoy the day knowing your belongings are safe.

### Steering wheel lock

A brightly colored steering wheel lock with a flashing light not only prevents people from actually driving your camper away from your park-up spot, but also it is an instant visual deterrent for anyone thinking that they might like to give grand theft auto a try.

Make sure to measure your steering wheel properly and get a steering wheel lock that actually renders your steering wheel unusable while locked into place.

### Wheel clamp

Some of you might be thinking, "Surely a wheel clamp is a little overkill." Still, as I said before, there's nothing worse than somebody stealing your home while you're on the other side of the world or miles and miles away from friends and family.

Wheel clamps are usually brightly colored in yellow and red, again providing a visual deterrent to potential thieves. They clamp around the metal center of the wheel and prevent anyone from driving away. The model I used was made of thick steel and both locked and chocked the wheel. It also meant that people didn't park around me because they thought I had been clamped!

### Lockable safe

Finally, if you're leaving your van for long periods of time, it's a good idea to keep your valuables locked up and safe in a hard-to-reach area. That way, if someone does manage to break into your camper, all the good stuff, such as your wallet, drone, Kindle, passport, and so on, will be out of the way in another secure location.

I installed my safe in the garage area of my van. That meant that someone would have to pick the Master Lock and the rear door lock and *then* break into the safe.

The safe I chose came with screw holes in the base and back panel of the unit. After drilling holes down through the floor of my van, I bolted it the through the floor and used nylock nuts to bolt to it into place before covering the exposed bolts on the underside of the van with expanding foam to prevent someone from tampering with them.

## Packing emergency equipment

In many places around the world, it's a legal requirement to carry the correct emergency equipment for when you break down at the side of the road. More than just a requirement, however, it's also just a sensible move to set out with as much equipment as you possibly can that might help you if you find yourself in a pickle. Here are some key pieces of emergency equipment you should consider taking with you on the road.

## First-aid kit

I bet 90 percent of you reading this book don't even have a pack of plasters or band-aids in your house, never mind a first-aid kit. I'm guilty of this, but accidents tend to happen when you live your life outdoors, so it's a good idea to have a well-stocked first-aid kit complete with bandages, eye cleaning solution, micropore tape — the works.

Don't forget to pack ibuprofen and paracetamol (acetaminophen) too. You never know when you might wake up with a sore head or fall over and find yourself with an inflamed foot!

## Recovery tracks

What happens if your van gets stuck in mud or sand? Do you wait for a local farmer who might happen to be passing by to come and tow you out? (You do if you're me.) Or do you place recovery tracks under your wheels to get some traction and get back on your adventures?

Recovery tracks like the ones made by MaxTrax include a shovel built into either end for removing excess earth or sand. They provide something for your tire to grip to no matter what terrain you're in and nestle neatly together when not in use.

## Spare tire

There might very well be a scenario where you burst a tire or get a puncture and need to replace it before you can carry on with your journey. If you have the space to mount a spare tire on the back of your van, then at least you know that, if push comes to shove, you can change your tire and continue your adventure without waiting for a breakdown service to rescue you.

Make sure to get the correct-sized wheel nut and a long breaker bar for removing your old tire. Picking a longer breaker bar will give you more leverage when pushing down to unfasten your wheel bolts.

## Puncture repair spray

Sometimes, however, changing a spare tire isn't always an option, or perhaps you've used your spare and have just got another puncture (sometimes the universe really wants to mess with you). Holts Emergency Puncture Repair spray is one type that reinflates tires and seals punctures, allowing you to safely drive to the nearest mechanic or repair station. It's available worldwide from eBay, so grab a couple of bottles and keep in your garage area in case of an emergency.

### European driving kit

Even if you're not driving around Europe, it's worth having one of these kits in your van. They contain all the compulsory equipment that some European countries require you to carry, such as high visibility jackets, wind-up flashlights, spare bulbs, warning triangles for when you have a breakdown, and other useful equipment.

### Tool kit

Having a well-stocked tool kit with wrenches, sealant, drill bits, and every other major tool you used while making your van will ensure that, if there is a problem with electrical wires or something falls down in your van or breaks, you can fix it on the go.

**WARNING**

As always, make sure your batteries are disconnected when working with your electrical system.

### Flashlight

A flashlight isn't just useful for making your way around your camping spot at night or for catching badgers in the act of trying to break into your cooler. Having the means of illuminating the area under your car hood or when peering into the back of your garage area is incredibly useful too. Flashlights can also be used to attract the attention of passersby using morse code if you're in danger.

### Snow chains

Snow chains slip over your tires and help when driving on snowy or icy roads. Even if you have all-weather tires, sometimes vehicles need a little helping hand when combatting slippery slopes.

# Being Self-Sufficient on the Road

There are two things you're going to need a lot of while traveling on the open road: water and power for your devices. Thankfully, it's easy to keep on top of both and make sure that you don't run out.

# Finding water

As I mention earlier in the section about useful apps and resources, many of the applications available to download on your smartphone show locations of water taps in your local area. In most cases, this is because other users or local authorities have uploaded this information for travelers. So if you come across one on the road that hasn't been added, it's always good to help other vanlifers out by logging it and adding the coordinates.

The beauty of having a simple water setup like the one I implemented with a removable freshwater jerrycan is that I could fill it up from anywhere. It didn't matter whether I found a water pump in the French Alps or a tap in a Sardinian village; by removing the canister or using smaller bottles to top it up if there was no parking nearby the water source, I could top up with water regularly and without any hassle.

Even if your water tanks aren't completely empty, it's always best to fill up whenever you see a water faucet. Being off-grid has so many advantages, but one of my biggest worries was breaking down and not having enough water. Sometimes areas might only have a couple of water points, especially if you're on a small island. My advice: Fill up regularly and don't chance finding another faucet en route.

Bear in mind that the water spots uploaded by other users might have been decommissioned, so don't rely on just one spot for your fill-up requirements, and check the comments to see when someone last used them.

If you have a tank that requires a hose to fill, then make sure to carry a long length of hose with you and a hose adapter set. Different countries around the world have different faucet threads and connector styles, so grab a universal set before heading out or do some research to see which connector you will need for the countries you're planning on traveling through.

Of course, you don't always need to get your water from faucets or plastic bottles at the supermarket. There are so many water filtration products out there on the market such as the LifeSaver Jerrycan and the Lifestraw Flex gravity fed water filter that you can use to safely filter water from natural sources. It might take a little longer to fill your tank up using this method, but having a backup on board in case you can't find clean water might let you sleep a littler sounder at night.

The Katadyn BeFree water filter bottle is a great product to take with you on walks or to make sure you have a method of keeping hydrated should you break down. At 1 liter, it's not ideal to use for filling up your water tank, but it's small enough to take with you to a water source a short trek away should the worst happen and you become stranded.

# Making the most of solar energy

I spent a lot of time talking about how to calculate your needs for solar energy and installing solar panels in Chapters 8 and 9, but it's not just a case of sticking them on the roof of your van and hoping for the best. Solar panels, as you probably are fully aware of after my constant rambling about them, use photovoltaic cells to convert the sun's rays into electricity. That means that they need sunlight and not just daylight to work properly.

If, for example, you are parked in a dense forest but need to top up your batteries, the limited sunshine under the shady boughs of the trees isn't going to be enough. Your panels need to be out of the shade and in direct sunlight, which means you should always bear in mind where you are parking during the day.

**TIP**

It sounds simple, I know, but sometimes the decision of securing a perfect camping spot can outweigh the need to do "basic van life admin" like topping up your batteries. Using the forest scenario again, consider parking on the outskirts of the forest or finding a large open gap in the trees so that your panels can soak up the sunlight. This might mean you have to reverse your van in line with the movement of the sun from time to time to keep your panels in sunlight, but that's a small price to pay for free energy!

## KEEPING YOUR SOLAR PANELS CLEAN

If you live in a rainy country, then chances are good your solar panels are going to get a nice rinse every now and again. Still, just like with every glass surface, and especially if you live in an arid climate with a lot of sand or dust, they're going to need cleaning by hand every now and again. Keeping your panels clean means that the sun doesn't have to fight through a layer of grease and grime to hit those all-important cells, making your panels much more efficient at converting light into electricity.

I traveled with a set of ladders in the back of my van for this very purpose and for cleaning the skylight I installed above the kitchen area. If you don't have space to store ladders, telescopic or otherwise, then consider attaching some ladders to your back door to create an access point onto the roof. This is much safer than trying to lean off a nearby wall with a sponge skewered onto the end of a broom handle, which is definitely what I used to do before I bought myself some ladders.

Chapter **17**

# Working Remotely from a Tiny Traveling Home

The idea of giving everything up and living on a shoestring budget may seem idyllic, but it's not always possible. In most cases, we still need to have a source of income dripping into our bank accounts whether we're living in a van in one place or traveling the world.

Perhaps you're torn between traveling and building a solid career that will stand you in good stead for years to come, or maybe you're sick of being an electrician and want to carve miniature bears out of driftwood for a living. Throughout the course of this chapter, you discover tricks, tips, and tools you need to take your job on the road or start a new career altogether. That's right; no more water cooler small talk ever again!

## A Beginner's Guide to Working Remotely

So many people have said to me over the years, "I wish I could do what you do; working and traveling is the dream." Okay, so there might have been a couple of different variations on that theme, but the general gist has always been the same.

The thing is — and this is what I tell everyone I speak to about remote working — working freelance or taking a job on the road isn't an impossible feat or something that requires you to steal three spiritual stones from the jaws of vicious monsters (spot the Zelda nerd in the room). It's simply a case of picking a goal and working toward it, making the right — and sometimes tough — decisions along the way, and giving it everything you've got.

I know you didn't pick up this book for a history lesson about Sebastian Santabarbara's life (that's me, in case you only skim-read the cover), but I thought it might help to give you a little rundown as to how I started working remotely. Hopefully, this will prove that there's no hidden wizardry going on anywhere.

I was working as a marketing manager in a music venue (an alternative opening line to The Human League's "Don't You Want Me Baby") when the idea of converting a van came into my head. When I began converting my van and posting content to the Instagram account I had created, friends and family slowly got involved, followed closely by a wider following of camper van and travel enthusiasts.

Toward the end of the conversion process, a friend sent me a tweet about an online magazine that was looking for writers. I got in touch and wrote a sample article titled "The Hardest Bits About UK Van Life." The owner of the website loved it and asked if I wanted to write a few more articles, and then a few more, paid this time. Eventually, we built Van Clan into a profitable brand with over five million weekly readers, giving me an income while traveling and a platform that kickstarted my writing career.

I wrote those sample articles on my lunch breaks and after work, spending what time I could to prove to the owner of the website that I was dedicated and that he needed me on board. Five years later, we've traveled to America to test camper vans, set up sister companies, and built a strong friendship, all from a tweet and a couple of free articles.

Now, some of you might have read that and thought, "But I can't do that," and in some cases, that might be right. I could just have easily taken my job as a marketing manager on the road had I fought my case, but I understand that for laborers, police officers, or people who have to be in a specific site for their occupation, it might not be as easy as grabbing a laptop and hitting the road.

With that in mind, I delve into how to take a job on the road over the course of this next section, along with how to potentially leave your current job and pursue a life-long passion, turning it into a career that you can earn money from while traveling the world.

**REMEMBER**

Before you get too excited and call your boss to tell them to shove their job where the sun doesn't shine, just remember that it takes a while for you to get set up as a freelancer. What's more, if you think you might be able to take your existing job on the road with you, you're going to need your boss firmly on your side, so keep the cussing to a minimum, alright?

# Turning a Passion into a Career

I'm sure a lot of you have heard the following quote: "Choose a job you love, and you will never have to work a day in your life." What the quote doesn't say, however, is that when you do something you love for work, you will have to work not only during the day, but also in the evenings and on weekends, and you'll likely think about work while you're sleeping too. Turning a passion into a career requires a lot of dedication and hard work, but when you finally get to a point when you can breathe and stand back to look at what you have created, it will be, and is, incredibly worth it.

There's no other advice that I can give you here apart from the three P's: practice, perseverance, and patience.

*Practice* your craft to the point where you feel so confident in your abilities that you could explain to anyone what you do and not be afraid to show them a sample. If you're too nervous to show a stranger what you're working on or what you're creating, then you're not ready. That's okay though; just carry on practicing and creating, continually working toward that moment where you feel you're ready.

Once you are ready to send samples to people or put yourself out there on the web or in market stalls around the globe, you need to *persevere*. You're going to get knocked back; that's a fact that I want you to take on board right now. I've had so many rejection letters for novels that I've written that I could probably wallpaper a room with them, but you've got to keep going. It only takes one person to say yes, and that yes will come at some point.

**REMEMBER**

If you don't believe in your work, then no one else will. Keep trying and stay positive. Don't be afraid to fail either. Those who don't try fail automatically; failure is a part of life that we learn from, so give it your best shot and keep persevering.

Lastly, have *patience*. It can take publishers months to get back to you, companies weeks to decide on artwork, and more emails back and forth about an idea that ultimately never happens than you've had hot dinners. Stay patient and don't throw in the towel. Remember the first two Ps and all the work that you've put in to get to this point.

# Creating a Business That Travels with You

I love being my own boss, deciding my own hours and from where I'm going to write on a day-to-day basis. One of the best things about my working style is that all I ever need to write books or articles is my laptop, meaning that my business can travel with me wherever I go (see Figure 17-1).

**FIGURE 17-1:** Working from home is even better when you've got a fantastic view out of the door.

Okay, so I appreciate that it's a lot trickier to take your business on the road if you work at a very specific research facility or own a premises in your home town, but there are lots of other remote work options out there that you could pursue if you're fancying a change of direction.

If you're looking to start a new career on the road, then the world really is your oyster, especially if you fancy starting up a mollusk museum. Let's take a look at some of the career choices you could embark on by turning your passion into a veritable income.

## Writing

A natural option, and perhaps I'm biased a little bit here because this is technically what I'm doing right now, is writing. Have you ever had an idea for a story?

Perhaps you're passionate about pastry and want to start a cooking blog, or maybe you love video games and want to write for a games magazine?

If you have ideas in your mind and think that you can convey your passion for a subject through your words to an audience, then writing is one of the most accessible and creative expressions you can turn into a career. I've spoken with people who would consider a 3,000-word article on Super Mario or camper van toilets one of the toughest things in the world to complete, never mind a whole book. Still, everyone has something they are truly passionate about, and there will always be others out there who want to read about it.

## Writing a novel

If you're thinking of writing a fiction novel, then unfortunately it's not a cut and dry procedure or a guaranteed form of income. For fiction, you have to write the entire book before getting in touch with an agent, so that's not something that's going to start earning you money straightaway. There are plenty of resources out there like the *Writers & Artists Yearbook* that list literary agents who might be looking for a book in your field, and you can apply to them at your leisure.

Nonfiction books don't require you to write the whole manuscript, rather three sample chapters or so and a full chapter plan, including a literary bio of yourself and why you're the one who should be writing the book. So if your job is currently in biomechanics and you want to a nonfiction book about a specific part of your field or a comedic take on your work in the same vain as Adam Kay's *This Is Going To Hurt*, then you simply have to put your proposal across in a succinct way and seek out the right literary agents to contact. Check out Figure 17-2 for a shot of me working away.

## Setting up a blog

Setting up a blog is perhaps one of the easiest writing forms to get going, though again, it's going to take a while to gain traction. This is essentially how the online publications that I've written for and still write for got started, building a social following alongside creative and engaging written content about a subject you're passionate about.

## Writing for a magazine

I've already given you a little insight into how I got into writing for a magazine above. In many cases, working for free is going to be your get-in to a magazine or online publication, especially if you're a full-time writer. The main thing you need to do, and this is something I'm going to write again and again through this chapter, is to make that editor or that manager think that they can't live without you. Write such incredible content that they realize what an asset you are and a what a fool they would be to let you write for somebody else.

## Photography

Like writing, photography is another passion you can turn into a career. However, before we go any further, I want to address something I'm sure all photographers will be thinking right now: that it takes more than a good camera to be a photographer. You need to know how to use your machine, how to work with it to get the best out of it, how to create the best shots, and how best to capture the scene in front of you to really portray the wonder of what you're witnessing for millions of others who might potentially view your work.

The scene. That's the most important bit, after all. Picking an interesting subject or vista and capturing the nuances of what your eyes can see is what photography is all about, a moment frozen in time that can speak a thousand words and prompt a thousand more questions.

REMEMBER

Still, if you're not a photographer right now, there's no reason you can't become one. One thing you'll find in common with all the creative ventures I discuss in this section is that practice makes perfect, and if you're traveling in your van on weekends to beautiful places or have a penchant for getting up to see the sunrise in areas of natural beauty, then take your camera with you and seek out interesting shots.

Companies are always looking for travel pictures to go with their products or articles. More often than not, they don't have the time to get out there and take them themselves, so having someone on the books who can provide them with pictures of fantastic locations, both with or without their products in them, will be a pleasing notion. However, you don't have to be a product or nature photographer to make money on the road. I know a vanlifer who earns money by photographing Iron Man competitions throughout Europe, driving from location to location and snapping the event for the organizers before setting out to explore the local area and heading for the nearest hot spring or lake for a well-earned swim.

As with creating a portfolio of your writing samples if you wish to be hired as a writer, create a photography portfolio of work you have completed and send it to as many companies as you can find. Be prepared for rejections, and always ask for some feedback that could help you improve. Companies love a person with moxie, so don't give up and show that you're keen.

Check LinkedIn for companies looking for photographers. It's a great tool and has lots of interesting opportunities.

## Writing jingles

Do you play a musical instrument? Writing jingles for adverts is a great way of making money remotely. As long as you have a laptop, a digital audio workstation such as Logic Pro or Pro Tools, and a USB microphone or method of plugging your instrument into your laptop, you can create songs anywhere in the world.

Check websites like Fiverr or Craigslist for companies or individuals looking for jingles. Put together a portfolio of sample work for companies to review and send it to as many people as possible. Talk about the benefits of having a jingle for potential radio articles and speak to companies that put jingles together for everything from YouTube videos to instructional videos.

## Illustration

Whether you're a wizard with a pen and paper or a master at Procreate, people always need logos and original graphics for products.

What's usually the first thing people want to nail down when they start a new company? The answer is a logo — something they can use to identify their company on a website and to print on handmade products, business cards, the works. Websites like Fiverr are great places to kickstart your illustration work and eventually build a portfolio of paid work that you can show others.

## Woodworking

If you're skilled with a blade and an axe, then woodworking is a great passion that you can turn into a career while on the road. Think about it; you're going to travel to beautiful places abundant with fallen wood for you to pick up that is only going to go to waste. It would be rude not to make beautiful creations out of it! Whether carving spoons or making little creatures from bits of oak or cherry, being creative with wood is a great, hands-on way to earn money on the road.

If this is something you could see yourself getting into, then you'll need to get yourself some carving knives, scoops, and a good apron. Now that you have your inverter hooked up too, you should bring your jigsaw along to help with cutting wood you find into blanks for spoons, necklaces, ornaments, and more.

## Online content creator

For many vanlifers, the pull of the passive income is one that fills their eyes with dollar signs. The Van Life hashtag on Instagram has grown dramatically over the past couple of years, with people around the world taking to social media to document their travels and work with companies as influencers.

I know many successful content creators who make a living from YouTube, and they will tell you instantly that their income is anything but passive. Making videos for YouTube is hard work; it requires incredible commitment, hours spent planning fresh videos and editing footage, traveling to events, and taking every opportunity thrown at you. You need to upload around two videos per week for at least a couple of years before you start to see any real income coming into your bank account, and you need to stand out from the crowd in order to get those all-important subscribers too.

TIP

There are thousands of YouTube channels out there that follow people's lives and the happy experiences that they are having on the road, so if you want to make an impact, you need to come up with something fresh and exciting. Find a niche that hasn't been covered and capitalize on it. Perhaps you're planning a big road trip and visiting unusual features along the way, or maybe you're thinking about carrying out specific events on the road and documenting them.

## RECEIVING MAIL WHILE TRAVELING: THE WONDERFUL WORLD OF POSTE RESTANTE

There's a little-known secret out there that digital nomads and traveling creatives can tap into, and it's called poste restante. Now, I know this sounds like Postman Pat's French cousin, but in actual fact, it's a nifty little postal service that many wandering makers tap into while traveling the globe. The poste restante service, known as general delivery in North America, allows anyone who does not have a permanent address in the place where they are traveling to still receive mail on the go. By addressing parcels to participating post offices and using poste restante or the country's equivalent on the front of the parcel, vanlifers can collect their mail safe in the knowledge that it's being looked after by a (hopefully) friendly postmaster.

*Posso avere I miei pacchi, per favore?* (For anyone reading this book while traveling in Italy.)

Poste restante is a great service for creators to use if they need to send supplies ahead or to restock up on supplies from their home country while working abroad. It allows people to receive goods to review on blogs or to collaborate with other makers in the same field who are also living the same lifestyle on opposite sides of the globe.

So if you're thinking about running a screen printing or jewelry business that requires arts and crafts supplies, then poste restante is the answer!

The same goes for your Instagram account. You'll need to make a consistent effort to post the same number of pictures per day, every day. If you choose to post one shot or reel per day, then you need to make sure you keep to this schedule, using relevant hashtags and swapping and changing them to keep things fresh.

# Taking Your Existing Job on the Road

Don't worry; you don't *have* to suddenly become a guitarist or learn to draw like Quentin Blake to earn money on the road. During the COVID-19 pandemic, many companies discovered that work can be easily done from home, no matter whether your home is made from bricks and mortar or a metal box on wheels. So many businesses have reported increased productivity since remote-working practices were brought into place in many parts of the world back in 2020, and of course, thanks to programs like Zoom and Microsoft Teams, coworkers can meet whenever, wherever at the touch of a button.

If you do any job that's centered around a computer or in an office environment, then there's no reason why you shouldn't be able to take that job on the road with you. In this section, I use my own experience of when I worked in music venue management before embarking on my writing career, and discuss how I would turn that job into a remote position. For starters, think about the main tools you need for your day-to-day role. In my case, this would be:

>> A computer with access to the Internet

>> A phone

That's it!

Let's break this down a little bit. One of the main things many jobs require is a computer to write up documents, work on spreadsheets, send email to clients, and more. I imagine most of you reading this chapter now have access to at least a laptop, if not a laptop and a tablet, as well as a smartphone that you use to answer your email on a daily basis, and plan to have access to these tools while on the road.

Thanks to the Internet, you can log into your company's intranet remotely from anywhere in the world, often gaining access to your work files and programs in the process. It doesn't matter whether you're a coder or an accountant, as long as you can access the system, you can still do your work perfectly.

As you discover in Chapter 14, there are many ways to get access to the Internet in your camper van, but hotspotting from a mobile phone is by far the easiest and most readily available. Providing you have an internet connection on your phone, you can upload documents, log into video chats with other members of the team, speak to clients, and do everything that you would have done while sitting in the office.

Your role will stay the same; it's just the view from your window that's going to change!

Speaking of your phone, if you have signal for internet connectivity, then you'll have signal for calls too. You can still speak to other businesses to set up advertising deals, contact clients or promoters, book customers, or troubleshoot problems with the program you're using with an IT wizard on the other end of the line.

The bottom line is that I know you could do your job from the middle of a Turkish mountain range, and so do you. The person you need to convince, however, is your boss. In this next section, I discuss how to present your case for remote working to your boss or the company as a whole.

No matter what happens, the worst thing they can say is no. No doesn't mean you have to be incredibly embarrassed or worry about finding a new job; it just means no. It might also mean "not now," though it might be a possibility in the future. But let's not get bogged down with that. You're only interested in one thing right now, and that's getting an amendment to your contract to say you can do that accounting spreadsheet with your toes buried in the sand and some sunscreen rubbed into your back.

## Approaching your boss about working from the road

Thanks to many companies adopting a work-from-home policy in recent times and seeing the benefits of a content and relaxed workforce, it might well prove easier than you thought to convince your bosses that you + travel = consistent output and an employee for life.

Over the course of this section, I delve into how to prepare, deliver, and ultimately convert your job into a remote position, all without breaking a sweat. Unless your job requires you to sweat; then I can't make any promises.

Making the case to your boss is all about diplomacy and doing your research thoroughly. You only get one shot at putting your point across and making the initial proposal for taking your work out of the office and into the big wide world, so make it count.

### Gathering your research

Fail to prepare, prepare to fail. That's the annoying phrase that used to be emblazoned on the windows and doors of my high school during exam season.

I guess it did its job, as it's stuck with me to this day. And in this instance — even more so than when 16-year-old Seb was getting ready to take his math exam — it's incredibly relevant.

Before you think about strolling up to your boss's office and slamming a 50-page dossier on the desk in a kind of work-place mic-drop scenario, you need to do some proper research. I'm not talking about which places would have the best view for your Zoom calls either; I'm talking about statistics on people who work while traveling, graphs showing productivity predictions, and charts with proposed work schedules and practices you will put in place to make sure your workload is done with the best possible standards.

**TIP**

One of the most impressive forms I've ever whipped out in a job interview is a SWOT analysis. It's essentially a piece of paper split into four sections covering strengths, weaknesses, opportunities, and threats. In this case, you're going to do a SWOT analysis on the proposed change to the business — you leaving to travel the world.

Let's take your strengths first. This is a good chance to show you have thought about the strengths that you bring to the company and how much of an asset you are. Lay this bit on thick; remember you're trying to sell yourself here. Talk about how you being in a certain place might help with international ties or creating the content I spoke about in the previous sections. Use your travels and new lifestyle as something that will help your productivity and bring something back to the company.

Don't see weaknesses as a bad point either; this is a chance for you to show that you've identified areas that you need to improve in and for you to bring it back around to say how you feel your new lifestyle could help to address these problems. The same goes for opportunities — how you splitting your working hours while seeing the world or spending more time with your family can only be good for the company.

The threats segment is a good chance for you to preempt everything your boss might come back with — every "what if" question — to show that you have given everything prior thought and come up with back-up scenarios for every problem you might face.

## Preparing your case

The main word I want you to take on board for this section is *meticulous*. Leave no stone unturned, dot every i and cross every t. Once you've done your research and are confident you have "all your ducks in a row," or everything in order as most people would say, then it's time to put everything together into a carefully structured proposal that will blow your boss away.

**TIP**

Make a copy of your research, SWOT analysis, and any other relevant information that you feel your boss needs to see so that you can give it to them in person, all displayed in a neat binder. Nothing says "I'm prepared" like a binder handout, and it will also give your boss a chance to take a look back over your proposal at a later date when deliberating or bringing the concept up with people higher up the company.

The key here is to put yourself in the position of your boss. What would your boss want to know? What kind of questions might they ask? Your job here is to answer any queries or questions before they arise, to show unequivocally that you have covered every scenario and that the results are incredibly positive.

The harsh truth is that, as much as your boss may like you and enjoy your quirky quips at the office parties, all they really care about is your work output and if you're doing your job properly. Whether you're sitting at a desk in Arkansas or writing from a mountain in Azerbaijan doesn't concern them; all they care about is making sure that when they report to *their* boss, they can say that everything is running smoothly and that there's nothing to worry about.

As long as you can convey that nothing is going to change apart from the company saving money on electricity from you not charging up your phone and laptop all the time, then you should be onto a winner.

## Presenting your case

Think about how you are going to approach your boss. Picture the scene: You approach your boss's desk, you sit down opposite them, and you open your mouth to ask a question that could potentially change your life.

Think about your language and your choice of words. Be respectful yet optimistic about what this could mean for you and the company. Your boss will appreciate your passion for the idea and your commitment to the company in not wanting to leave all together, a factor that would ultimately create a time-consuming hiring process to find a replacement for you.

Don't waltz into their office and stick your feet on the desk while proclaiming that you've outgrown the losers you work with and are looking for pastures new, all while chewing gum. For once that niche reference is not something I did, but it *is* the kind of thing that would get you fired faster than a speeding bullet.

If your boss is a little on the fence about whether to go ahead with the plan or not, then consider suggesting a trial period of a predetermined number of weeks to see if anything changes with regard to your work output. This is a bit of a safety blanket for you both and a chance for each party to discover how this new working arrangement might work without immediately making any big decisions.

# Converting your job into a remote job

When you've got the go-ahead from your boss (that's right; *when*, not *if*), the next step is simply to head to your new office, situated either in bed with the rear doors open looking out at one portion of a beautiful landscape, or at a table by your sliding door looking out at the opposite side of said stunning vista, and start working! Of course, you might need to do a few things before leaving the office, including signing that birthday card for Janice in accounting.

To make sure your move from a fixed location to remote working goes as smoothly as possible, take the time to double-check that you have all your passwords, intranet logins, and any affiliate codes, templates, or anything else integral to your role stored away somewhere on your laptop.

Don't just abandon ship and not tell your clients, either. Spend time reassuring the people you work with that you'll still be contactable and that nothing with their accounts, books, or any element of their working relationship with you is going to change bar the sounds of birdsong in the background of your Zoom chats instead of next door's vacuum cleaner, or the tranquil sounds of someone banging the photocopier to try to solve a paper jam.

TIP

If you are planning on working in your camper, make sure you have made the necessary adjustments to your electrical calculations back in Chapter 8 to ensure your batteries can handle any extra charging or use of external devices that you might need for your role.

## Finding examples in your field

Don't forget that the van life community is a thriving global neighborhood with many different moving parts, and you should definitely seize the opportunity to chat with other people in your line of work to ask how their transition into remote working went. One of the best places to find people who have made the same jump as you by taking their existing job on the road is social media, namely Instagram. Through Instagram I've come into contact with doctors and nurses, flight attendants, coders, architects, and more, who work remotely while living in vans, all traversing the globe in tiny homes.

Not only will talking with others help you to feel more confident in taking the plunge and prove that your remote-working dreams are entirely plausible, but it will also help you to connect with people who could one day potentially become clients, business partners, or just friends whom you can bounce ideas off of while on the road.

Just don't forget to invite me to your rolling office Christmas party, alright? I'll bring the red cups.

# 4

# The Part of Tens

Discover ten van life kitchen hacks that make cooking in your van a piece of cake.

Find out what items to consider bringing along with you to complement your van life adventure, from portable speakers, camping chairs, and an extra battery power pack to board games, beach towels, and more.

Get an idea of monthly costs you might incur when living in a van part or full time, and how to keep those costs to a minimum.

# Chapter 18

# Ten Van Life Kitchen Hacks

The way each one of us lives our van lives might be different in terms of how outdoorsy we are or how long we intend to spend in our vans. But one thing remains constant: We've all got to eat. The kitchen was the epicenter of my van. Whether I was whipping up smoothies for breakfast, making sushi for lunch, or cooking up hearty stews with fresh bread for dinner, it's one of the places where I spent the most time in my build and definitely the place that housed the most equipment.

If, like me, you like the notion of cooking up your favorite meals while parked by a lake or halfway along a mountain pass, then these ten kitchen hacks should make your van life cooking exploits a heck of a lot easier.

## Use an Omnia Oven

If you're a huge fan of freshly cooked bread or roast potatoes (and let's face it, who isn't?), you don't need an oven to be able to enjoy them in your camper van. The Omnia Oven is the perfect solution for cooking all your favorite oven-based meals right on your stovetop, and it stores away in a handy carrying pouch when not in use. Over the years, I've cooked everything from cinnamon buns to shepherd's pies in my Omnia Oven. You can either cook straight in the metal dish it comes with or use the different silicon molds available.

TIP

I used one silicon mold for savory items such as olive and sundried tomato bread and another for making sweet items such as the chocolate cake I made on a weekly basis . . . which thinking back now probably can't have been that good for me. Omnia also makes a bun mold that is great for making buns and small Yorkshire puddings.

## Use a Fruit Hammock to Keep Your Workspace Clear

When you live in a van, worktop space can get cluttered far too easily. If you want to eat fruit and vegetables but not have a big bowl taking up a large portion of pizza-prepping space, then attach a fruit hammock to your wall! I know, a banana hammock is something you probably didn't think you'd ever own, but this one is actually a practical solution for storing your fruit and vegetables, and in my case, crisps and biscuits, while keeping the worktop below clear.

TIP

Bananas release ethane that makes other fruits ripen much quicker, so if you're storing other fruits alongside your bananas in your fruit hammock, then they will go off much faster than usual. I went through far too many clementines in Spain before I realized this. On the plus side, if you have a piece of fruit that you want to ripen more quickly so that you can chomp it down, then place it in a drawer with your bananas overnight and it'll be ready the next day!

## Glue Jam Jar Lids to the Bottom of Your Spice Rack or Cupboard

Unless you're planning on creating a contemporary art piece on your wall above your worktop and below your overhead cupboard, then it really is wasted space that you could do something with, such as storing spices and other dried goods. By gluing jam jar lids to the bottom of your cupboard or spice rack, you can screw jars filled with pasta, rice, spices, flour, or any other dried good into place, keeping them secure while driving and also creating that contemporary art piece I spoke about at the same time!

# Create Hidden Undercounter Storage

This is a bit of a niche hack, but hear me out. I made an L-shaped kitchen in my van so that I had as much worktop space as possible. The problem was that apart from the gas bottle and drop-out vent that I placed under the counter against the wall of the van, I couldn't get much storage out of the corner of the L.

The solution? I cut a portion of my worktop out and attached hinges to it to make a flip-up piece of worktop with a hidden compartment underneath. I used this little hidey-hole to store my expandable draining board and large kitchen tools such as my tongs, rolling pin, and the gigantic pancake flipper I bought on a whim one pancake day.

# Create a Cutting Block with the Extra Worktop Cut Out for Your Sink

I meant what I said when I wrote that worktop space is incredibly important in a van. It's basically the holy grail when it comes to cooking on the road, and I guarantee you'll end up cooking yourself into a little corner without even realizing it until your bowl of chickpeas topples onto the floor. To help solve this lack of counterspace, I kept the slice of worktop that I cut out for my sink and used it as a cutting block that fits back into my sink for extra worktop space when I'm not using the faucet. Is that genius or what?

When you cut out the hole for your sink, keep the chunk of wood from the middle, resize it, and slot it in the top of your sink like a giant plug to create even more worktop space when you're not using your sink.

**TIP**

Remember to seal the wood with food-safe worktop sealant if you're going to prep food on top of it.

# Use an Expandable Draining Board to Dry Dishes

Perhaps some of you won't have even realized that expandable draining boards existed and now you've read this word three times in the past 30 seconds. Joseph Joseph makes a great unit that when extended has a place to dry cups and a section for drying plates, pans, and cutlery.

The great thing about these expandable racks is that you can either open the spout to let the water run down into your sink or keep the spout closed and, providing you've used eco-friendly washing-up liquid, dispose of your wastewater outside.

TIP

Some of you might be thinking, "Just use a tea towel," but draining your dishes first means you won't be carrying a sopping wet towel around for days with you. It's not as easy to dry towels in a van, especially in the middle of winter, so try not to get you tea towels too soggy and they'll dry a heck of a lot quicker.

## Wipe Dishes Before Washing

How many of you just leave the tap running when you're washing up? We're all guilty of it when we live in a house because water just keeps on flowing. But in a van, every drop of water counts, especially when you're living off grid and not near a water source that you can filter.

By wiping plates down with a paper towel first, you reduce the amount of washing that you actually have to do. I could manage to wash plates with a half pump from my foot pump to "pre-rinse" and then a full pump after to rinse the suds off.

REMEMBER

I know this sounds like quite a pedantic hack, but how much water you have is one of the main factors that dictates how long you can stay in a certain place, so go easy on the washing up and conserve your reserves!

## Use the Cab Area to Prove Bread Dough

Thanks to that big ol' windscreen at the front of your van, your cab often ends up being one of the warmest places in your van. That means that it's the perfect place for proving dough when you're cooking bread or making pizzas and calzones. I once left some bread to prove in the front of my van and came back to find the dough pushing the top of the container clean off like something from a horror movie!

# Use a RidgeMonkey to Make Pancakes, Yorkshire Puddings, and More

If you haven't already guessed from this short chapter or all the other heavy hints that I drop in the main body of this book, I get hungry quite a lot! I find cooking a good way of relaxing, and getting to make the food that I grew up with on the other side of the world while living off grid is something that will never grow old.

Even without an oven, you can use a RidgeMonkey sandwich toaster to make a large Yorkshire pudding or a toad in the hole. (That's sausages in Yorkshire pudding batter for anyone who didn't grow up in the U.K.) I've also made pizzas, frittatas, enchiladas, and lots of pancakes in the RidgeMonkey, too, as well as my world-famous fried eggplant, pesto, cheese, olive, and sundried tomato toasties. Okay, they're not world famous yet, but after this book has been out a while, they might be!

# Make a Meal Plan Before Shopping

My final kitchen hack is to make a meal plan before going shopping. Hitting the grocery store while hungry is a terrible idea, especially when you live in a van and have limited space for food storage. The solution: Make a meal plan and decide what ingredients you are going to need before you even set foot in the store. For example, if you're making a pasta dish with broccoli and mushrooms on Monday, use the leftovers in a stir-fry on Wednesday. If you're roasting a butternut squash in your Omnia Oven for butternut squash risotto on Tuesday, then make sure to leave some aside for a curry on Thursday or Friday.

REMEMBER

Making a meal plan reduces the amount of waste that you throw away each week. It's also a really useful way of budgeting. Cooking meals in your tiny home is much cheaper than going out every night, and if you can save money by making multiple meals out of the ingredients you buy, then you can spend your hard-earned cash on other important things like fuel or exciting excursions.

Chapter **19**

# Ten Essential Items for the Perfect Road Trip

A re you ready to hit the open road? I'm betting at this point you're already making a Pinterest board of places you want to visit and researching how much ferries and van shipping costs so that you can traverse the entire globe.

Packing for a road trip is a fine art; you don't want to forget the important stuff, but you also don't want to be tripping over novelty gnomes or other items you have no use for. In this chapter, I share with you my top items to bring on a road trip to complement your adventures, all picked up from my experiences as a full-time vanlifer!

## Portable Bluetooth Speaker

Music and road-tripping go hand in hand. Whether you get pumped up listening to metal music or enjoy relaxing to the sweet sounds of jazz, having a portable Bluetooth speaker on board that you can take out of your van on a walk to the beach or to a firepit with newfound friends is essential to get the party going.

I listened to a lot of podcasts and audiobooks while out on the road too, and having a portable speaker meant that I could clearly hear everything that was going on from any point of the van, especially if I was in the back doing my electrical system checks or spring cleaning.

# Camping Chairs and Beach Towels

Nature is beautiful, but it can also be uncomfortable. Taking some comfortable camping chairs with you is a must, especially if you're planning on working outside on a laptop or doing something creative like drawing or carving. I took some moon chairs with me on the road that were extremely comfortable, perfect for an afternoon snooze in the sun.

In addition, beach towels are a great idea to prevent getting sand on all your clothes if you're sitting at the beach. Sure, rolling around in the sand is fun, but it's also a surefire way of bringing sand back into your van and eventually your bed (it's going to happen at some point, so be prepared for it).

# Dustpan and Brush

Boring, but after all that sand, you're going to thank me for sliding this one in-between the exciting stuff!

# Omnia Oven

I don't think I could go on a road trip without the Omnia Oven anymore. What is a world without homemade cake to order? Whipping up fresh bread on the side of a mountain never gets old, and with an Omnia Oven and the necessary ingredients you always have a food staple no matter how far off-grid you are. The Omnia Oven is perfect for cooking up everything from cinnamon buns to beef stew. I never travel without one.

# Scrubba Wash Bag and a Clothes Line

Washing your clothes while off-grid doesn't have to be a chore. I used the Scrubba wash bag for everything from socks to T-shirts while out on the road, and then ran a clothesline around my seats, through the hatch into the living area, and around my guitar hanger in order to create enough space to hang everything to dry. I definitely received some odd looks — all from people who were just jealous they didn't have fresh socks drying on their steering wheel . . . probably.

# Battery Power Pack

Power packs aren't just a great for working outside away from your van. Keeping a power pack topped, be it a smaller battery bank or a bigger pack like the PPT Powerpack 450+, means that you have power should anything go wrong with your in-built electrical system. You can charge them up using an external solar panel or by plugging them into the plugs linked to your inverter and leisure batteries.

On overtly sunny days, I would charge portable pocket power banks in the van for taking on long walks with me. At least if anything went wrong, such as I became injured or got lost, I could charge my phone up to call for help or use the translation features to converse with locals to find out how to get back to my van.

# Water Flask

Don't take plastic bottles everywhere with you! A good metal flask like the Hydro Flask that can cope with hot drinks and keep cold drinks cold for long time periods is all you need while out on the road.

TIP

If you think you're going to spend a lot of time off-grid and not going near towns, then consider getting a portable water filtration system to filter your own water while out on the road.

REMEMBER

Regardless of how long you are planning on staying off-grid, always take more water with you than you think is necessary. I carried two extra 10-liter water cannisters in the back of my van in case of emergencies, and I was always glad I did when the weather was incredibly hot.

# Portable Solar Shower

Carrying extra water, as I note in the previous section, also comes in handy for use with a portable solar shower. While it's nice to freshen up in hot springs and lakes using eco-friendly soaps, getting a good shower while looking out at a beautiful vista never gets old. Portable showers provide just as good a clean without faffing around with plumbing a shower into your van and are a good item to have onboard just in case you find yourself off-grid and in the need of a freshen-up.

# Board Games and Cards

Even if you're traveling on your own, nothing beats a game of patience while listening to Stephen Fry reading *Harry Potter* on your Bluetooth speaker! On an optimistic level, it's quite likely that you will come across other vanlifers on your travels who will want to chat and hang out during the evening. I've met some of my best friends from traveling in a van and spent hours playing games like Ticket to Ride and Exploding Kittens with them in car parks and beachfront park-ups. If you have games, friends will come.

I connected with a lot of vanlifers on Instagram and met up with a few on the road. Many of them were also from the U.K. and were out traveling in places nearby to me.

REMEMBER

If you're unsure about meeting someone, arrange to meet in a public place where you feel safe.

# GoPro Camera

What's the point in getting your phone out all the time while you're on a road trip? You don't want to see notifications about work emails or that someone in one of your WhatsApp groups got a high score on Candy Crush while on the train. Take a GoPro camera out with you and leave your phone off in your bag where it belongs. Plus, sticking a GoPro underwater to take pics of jellyfish feels less scary than sticking your phone under the waves.

# Chapter **20**

# Ten Tips for Budgeting While on the Road

B elieve me when I say that living in a van is not expensive. However, it doesn't matter whether you are planning the road trip of a lifetime, considering a short-term off-grid adventure, or thinking about living in a van in one place for a long length of time, there are still costs related to van life that you need to cover on a monthly basis. In this chapter, I break down how much money I spent per month while traveling full time in my van to help you determine how much you want to budget for your next van life road trip.

I spent 15 months continuously traveling around Europe and visited 14 countries during that time. From two weeks in Slovenia to three months in Sardinia, I spent my time wild camping in beautiful locations and soaking up as much of the local culture as possible while writing books and articles along the way. It was an incredible time and a journey that taught me how to think big while living small and by my means.

What follows is a snapshot of my monthly van life costs while traveling around Europe, along with information about how to keep said costs to a minimum while enjoying and experiencing everything your road trip has to offer. While cost types might vary if you opt to stay in campsites as opposed to boondocking or fancy traveling with a pet in tow, my experiences will give you a general idea of just how little you can spend while living the van life full time.

# Food, Glorious Food

Of course, being of Italian origin, I'm jumping right into what I spent on food. Food might be an essential part of daily life in order for us to survive first and foremost, but to me, it's so much more. I love cooking food almost as much as I love eating the food I have cooked. Cooking fresh and buying local ingredients from the places you travel through is one of the best ways to immerse yourself in local culture, and if there's one thing I didn't have to worry about while on my travels, it was going hungry.

I hit the nail on the head with cooking fresh: If you're going out for food every night while on the road, then your budget will skyrocket faster than you can spell taramasalata.

TIP

The best way to keep costs down when you enter the supermarket is by sticking to the shopping list code: "If it ain't on the list, it ain't going in the cart!" Better yet, consider making a food plan and map out what you are going to eat that week to avoid wasting ingredients.

I spent around £30 ($36) on food every seven to ten days, and that stocked up my drawers with dried goods, beans, chocolate, crisps, fruit, and filled the fridge to the brim!

If you haven't been inventive with food before, then now is the time to start trying your hand at new stuff. When in Rome, eat pizza. But when in Slovenia, it's fine to make your own calzones in the XL RidgeMonkey or the Omnia Oven. Similarly, an all-you-can-eat sushi bill might set you back $80 with drinks included, when boiling sushi rice and wrapping your own sushi-grade fish in seaweed doesn't cost nearly as much, and you can make as much as you want!

TIP

I'm not telling you how to live your life, but buying alcohol also pumps your bills up dramatically too. I drink and I eat meat, but I lived on a predominantly fish- and vegetable-based diet while traveling full time, and I had beer on special occasions. When you have a small fridge, you have to prioritize your refreshments, and Pepsi won every time.

**Average monthly food total: £120 ($144)**

# Fuel

Having the ability to take your house anywhere in the world is amazing, but it comes with a cost. More specifically, the cost of fuel as you pass through regions, states, and countries. When I first began living in a van, I lived in the same city for 13 months. I parked in about four different locations, each with cool code names that I allocated to them to make me feel like I was part of the A-Team. As such, I hardly spent anything on fuel, but once you start crossing state lines or powering along highways through the mountains, you'll see that fuel meter depleting much faster.

Fuel prices fluctuate more than the state of the weather. In mainland Europe, fuel is much cheaper than in the U.K., and I found gas prices in the U.S. to be much cheaper again. Like food, this cost can't be avoided if you want to move around and see the world, but it doesn't mean that you can't budget accordingly and account for your fuel just like you would every other aspect of your van life journey.

TIP

One of the best ways to save on fuel is to slow down and stay in places longer. I know that sounds like a cop-out, but it's true. To make your trip last longer, spend more time in beautiful places and less time on the road. I spent three months in Sardinia, often parking in beautiful locations for eight to ten days at a time, writing on the beach with my feet in the ocean. As Treebeard says so often, "don't be hasty."

**Average monthly fuel total: £150 ($180)**

# Tolls

Whatever satnav you choose to use, make sure you have the toll-free option selected. The TomTom Go Camper GPS navigation system is one of the best for picking scenic routes away from toll roads, and I can honestly say that I've seen some of the best places en route because of it. Tolls might not seem that bad when they're the odd one here and there, but I once spent €140 ($148) in one day on tolls in France, and that cut me deep. Google and Apple Maps have toll-free route options, but be warned that these apps don't always pick van-friendly routes.

**Average monthly tolls total: £30 ($36)**

# Everyday Bills

But I don't live in a house anymore, why am I paying bills?

Well, the amount of bills you do have to pay while living in your van will undoubtedly have gone down, but there are costs to companies that can't be avoided, especially if you're planning on working on the road like me. The good news is that thanks to your solar panel setup, you won't have to pay an electricity bill anytime soon, and propane or butane gas bottles are as cheap as chips too. I ran a 12-volt refrigerator on free electricity for almost five years, which I think you'll agree is pretty good going.

Let's start with the mobile phone bill. Yes, you can go off-grid, but your mother or uncle will still want to know where you are and if you're safe once every three days (or three hours, in my case). My phone plan was with a company called VOXI. For £20 ($24) I received 45GB of data to use for streaming and sending email, and all my social data (Instagram, Twitter, WhatsApp, and so on) was free.

**TIP**

Download your shows when streaming rather than watching them in real time. Downloading uses less data and won't cause you to run out out mid-month.

Apart from accessing the Internet and making calls, the main bills I racked up were for Netflix and Spotify. Okay, there are going to be some of you who have thrown this book down in disgust at the thought of my sitting inside watching *Seinfeld* instead of being out and about in the countryside, but hear me out.

I am a very outdoorsy person; I spend a lot of time walking, paddleboarding, reading in forests . . . you get the idea. Still, there are times where all a person wants to do is just kick back and watch *Lord of the Rings* with a cup of tea, and that's totally fine. As I've said before, there will be times when you are ill, and there will be times when you are tired or just don't want to get out of bed. Don't feel as though you have to follow expectations set through the view of every vanlifer on Instagram; how many of those accounts show what it's like to have the flu in a van or talk about days when your mental health is bad even when you're in a beautiful location? Go at your own pace and make your own schedule factoring in downtime to recharge.

**Average monthly bills total: £44 ($53)**

# Washing Clothes and Showering

In the half-decade I lived in a van, nobody ever said that I smelled or had dirty clothes. That wasn't because I kept away from people; I just looked after my personal hygiene like any normal person would.

Getting water to fill up solar shower bags or washing clothes isn't as hard as you might think. In pretty much every country other than the U.K., it's easy to find a tap to fill up from, making washing clothes and your body a simple task.

When showering, either leave your solar shower bag in the sun to warm up or fill with two warm kettles and one cold for the optimum water temperature.

If you can plan a visit to a hot spring or a place where hot spring water is rife, then earmark that as a spot to wash your body and clothes. I stopped at a town in Sardinia that had an old outdoor laundry spot that was still used by all the locals. And I mean *all* the locals; one regular was a laundry company that brought people's belongings there to clean. I guess free hot water is free hot water!

When it comes to washing clothes, you can't go wrong with the Scrubba wash bag, a portable washing machine big enough for underwear, T-shirts, and shorts. It's essentially a plastic bag with a washboard in it and requires a bit of elbow grease when scrubbing, but with some hot water and detergent, you can clean smaller items with ease without having to spend a fortune in the laundromat. That being said, spending £20 ($25) a month at the laundromat isn't going to break the bank, especially when food smells can quickly seep into larger items like bedding and blankets.

**Average monthly washing total: £20 ($24)**

# Gas (Propane, Butane, LPG)

I did a lot of cooking while out on the road and usually changed a 15-kilogram butane bottle every six months. And when I say cooking, I don't just mean whipping up pasta either; I baked bread and cakes in my Omnia Oven and often cooked using three pans at a time on my Vango three-hob burner, making everything from katsu curry to risotto, donburi dishes, and more. The average cost of a 15-kilogram butane bottle here in the U.K. is £45 ($54).

TIP

Your costs will go up if you have to keep buying new regulators for any different countries you might pass through, so make sure to grab the relevant regulators or a conversion kit before you set off on your travels.

**Average monthly gas total: £7.50 ($9) (Yearly cost of £90 [$107])**

# Specialized Health Insurance and Breakdown Coverage

No one wants to think about the worst-case scenario all the time, but it's a good idea to have a plan in place in case something does go wrong, giving you peace of mind while you're out and about on your travels.

Insurance is key when traveling in a van — both medical insurance and vehicle insurance. Some companies, like SafetyWing, cater to vanlifers and nomads without fixed addresses too, offering medical care and custom policies tailored to your travels. Explorer Backpacker Travel Insurance is another good option too, especially if you're thinking about getting sucked into some winter or water sports while you're out exploring.

REMEMBER

Don't forget that vehicle insurance is an essential part of living and traveling in a van too. I paid for my camper van policy up front, and if you've been reading this book cover to cover, then you'll already know that it only cost me a couple of hundred pounds for the entire year.

TIP

Shop around when trying to find the best quote and don't be afraid to tell other companies the prices you have received already; everyone wants to outdo the competition, and a good deal is never far from reach.

Lastly, I want to speak about breakdown coverage. Some countries don't have any options for roadside recovery or onward travel, but I took the plunge and signed up for the RAC European Breakdown Cover package before heading out on my adventure and boy am I glad. When my diesel pump was being fixed, my RAC coverage paid for three weeks of Airbnb stays as well as train travel for me to keep exploring while my van was in an Italian garage, all for a one-off cost of £320 ($382). In my case, that cost was for travel away from home. If you're just staying in one city, then expect to pay around £10 ($12) per month on average.

**Average monthly insurance and breakdown total: £40 ($48)**

# Social Activities

It's very likely you'll make some friends while out on the road; likeminded souls tend to flock together, and that's definitely true with the van life community. New neighbors you park up next to on a night often become friends come the morning, which in turn leads to heading out into town for meals or traveling to tourist attractions together.

What starts off as a quick trip to get ice cream can also lead to one of your party going to a restaurant at 11:50 p.m. to get pizzas while you sit around a firepit. And if that sounds niche, that's exactly what happened when I met my friends Dave and Ilse (everyone needs a pizza-grabbing Dave in their group).

TIP

Cooking fresh and making BBQ food is the key to keeping costs down when eating with friends. Turn cooking into a fun activity for everyone to enjoy and keep the leftovers for lunch by the ocean the following day. Also, if heading to an attraction, look for a group ticket price to keep costs down or check which days have cheaper admission.

**Average monthly social life expenditure total: £30 ($36)**

# Nonessential Items

I could also call this section, "Things you don't need but would like" to encompass the stuff that you don't factor into your grocery shopping but that still has a place in your van.

I took lots of Polaroid pictures while out and about and often had to replace the batteries in the LED lights over my bed, so film and batteries were something I sought out on a semi-regular basis.

TIP

Buy rechargeable AA batteries. You'll be saving the planet and saving money at the same time!

**Average monthly nonessential items total: £4 ($5)**

# Tourist Attractions

I'm going to be honest here: I'm not one for tourist attractions. I don't need to see the inside of another stately home when the gardens outside are way more impressive. That being said, there are some things that you just can't miss. What would be the point in going to Lisbon without seeing St. Georges Castle or to central California without going into Yosemite National Park?

More often than not, it's the actual city parking that costs more than the attractions themselves. There are tons of free things to do in cities (check out Atlas Obscura for the place you are visiting), but getting to them can be tricky. Use apps like Park4Nite to find places to park on the outskirts of cities and utilize public transport to get into the center. For two weeks I did this in Barcelona and used the train to get into the city. I bought two weekly rail cards for a total of around €20 ($20).

**Average monthly tourist attractions total: £10 ($12) every other month**

## COSTS SUMMARY

For my travels, I spent an average of £450 ($538) a month to travel full time and see the world. Compared to a package holiday that might cost you £500 ($598) per person for a week, I think you'll agree that van life is an affordable way of seeing the world.

Of course, if you're planning on just living in one place and not traveling around, then your costs will almost halve. Van life is what you make it, and you can live as frugally or as extravagantly as you like. The important thing is that you have fun and don't miss out on exciting opportunities that you want to embark upon along the way.

I always recommend storing up a stockpile of cash before heading out on your adventures. That's why I worked and lived in a van in the same place for 13 months before setting off on the road. I knew then that, if there was an emergency or if work dried up, I had a slush fund to dip into to help me out. It takes the pressure off and means you can go a little over budget here and there if you need to.

# Index

## A

absorbed glass mat (AGM) batteries, 110

AC unit
  BTU ratings, 229–230
  choosing, 229–230
  installing, 230–233
  powering, 230

activities compatible with van life
  art, 260
  board games and cards, 340
  cooking, 261–262
  gaming, 260
  music, 259–260
  playing instruments, 260–261
  TV, 258–259
  wood carving, 260
  working out, 260
  yoga, 259

AGM (absorbed glass mat) batteries, 110

aires, 303–304

airflow and heating, 238

allemansrätten, 305

aluminum floor trim, 70

aluminum sheeting, chimney, 240

amps, 119, 126–127

angled L brackets, 204

AWG chart, 128–129

awnings, 253

## B

bathroom
  emptying grey and black waste, 282–284
  managing waste, 281–282
  odors, 280–281
  showers
    budgeting and, 345
    Hozelock PortaShower, 278
    overview, 277–278
    portable solar shower, 340
    RinseKit, 277
    RoadShower, 278
  toilets, 278–282

batteries
  calculating storage and supply, 123–124
  hooking up terminal clip connectors on, 138–139
  installing, 141–143
  types of, 108–110
  wiring up to solar charge regulator, 150

battery power pack, 339

beach park-ups, 300

bedroom
  beds
    building, 198–200
    internal conversion criteria and, 254
    mattresses, 200–201
    types of, 201–204
  decorating, 265
  overview, 197–198

Bialetti moka pot, 275

bills, budgeting, 344

bin storage, 211

BioLite kettle set, 275–276

blade fuses, 114–115, 161–162

BLM (Bureau of Land Management) land, 302–303

bluetooth speaker, 337–338

bolt terminals, 138

bonded windows, 93

bonding sealant, 92

boondocking, 292–295

breakdown coverage, 346

Brit Stops, 304

BTU (British Thermal Unit), 229–230

budgeting. See cost and expenses

bulkhead walls
  framing false wall against, 83–85
  utilizing as storage, 212

Bureau of Land Management (BLM) land, 302–303

butane gas bottle, 239–240, 345–346

buying vehicles
  dealers, 48–49
  financing, 36
  mileage, 51–52
  negotiating price, 50, 51
  overview, 47–48
  private sellers, 49–50
  used, 52–54

# C

cable conduit, 106
campers. *See also* vehicles
  legally converting van to, 253–254
  overview, 44–47
camping
  boondocking, 292–295
  chairs, 338
  in Europe, 303–305
  overview, 299–300
  self-sufficiency and, 312–314
  in U.S.A., 302–303
CARFAX, 52
Celotex (insulation), 182–183
cement, 239–240
cement board, 83
chargers
  calculating storage and supply, 124–126
  overview, 108
  wiring, 170–172
chemical toilet, 280
chimney, 192
circuit breakers, 115–116
circuits, electrical, 129–132
city park-ups, 300–302
cladding
  building cupboard door with, 195–196
  chimney and, 192
  choosing, 188
  curve of roof, 191–192
  installing, 187–192
  lights and, 192–194
  tools, 188–191
Class A vehicles, 40
Class B vehicles, 40–41

Class C vehicles, 40–41
clothes and shoes, 263–264, 339, 345
composting toilet, 279–280
condensation, 201, 204, 284–285
contents insurance, 251
conversion criteria, 254
cooking facilities
  Bialetti moka pot, 275
  BioLite kettle set, 275–276
  burners, 273–274
  handheld food processor, 276
  handleless pans, 275
  internal conversion criteria, 254
  knife set, 276
  managing kitchen space, 332, 333–334
  meal plan, 335
  nesting bowls, 275
  Omnia Oven, 261–262, 274–275, 331–332, 338
  overview, 37–38, 272
  RidgeMonkey sandwich toaster, 261–262, 274, 335
  spice rack, 332
  stoves, 272–273
  tips, 274–276, 331–336
  tips regarding, 274–276
cooling, 229–233
cost and expenses
  bills, 344
  buying vehicle, 33–34
  food, 342
  fuel, 343
  gas, 345–346
  insurance, 346
  overview, 27–29
  purchases, 347
  showering, 345
  social activities, 347
  summary, 348
  tolls, 343
  tourist attractions, 348
  washing clothes, 345
cupboards
  above toilet, 212–216
  building, 209–211
current, electrical, 117–118
curtains, 266–267

ground fault circuit interrupter (GFCI) plugs, 116–117

grounding electrical system, 131–132, 136–138

# H

HardieBacker, 83

hatches, 87–88

heating

  airflow and, 238

  connecting to electrical system, 235–236

  diesel powered, 234–236

  overview, 234–237

  stoves

    aluminum sheet, 240

    fire rope, sealant, and cement, 239–240

    flashing, 239

    installing, 241–244

    overview, 237

    parts, 238–240

    potbelly stove, 239

    rain cap, 240

    stand and stone, 240

    twin insulated flue, 238–239

    wood stove, 236–237

high-top roof, 253

hinged caravan/trailer windows, 94

hotspotting, 257

Hozelock PortaShower, 278

# I

illustration as suitable van life career, 321–322

installing

  AC unit, 230–233

  batteries, 141–143

  cladding, 187–192

  electrical system before insulation, 106

  faucets, 227–228

  gas drop-out vents, 220–221

  insulation

    deciding on amount, 77–78

    methods for, 186–187

    overview, 62–67

  plug sockets, 163–166

  plywood subfloor, 62–67

sinks, 225–227

stoves, 241–244

USB sockets, 163–166, 169–170

water pumps, 227–228

windows

  overview, 96–98

  rooflight vents, 99–101

  skylights, 101–104

insulation

  Celotex, 182–183

  choosing, 186

  deciding on amount, 187

  expanding foam, 65

  flooring and, 61–62

  general-purpose, 76–78, 180–181

  glass mineral wool, 181–182

  installing

    deciding on amount, 77–78

    methods for, 186–187

    overview, 62–67

  Kingspan, 182–183

  recyclable materials, 185–186

  sheep's wool, 183–184

  soundproofing tape, 64

  spray foam, 184–185

  types of, 180–186

  vapor barrier, 66

insurance

  benefits of, 249–251

  budgeting for, 346

  changing vehicle's classification, 248–249, 251–254

  discounts, 250, 251

  external conversion criteria, 253–254

  increased speed limit, 250–251

  internal conversion criteria, 254

  legal requirements, 249

  legally converting van to camper, 253–254

  V5 form, 248

internal conversion criteria, 254

internal structure. *See* modifying vehicle

Internet, connecting to, 256–257

inverters, 111–112, 162–163

iOverlander, 296–297

isolator switches, 116, 141

Isopon Fastglas Glass Fibre Kit, 56

# About the Author

Sebastian Antonio Santabarbara is a writer from Yorkshire, U.K. His first break-through role came as the Head of Written Content for Van Clan, an online media brand documenting the van life movement with a weekly reach of over five million readers. This role led to Sebastian being head-hunted to write several inspirational nonfiction books on alternative living and this very book you're holding in your hands. He is also the Editor in Chief for Retro Dodo, a media company with a monthly reach of one million people.

A keen alternative-living enthusiast, Sebastian has built up an exciting catalogue of Middle Grade and Young Adult novels written during his adventures across the globe. He has worked closely with industry professionals to hone his craft, liaising with leading agents and publishing editors who have described his novels as punchy, slick, and filmic, with strong leads and memorable character camaraderie throughout. His adventures provide the inspiration for the vibrant worlds and immersive plotlines in his stories, with Sebastian regularly posting updates to his 30,000-strong personal social media following along the way.

# Dedication

To Jane and Tony (a.k.a. Mum and Dad), for teaching me to dream big, to never give up, and how to cook perfect pasta.

# Author's Acknowledgments

My first thanks goes out to you for buying this book, and I'm really pleased you've taken the first steps toward living a new and exciting lifestyle wherever you are in the world.

Jane and Tony, I'm sorry I put you through so much stress when I was out traveling for all those years and continually forgot to text you back, but all those adventures have certainly paid off now. Thanks for your unwavering support and for always believing in me.

A huge thank you to my friend Brandon for giving me my first writing break with Van Clan back in 2017. We've had some incredible adventures, especially you leaving me with no food or kitchen tools and me ending up spilling tuna fish oil on my clothes in bear country — a story I'll never let you forget.

Big thanks to the legendary Dave from Stray Vans for reading through the technical elements of this book and giving me his expert opinion on all things electric, and to Ilse for reminding me to take breaks when things get tough and to slow down, even when I don't listen.

Thanks to Josh, Lauren, Ryan, Kelsey, and Danny from Adara Tattoo Collective, and to Chris and Alex from Alpher Instruments for giving me a creative space to write in and for supporting me through all my ventures. You guys are incredible friends and a pleasure to both work and celebrate with, especially when you make cups of tea. When things get tough, you've always got my back.

Thank you to my friends across the pond, Dan and Lori Welty, for always being so hospitable to me whenever I'm over in California, and to my friend Andy for the countless hours of support he's given me over the years while both building and traveling in my van.

Thanks to Theo and Bee from the Indie Projects for always being around for a chat when things are tough, to Nathan for beating me on Mario Kart whenever I take a break from writing, and Fliss for keeping the cats off my laptop.

Lastly, I want to thank Katie from Wiley for her constant belief in this project, for all the "Britishisms" she's learned along the way, and her patience at my refusal to take the second "i" out of aluminium. None of this would have been possible without you; you've kept me on my toes, and I think we've made a better book because of it.

Here's to all of you taking more adventures and making incredible memories wherever you go.

*All we have to decide is what to do with the time that is given us.*
— J.R.R. Tolkien, *The Fellowship of the Ring*

## Publisher's Acknowledgments

**Executive Editor:** Steven Hayes

**Senior Managing Editor:** Kristie Pyles

**Project Manager and Development Editor:** Katharine Dvorak

**Technical Editors:** Cassandra Michelle and Dave de Vries

**Proofreader:** Debbye Butler

**Production Editor:** Mohammed Zafar Ali

**Cover Image:** © View Apart/Shutterstock

# Leverage the power

*Dummies* is the global leader in the reference category and one of the most trusted and highly regarded brands in the world. No longer just focused on books, customers now have access to the dummies content they need in the format they want. Together we'll craft a solution that engages your customers, stands out from the competition, and helps you meet your goals.

## Advertising & Sponsorships

Connect with an engaged audience on a powerful multimedia site, and position your message alongside expert how-to content. Dummies.com is a one-stop shop for free, online information and know-how curated by a team of experts.

- Targeted ads
- Video
- Email Marketing
- Microsites
- Sweepstakes sponsorship

**20 MILLION** PAGE VIEWS EVERY SINGLE MONTH

**15 MILLION UNIQUE** VISITORS PER MONTH

**43%** OF ALL VISITORS ACCESS THE SITE VIA THEIR MOBILE DEVICES

**700,000** NEWSLETTER SUBSCRIPTIONS TO THE INBOXES OF

*300,000* UNIQUE INDIVIDUALS EVERY WEEK

# of dummies

## Custom Publishing

Reach a global audience in any language by creating a solution that will differentiate you from competitors, amplify your message, and encourage customers to make a buying decision.

- Apps
- Books
- eBooks
- Video
- Audio
- Webinars

## Brand Licensing & Content

Leverage the strength of the world's most popular reference brand to reach new audiences and channels of distribution.

## For more information, visit dummies.com/biz

# PERSONAL ENRICHMENT

9781119187790
USA $26.00
CAN $31.99
UK £19.99

9781119179030
USA $21.99
CAN $25.99
UK £16.99

9781119293354
USA $24.99
CAN $29.99
UK £17.99

9781119293347
USA $22.99
CAN $27.99
UK £16.99

9781119310068
USA $22.99
CAN $27.99
UK £16.99

9781119235606
USA $24.99
CAN $29.99
UK £17.99

9781119251163
USA $24.99
CAN $29.99
UK £17.99

9781119235491
USA $26.99
CAN $31.99
UK £19.99

9781119279952
USA $24.99
CAN $29.99
UK £17.99

9781119283133
USA $24.99
CAN $29.99
UK £17.99

9781119287117
USA $24.99
CAN $29.99
UK £16.99

9781119130246
USA $22.99
CAN $27.99
UK £16.99

# PROFESSIONAL DEVELOPMENT

9781119311041
USA $24.99
CAN $29.99
UK £17.99

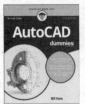

9781119255796
USA $39.99
CAN $47.99
UK £27.99

9781119293439
USA $26.99
CAN $31.99
UK £19.99

9781119281467
USA $26.99
CAN $31.99
UK £19.99

9781119280651
USA $29.99
CAN $35.99
UK £21.99

9781119251132
USA $24.99
CAN $29.99
UK £17.99

9781119310563
USA $34.00
CAN $41.99
UK £24.99

9781119181705
USA $29.99
CAN $35.99
UK £21.99

9781119263593
USA $26.99
CAN $31.99
UK £19.99

9781119257769
USA $29.99
CAN $35.99
UK £21.99

9781119293477
USA $26.99
CAN $31.99
UK £19.99

9781119265313
USA $24.99
CAN $29.99
UK £17.99

9781119239314
USA $29.99
CAN $35.99
UK £21.99

9781119293323
USA $29.99
CAN $35.99
UK £21.99